Innovation

Practical Books for Smart Marketers from PMP

Now you can equip all your sales and marketing people with **Innovation**. It will help them introduce new solutions to your existing customers and open the doors for new business development. You may also want to distribute the book to potential customers to help them understand the size and purchasing power of this market and its implications for their industry.

A customized edition, with "**Compliments of Your Company Name**" on the cover is available with orders of 200 or more copies.

Call us toll-free at **888-787-8100** for quotes on quantity orders.

For more practical books for smart marketers, go to our website, **www.paramountbooks.com.**

Innovation—

Myths and *Myth*stakes

Tim Coffey

Dave Siegel

Mark Smith

PMP

Paramount Market Publishing, Inc.

Paramount Market Publishing, Inc.
950 Danby Road, Suite 136
Ithaca, NY 14850
www.paramountbooks.com
Telephone: 607-275-8100; 888-787-8100   Facsimile: 607-275-8101

Publisher: James Madden
Editorial Director: Doris Walsh

Cataloging in Publication Data available
ISBN 978-0-9801745-7-1

Cover design: Bethany Barr

CONTENTS

THE AFTERWORD
Formerly, The Foreword

"Always speak the truth, think before you speak, and write it down afterwards."

—LEWIS CARROLL

THIS IS NOT OUR FIRST BOOK, so we certainly know that this is where the Foreword is supposed to go. And we know that someone other than the author always writes it . . . until now!

As you will learn in this book, real break-through innovation comes best from first undertaking an exploration—an exploration to discover new opportunities, which will lead to new ideas. So, practicing what we preach, we too, went on an exploration—a journey that, afterwards, led us to having a book unlike we had first envisioned. And who best to explain this? US! And where? Upfront, of course . . . right where the foreword belongs.

In our well over 100 years combined experience consulting, we've observed that many of today's executives and organizations have numerous misconceptions regarding the subject of innovation—**Myths** that not only hamper innovation, but lead to costly mistakes. We've also observed many instances where truths about innovation are misapplied by many of today's practitioners. We call these *myth*stakes. And innovation *myth*stakes are highly destructive as well.

We set out on our own search to study the entire field of innova-

tion, looking to uncover and expose many of the numerous **myths &
*myth*stakes** that we have seen do damage. We then set out to write
a book about the findings of our excursion so that our readers could
become truly world-class, successful innovators.

Then, just as with true innovation, our journey led us to discover
things we weren't expecting, new insights, new opportunities, and as
a result, after we finished our book, we realized that it was different.
Make that, more innovative, than we envisioned.

There are already scores of books on the subject of innovation, and
more on the way. A quick look at Google Alerts confirms what you
already know—that there are over 20 new writings on the subject of
innovation every day.

Not to mention the blogs.

Okay, we'll mention the blogs. Visit *http://innovation.alltop.com/* to
see who is featured today as the "best-of-the-best" bloggers on innovation. And as of this printing, there were more than 50 of them.

Admittedly, the topic of innovation has never been hotter. Companies are talking innovation; entire countries are talking about the need
for innovation. Our latest president won the election by extolling the
need for innovation and change.

So innovation is a big deal, and that's why we set out to do a different type of innovation book. Goodness knows, the world could use
one.

Our book is different because it capitalizes on all of the previous
work of others on the topic. We have read virtually every book on
innovation while monitoring most of the innovation blogs. And this
little tome draws upon *much* of that learning.

This is a better book on innovation because of our specific experience in the field. In fact, there are three things that make *this* book different from all the others: Coffey, Siegel, and Smith—the three authors
who hope to inform and entertain you throughout. That's because
we're not academicians in an ivory tower some place. We're actual
innovation practitioners and consultants with a long list of clients

and success stories including Kellogg's, Sara-Lee, Nestlé, Norvartis, Purina, Hasbro, Tate & Lyle, PNC Bank, Kraft, UniLever, KAO Brands, and dozens of others. We have been instrumental in the development of innovations ranging from the world's #1 leisure product in its hey-day, the Super Soaker Water Gun, to well over a billion dollars in Kellogg's fruit snack line sales. We're even responsible for Heinz Green Ketchup—the category's first big grower of this century. Oh yeah, we're also all trained hypnotists! And you'll see what that brings to ideation later in the book, provided you're not asleep already.

We wanted to guarantee a superior book on innovation because, as you will learn, successful innovation requires both knowledge and imagination. Now, for full disclosure, it should be pointed out that as authors, we bring a dual-dominant (both a right- and left-brain) perspective to the proceedings. Coffey, Siegel, and Smith have classical package goods marketing experience *and* creative advertising backgrounds. We approach every challenge with both sides of the brain (kind of like a cello player who can balance a check book).

We wanted **Innovation—Myths and *Myth*stakes** to be a book that not only explained what to do, but also how to do it.

Now that our exploration is complete, we found that, for the most part, our book *does* do everything we intended it to do.

But now it also does much more.

We found that so many myths involved the "business" part of innovation—the ROI, the marketing strategies, the validation tests, the translation of ideas (concepts) into "consumer speak," the inter-office communication of ideas, and so on.

We found that *no* book has really looked into this.

Why is this so important? Well, here are just a few questions for you to contemplate before delving into the book:

- Is it better to pursue the development of a new product concept that scored extremely high in consumer concept testing, or one that scored lower *but* is something your competitor cannot do?

- Is it always better to be first to market?

- Why is it that truly breakthrough ideas tend to fail in traditional consumer research?

- Why is it that so many product ideas that test well in consumer research, wind up failing in the real world?

- Is it better to try developing the very best new product, or one that is just "good enough?"

- Is there a limit as to how much innovation makes sense?

We'll bet that no one else has asked you these questions. We'll double-down that no one else has tried to answer them. But the answers to these types of business questions have huge implications as to whether or not your innovation will be successful. The truth of the matter is that it may all start with a great idea, but it can all stop with a poor business decision.

ABOUT THIS BOOK

We'll start off with a general overview of innovation. Why it is now more important than ever, and why it is so difficult to do.

Our first four myths deal with overall investments and risks associated with innovation. For instance, you've long heard that 80 percent of all new products fail, right? Guess again.

Myths #5 thru #8 will be shattered to present some eye-opening truths that will help you to better understand how to uncover opportunities. Want a taste? Think that the consumer is king?

Myths #9 thru #13 will get you to think about ideation in ways that will make your brains fall out. How? Do you think that brainstorming works? Ha!

Basic marketing issues surrounding innovation are presented in myths #14 thru #20. For example, we all know that the most important thing is for consumers to like your new product right? Well if you said yes to this, chances are you are batting 0-for-4.

Myths #21 thru #23 uncover some interesting myths regarding process. Should R&D lead the way?

Then we explore some wonderful case studies. In Myths #24 thru #26 you'll read the true stories of some great innovation in action. We can promise that you will not find these to be the typical "New Coke" type of case studies that have been presented so many times, they've lost their fizz.

Lastly, our final myth (for now), #27, will discuss how or whether to keep innovation going.

So if you're ready to explode the myths and avoid the *myth*stakes, then read on and improve the overall success rates in your quest for positive, productive, and profitable change.

And to close (or open) with Lewis Carroll once again: *"Begin at the beginning and go on till you come to the end; then stop."*

—TIM COFFEY, DAVE SIEGEL AND MARK SMITH
MARCH 2009

The Situation

Why all the commotion?

Come gather 'round people wherever you roam
And admit that the waters around you have grown
And accept it that soon you'll be drenched to the bone.
If your time to you is worth savin'
Then you better start swimmin' or you'll sink like a stone
For the times they are a-changin'

—Bob Dylan, 1965

How prophetic. Dylan's words were so true some 40+ years ago, but now they are even more "in tune."

The acceleration of change in the world today is unprecedented. On the plus side, it creates head-spinning opportunities. On the downside, it threatens one with obsolescence. Innovation is risky, but in today's world, the risk of *not* innovating is even greater.

Thanks to technology, and especially the Internet (a huge game-changing innovation by itself) the ability of today's companies and services to innovate is faster and better then ever. Now, those looking for new ideas and solutions can access billions of minds easily and at little cost.

The rate of innovation and change on the part of today's companies and services is accelerating at unprecedented rates. And guess what?

These new changes cause the need for other new changes!

After all, if your competitor has a new, differentiated offering that is perceived to be a better value than yours, you better get off your butt and out-innovate it or face loss of business. In fact, this alone has been a key reason for many retailers to keep a #2 or #3 brand on their shelves. They have come to realize that as long as they keep this competitive threat alive, the #1 brand will not dare to stop innovating.

But beware! You know the old saying: "First comes the innovator, then comes the imitator, then come the idiots." Being third-to-market is being first to the graveyard.

That's why continuous innovation is critical. Without it, brands and companies can fall victim to significant business erosion or at the very least commoditization, and the funny thing about commodities is that they tend to sell at commodity prices, which destroys margins.

A few short years ago, the world got its drinking water out of a tap, or even a garden hose, before *it* became dangerous. Now there is an *entire* retail shelf devoted to bottled water. And yes, soft drink manufacturers quickly introduced theirs as well. Where once there was simply a TV set that captured three off-air TV networks, now there is a thousand-channel HD satellite universe, the MP3 player, laptop, PDA, Internet, YouTube, TiVo, and even the mobile phone. By the way, virtually all of this technology occurred in just the past decade.

Our marketplace has moved not only to one of constant change but to one of global competition as well. No longer must we be concerned only about defending, or out-marketing competition from within our own country but now, from competition anywhere in the world. As William D. Green, chairman and CEO of Accenture and chairman of Business Roundtable's Education, Innovation & Workforce Initiative stated: "Competition is relentless and can come from anywhere and any time, no matter the industry."

In high-tech, we have witnessed Salesforce.com becoming a threat to once market-leading Siebel in just a few years. We saw MySpace feeling the pressure of a new upstart—Facebook—in what seemed to be the blink of an eye. Using its value innovation program, we observed

Samsung, originally just a maker of inexpensive black and white TVs, take the leadership of the flat-screen LCD and with it the consumer electronics industry away from once dominant Sony.

The debacle concerning U.S. automakers resulted from failing to stay competitive with global rivals in the realm of advanced principles of design and manufacturing—principles that exploit global, peer-to-peer information platforms to increase the variety of huge hits a firm might produce.

No wonder that governments around the world are concerned about keeping and motivating their industries and workers to be innovative. The more unique, relevant, and better-valued a country's products and services are perceived, the more their countries' economies can succeed in today's global marketplace.

Witness our own unfortunate U.S. situation. A few decades ago, it was laughable to buy anything "made in Japan." Japanese goods were cheap, inferior, and very low quality. Now Japan owns our auto industry. Toyota surpassed GM for the most cars sold in a year. Our once highly valued manufacturing workforce no longer has the perceived superiority to workers elsewhere, and thus, it is only natural that companies, including our own, go elsewhere for the best perceived value while touting the "Free Trade" banner.

It may not help when Europe imposes a 15 percent value-added tax on U.S. imports and rebates the VAT on exports to the United States. Or when China devalues its currency 45 percent, as it did in 1994, and sucks jobs and factories out of the United States. Or even when Japan manipulates its currency, preaches economic nationalism to its people, and shelters its market for TVs, autos, and steel, while dumping into and capturing ours. But like it or not, that is what masquerades as "Free Trade" today. As a nation we'll have to innovate our way out of it.

In Uganda, AllAfrica.com reports students calling for innovation. The Press Association reports an award program to help Scotland's global competitiveness. On July 2, 2008, the *New York Times* online reported: "Japan determined to boost innovation." Australia, New Zealand, and others have opened up centers for innovation. India wants to draft an India Innovation Act focusing on increasing research investment, strengthening education opportunities in math, science, and technology, and developing an innovation infrastructure.

The first week of 2009, Welcomeurope.com boldly announced: "We have entered the European Year of Creativity and Innovation 2009! A slogan, 'Imagine. Create. Innovate' has been chosen to illustrate the official launch of the European Year of Creativity and Innovation 2009 that will be done by the Czech Presidency of the EU on 7 January. The objective is to promote creative and innovative approaches in different sectors of human activity and help the European Union to face the challenges of the globalization."

It is also no wonder that the basic driver of the U.S. presidential race was the cry for "CHANGE!" One candidate became the party's nominee based on the promise for change, while the other obtained the mantle based on a promise of reform. And, the number one question asked to both candidates by the Science Debate 2008 was, "What policies will you support to ensure that America remains the world leader in innovation?"

After all, significant innovations like the personal computer, cell phone, and Internet have driven major cycles of U.S. growth. What's next? In her recently published book, *The Innovation Gap*, Judy Erstin stated, "Today, more than ever, our role in the future depends on our ability to sustain a culture that supports and promotes the ability to innovate."

The U.S. has been on top for so long largely due to its spectacular run of world-beating innovation based, in part, on out-educating the rest of the world and providing the right economic incentives. But studies show a drop in our educational attainment.

Test scores for high school students have been falling now for 20 years. Witness the performances of high school seniors on the National Assessment of Educational Progress exams known as the "nation's report card." An NAEP test of 12th-grade achievement was given to what the *New York Times* called a "representative sample of 21,000 high school seniors attending 900 public and private schools from January to March 2005."

WHAT DID THE TESTS REVEAL?

Since 1990, the share of students lacking even basic reading skills has risen by a third, from 20 percent to 27 percent. Only 35 percent of high school seniors have reached a "proficient" level in reading, down from 40 percent.

The ultimate test is how American kids stack up in a world where leadership in math and science eventually translates into innovation and global dominance. In all recent world tests where they have competed, Mainland Chinese, and students from Hong Kong, Singapore, Japan, and Korea come in at or near the top, whereas Americans bring up the rear.

A 2006 multinational study (the OECD Programme for International Student Assessment) showed the U.S. scoring lower than average on math and combined science.

As we speak, China and India are becoming major innovation competitors to the United States. Chinese and Indian children take more science courses than U.S. students. Presently, only one in twenty U.S. college graduates have engineering degrees, compared with more than one out of every three college graduates in China and India.

Consumers are changing as well. They are not only adapting to this rapidly changing world, but they actually embrace it. Here too, the Internet is playing a significant role. Consumers today are better connected than ever before and talk about new products through blogs, forums, twitters, and online communities. What is good? What is bad? What they recommend. And *they are trusted!* Recent surveys show that the most trusted source for consumer product information after family and friends was *strangers with product experience.*

The desire for change by consumers wanting the next best value, by companies wanting to beat their competitors, and by countries wishing to protect and grow their economies, has become so great that, to the companies, services, and even countries that do it best, will go the spoils. Those that do not win face not only lost business or lost jobs but, in some cases, even obsolescence. We now have a business environment in which the need for companies, services, and countries to innovate is constant. Unless a business constantly reassesses how it can improve, it risks losing out to more innovative competitors.

Plus if a company is going to grow, it virtually has to employ innovation. Product Development and Management Association (PDMA) studies revealed that on average, new products account for about one-third of a company's sales. It is no wonder that for some companies, such as P&G, innovation has become the central driving force for their businesses. Innovation expands brand value, enhances relevancy with customers, and even empowers the workforce. As A.G. Lafley, CEO P&G and author of *The Game Changer,* puts it: "The best way to win in this world is through innovation."

Just as we were writing this book, David Mackay, President, CEO of one of our favorite clients, Kellogg's reported, in the Q3, 2008 Earnings call that:

"Our solid performance came from *innovations* like MiniWheats Blueberry Muffin . . . We achieved double-digit frozen food sales growth due to the trend toward in-home food consumption as well as strong *innovation* and advertising. Eggo sales grew in double digits, driven by strong price realization and *innovations* like Bake Shop Swirlz and Bake Shop MiniMuffin Tops." Makes us proud.

In the 2008 best practices study, *The Making of World-Class Innovators* (Prophet), 70 percent of corporate leaders surveyed now count innovation as one of their top three growth-driving priorities. Additionally, some three-quarters of survey respondents say the huge amount of media attention devoted to innovation has raised their companies' awareness of the importance of innovation.

The authors have witnessed a significant change within current and potential clients. Where once there was a brand manager or two or at the very best a new products development group interested in innovation, we now find entire insight and development divisions within companies. In fact, in one particular pharmaceutical client's hallway, we found banner after banner hanging from the ceiling extolling everyone to innovate . . . innovate . . . innovate.

A successful innovation can even turn an entire company around. For example, in the late 1990s Motorola was in serous trouble as a result of its pride and lack of consumer focus. Then it introduced the RAZR mobile phone. Not only did consumers around the world begin to consider the company cool again, but also, as its CEO Ed Zandler stated; "You start getting employees believing again that you can win."

And new innovations don't mean turnarounds just for big companies, but also for smaller ones. Earlier in the 1990s, one of our authors had the chance to help a small leisure products company by the name of Larami. The company seemed so down and out that the CEO, Mr. Myung Sung, made it a point to explain that everything, even its very old, worn, and rickety conference table was rented. But the firm possessed an unusual water-toy. The item was passed over by every other toy company that had a chance to acquire it. It was very large, kind of expensive, and very different from the category at that time. With some coaxing and planning, Larami was persuaded to launch the item, mortgaging itself further for modest support funds. The result? Super-Soaker. Larami became the darling of the leisure products industry worldwide. Its VP of sales said he felt so famous that he thought he was a celebrity. Kids stopped him in the street wanting his autograph! And, oh yes, Mr. Sung eventually sold his little company for a reported $90 million profit.

There you have it! We now have an environment where consumer's demand for change and innovation is at an all-time high and companies' desire and capability of filling this demand is faster and better than ever. Add to this the significant competitive and governmental pressures that will be put on companies to innovate even better and *bang!* What a situation!

So, to put it bluntly, *"you better start swimming, or you'll sink like a stone!"*

WHAT EXACTLY IS THIS THING CALLED "INNOVATION?"

Merriam-Webster defines innovation as the introduction of something new, a new idea, method, or device. Others have defined innovation as the process of making improvements by introducing something new. But for businessmen, innovation must also be something that actually reaches the marketplace and generates revenues and profits. Anything short of this is merely a "nice idea."

Too often we hear firms telling us: "Oh, we already do innovation—we have held lots and lots of ideation/brainstorming sessions."

While many think of innovation primarily as idea generation, it is far more. It is the understanding and gathering of insights, needs, and opportunities. Then it is the idea generation based upon this understanding. It is the refining and sharpening of these ideas and the development of a go-to-market strategy. And, finally it is the mass adoption on the part of the consumers.

Innovation is not limited to the ideation and development of new products and services. Rather, innovation could include new, different business models, supply chains, and operations. It could involve new products, new methods of production, new sources of supply, the exploitation of new markets, new people to serve, new ways in which to go to market, price your offerings or make money. It could also involve finding a new application for a dying or dead product.

A 2008 best practices study, *The Making of World Class Innovators*, found that although executives say that breakthrough innovation has the most likely positive effect on corporate performance, they also admit that their companies focus innovation only in areas of product or service development. Only one-third reported innovation as part of everything the organization does.

Essentially, innovation can take place in any area that the company works. Areas like:

Who does the company serve?

What does it provide?

How does it provide it?

How does it make its money?

How is it different?

For example, consider the ways in which Target innovates against Wal-Mart. It provides different, exclusive products by fashionable designers, and offers a different more pleasant shopping experience.

Some of the world's most profitable companies, such as Apple and Google, have built their success on innovative approaches to existing technologies and products. Others, such as Quaker, reportedly missed some big opportunities by not looking at innovations apart from product. Specifically, in the 1990s, Quaker missed out on the opportunity to innovate its distribution by not taking advantage of smaller, health-oriented outlets used by its Snapple beverage acquisition. Likewise, it lost out on a chance to introduce Tetra-Pak's paper bottles by letting Ocean Spray lock up an 18-month exclusive license. Ocean Spray had a more eclectic innovation strategy including idea forums to explore innovations in any domain, while Quaker busied itself tweaking minor product improvements.

Another recent example of business process innovation is P&G's move to change its production and distribution model. As a result of increasing cost of oil and rising salaries in some of the countries the company uses for outsourcing, transportation, distribution, and production have suddenly become quite expensive. P&G, being a smart innovator, is now reconsidering how to best use it 30,000 trucks and 145 manufacturing plants to make production and distribution more local.

Importantly, innovation not only can occur at any part of the marketing mix but it can also come in different degrees. In some cases, it can be a modest product improvement or line extension. In others, it can be a huge, game-changing move that changes social practices, the way we live, the competitive arena, or creates an entirely new consumption. For one company, innovation can mean bringing a dramatically new product to store shelves. For another, it can mean adding a tiny new button on a website.

The degree of innovation being sought depends on a company's objectives and risk tolerance. That firm, whose objective is one of playing to win or seeking substantial sales or profit growth, requires bigger "disruptive" innovations. The bigger the innovation, the more radical it will be and the greater the opportunity will be for a huge win over competition. However, the bigger the innovation, the more money, time, and risk will be involved. The authors of *Blue Ocean Strategy* found that just 14 percent of the new product launches they studied qualified as true game-changers. But these 14 percent accounted for 61 percent of total profits generated by all launches.

Less glamorous, smaller, closer-in innovations such as line-extensions, new flavors, and smaller product improvements also play an important role within today's organizations. These types of innovations, typically called "sustaining" innovations do just that—they help companies sustain or modestly grow their market share by providing "new news" and excitement for their businesses. Remember that today's consumers are actually looking for and embracing news, and smaller innovations can help sustain consumer, sales force, and retailer excitement over a brand. *Blue Ocean Strategy* authors found that line extensions accounted for the vast majority of all new launches (86 percent), yet only a small percentage of total profits (39 percent).

Ideally, most look for a balance between innovation programs. Firms need programs that deliver big, significant innovations that can provide them with a sustainable competitive advantage and significant revenue growth. However, firms also need a program that helps them meet specific, growth and financial targets in the short term and enable them to remain new and exciting in the eyes of their customers—all while allowing them to spread their risk.

SO WHAT'S THE PROBLEM?

If is so much good that can come from innovation and, there is so much need for innovation, what holds it up? Why isn't every firm innovating its head off? What are the roadblocks?

If we understand the challenges, perhaps we can all be better, smarter, more-aggressive innovators. Better yet, once we properly define the problems and the needs, we can *innovate* our way into a better way to innovate.

New is scary

Unfortunately, many times, "better the devil you know than the devil you don't" rules the day. The challenge with innovation is that its outcome is always something new and while one can try to predict the results of something new, there is certainly no certainty. While innovators try their best to predict the future, it is impossible for them to truly do so. Even the most popular futurists are wrong most of the time, or there would be far more lottery winners walking around.

While change is a constant factor in life, we as human beings are still afraid of it. Accepting innovations, not just from a consumer point of view, but also from a management point of view, requires faith in the unknown. We can't tell you how many clients have asked us for help in identifying break-through, game-changing, innovations only to select the safest, closest-in option to increase their certainty. The simple fact is, the bigger and more different the idea, the harder it is to get people to go with it.

Investors are generally skeptical about any new strategy. Most only understand what has been done before. More recently, even venture capitalists—investors with a reputation for funding "ventures"—have become risk averse. Judy Estrin, former Chief Technology Officer of Cisco and author of *Closing the Innovation Gap*, laments:

> "The attitude towards failure in the Valley has shifted. It used to be that if you had tried to start a company and it had failed, you would be looked upon by the VCs more favorable than someone who had never tried. Today that's not necessarily true."

One of my first enlightenments on this subject came at the start of my marketing career. Many years ago, I interviewed at P&G at a time when that company was known for its stellar marketing and not-so-stellar innovation. At the time of my interview, one of the key decision makers told me: "You may be crazy or you may be creative, but it doesn't matter since we don't have either here in the company—so you're hired!" It didn't take long to find out why they didn't have people like me staying in the company when, in my first written recommendation as a marketing assistant, I was told that for me to get a proposal approved by management, it would *have* to be based solidly on the fact that what I was proposing *was done successfully before!*

There is a price to pay

Many innovations fail! There have been many reports over the years citing a new product failure rate of 80 percent. (We'll see later on, however, if this is a myth). It is nice to rally around a battle cry of "Innovate or Die" as we have heard from many a guru of innovation, including none other than the CEO of P&G. But, it's awfully hard to keep marching towards this command when you think that you will most likely fail.

Whether or not the failure rate is this high, one thing that simply cannot be disregarded is that innovation does have a price tag, not just dollars, but also time, friends, job, and sometimes family too. If your key role, whether within a company or as a consultant, is to lead its innovation you'll no doubt feel the pressure of having to deliver. After all, others are counting on you to find the next big new product idea and unfortunately, you're only as good as your last success.

Dollars are also a drawback. Unfortunately, innovation is guaranteed to cost something, yet you cannot guarantee there will be any income from it whatsoever. In May 2007, *BusinessWeek* reported that less than half (46 percent) of senior executives are satisfied with returns on innovation.

Lack of time

Time is on my side ... yes it is
Time, Time, Time is on my side ... yes it is
                                —THE ROLLING STONES, 1964

No it isn't!

Innovation takes time, not just to come up with the big breakthrough idea, but also to develop the final product and to build manufacturing capacity and inventory. Today's management is often pressured to have a short-term earnings orientation that makes investments in risky, long-term innovation that much more difficult. In *Closing the Innovation Gap*, Judy Estrin blames America's obsession with quick fixes, the quick buck, the pump-and-dump mentality now present among today's entrepreneurs and venture capital firms along with the "build-it-to-flip-it" attitude as the root cause of a drop in real significant innovation.

Presently, America is facing a significant economic downturn (ironically, somewhat caused by a cutback in innovation). Will top executives have to further scale back on innovation expense in order to achieve their quarterly income goals?

"Lack of time" is, in fact, one of the most common responses management gives for being the barrier to innovation. The financial community, and most shareholders, place huge emphasis on a company's short-term profits. Sadly, one consequence of this is that a great deal of pressure is being placed on today's firms to get the most day-to day productivity out of their employees. What used to be the job of two people is now, at times, the job of one.

Add to this the new business workplace where workers are constantly distracted by e-mails, IMs, cell phones, and meetings and it is just too darned hard to carve out creative "what if?" time. Heck, its even getting difficult to play a round of golf or take a much-needed vacation without having to check e-mail and answer mobile calls from the office!

Innovation as well as any creativity, requires time. And the sad truth is, many companies barely staff themselves adequately enough to handle their current business, let alone plan and ideate for the future.

Corporate culture

Top managers generally agree that the most important drivers of innovations in any organization are its culture and people. But the simple truth is, it is the organization's culture that generally either attracts or scares away the right, innovative people.

Since innovation is somewhat scary and risky, a corporate culture is needed whereby employees at least feel free (better yet, are motivated) to take on the challenge and to feel that it is okay to be wrong. Companies need to send a clear message that it is far better to try and fail than to fail to try.

Unfortunately, in most companies the deck is stacked against encouragement of innovation, especially disruptive innovation—the kind that leads to major changes within the business or marketplace. The sad truth is: an innovator's desire to improve the world or to create new solutions is rarely supported by those they hope to help.

Too often companies actually discourage talented employees from pursuing innovation. They offer limited incentives, if any, are often risk-averse, and have no plans for dealing with failure. In fact, in the 2008 McKinsey survey *How Companies Approach Innovation*, 33 percent of top managers say leaders hinder innovation by maintaining a fear of failure.

While the wrong corporate culture greatly impedes the ability to attract innovative people, the same, unfortunately can be said for a country's culture. Specifically, while there is a strong desire on the part of Asian countries to encourage innovation and entrepreneurship to boost their economies, their society is not geared to encourage it. In the July 2008 *New York Times* online article mentioned earlier, "Japan Determined to Boost Innovation," the chairman of the policy council of the ruling party in Japan pointed out that the stigma attached to business failure and bankruptcy is still a problem in Japan. Separately, when one of our authors recently spoke in Singapore, representatives of that government tried to ascertain his interest in teaching Singapore individuals to be more open to risk and entrepreneurship.

Corporate politics and ideologies

Inter-company politics and other social barriers can inhibit people within the organization from connecting on ideas, making innovation even riskier. Corporate operating divisions and departments can be a special culprit here. Many times we have seen different divisions within the same company working on the same initiative—duplicating costs, duplicating valuable time, and halving the intelligence!

Believe it or not, often companies lose out on a big new product idea because the division or department within the company that discovered it would have to turn the idea over to a different operating division. Rather than turn the revenues and profits over to a different division, the original group buries the idea! For example, in one company, we witnessed the discovery of a potentially big new product concept identified by this firm's "Morning Snacks" Division. The only problem was, the concept was more of a "Breakfast Item" rather than a "Morning Snack." And that meant that the idea would have to go to the "Breakfast Foods" Division, not the division that discovered the concept. Guess what? They buried it!

Further, in several instances we have seen the potential of specific brands to innovate across several different categories. Here too, these opportunities were dropped because the sales and profits would wind up going to different category managers and not to the original brand.

Which comes first, the company or the brand? You can bet that to the Brand team, the answer is the brand!

On a broader issue, ideologies have been shown to hamper innovation. After all, beliefs, values, and opinions that shape the way an individual or his manager thinks, acts, and understands the world certainly impact the ability to accept something new and different. Ptolemy's astronomical theory lasted more than a millennium, then was replaced by Newton's theory, and more recently by Einstein's theory, which in due course will be found wanting and replaced. Each theory, however, does have pieces of the truth, which are amplified in subsequent theories. For example, there have long been conflicts between religion and science, even though science and religion are by nature compatible. As Pope Pius X said, "True religion and true science should never be at odds, as both are based in truth." But no matter which side one is on, the fact is, conflicts such as these cause inactivity. In Science Debate 2008, one of the candidates for President was asked his position on government regulation and funding of stem cell research because the ideology of the past President was felt to have handcuffed U.S. scientists and hindered the country's ability to compete with other nations.

Corporate structure

In too many companies, silos and turf wars and battles over who owns the innovation process are the norm and where there are silos and turf wars there is a poor likelihood of successful innovation. For innovation to have the best chance of working, collaboration between people and departments is a must and managerial hierarchy must be careful not to present a barrier to collaboration.

Silos can occur between innovation departments and marketing departments. In some organizations, a separate innovation team handles the entire up front innovation effort, from insight, to ideation, to conceptualization, and even prototyping. The result of their efforts is then handed off to a separate brand team, package designer, and advertising agency. Sadly, too many times we have seen the latter groups disregard much of the upfront thinking of the innovation group and this, in turn, results in packaging or commercials that fail to communicate the true drivers of the concept that were uncovered in the first place. Importantly, BASES (a world renowned, new product testing company which we talk about later) has labeled the lack of cohesiveness between the originally tested concept and the go-to-market communication, in either package or advertising as being a key reason for new product failure.

One particular case in which we were involved included innovation efforts undertaken for Hot Pockets. The Innovation Team uncovered the insight and opportunity for creating a Hot Pocket sized and shaped for younger kids. Younger kids were not consuming Hot Pockets because they were too big for their hands and mouths. The development of a Hot Pockets for kids would mean totally new consumption for the brand and category—a potentially break-through innovation.

The innovation team created a twisted stick type of Hot Pocket, shaped and sized for kids. This would have been fine. But when handed to the Brand team they saw this as a neat new shape for Hot Pockets in general, not caring about the original insight. As a result it was packaged as a typical Hot Pocket (adult look), and treated as part of the Hot Pockets line. What did they do? They took a potentially break-through "disruptive" innovation that would appeal to a totally new consumer and bring with it new consumption, and turned it into a "sustaining" innovation—a variety to their base brand. Nice, but certainly not break through.

Another silo can occur between R&D people and marketing people. R&D people study and shape ideas and tend to be internally focused. Marketers are more externally focused. They understand the consumer, the prospects, and the markets. They understand where potential new products could go and why and how consumers may want them.

Both must work together for the innovation process to succeed. Sometimes the ideas can come from marketers seeing a consumer need or opportunity and R&D then finds a way to deliver a product that meets this need. Many times R&D comes up with some very interesting new technological solutions. However, without marketing's help in determining why or how consumers would be interested in these discoveries, too often these new solutions will be ones that nobody wants. 3M's widely acclaimed success with its Post-It Notes is a nice example of what can happen when everything works together. R&D discovered this unusual glue and marketing married it to a consumer need.

Leadership

Naturally, much of corporate culture comes from leadership, and if the CEO or top management is not fully committed to innovation, the rest of the company will act accordingly. According to the McKinsey Global Survey on Innovation, some 70 percent of corporate leaders say innovation is among their top three priorities. But, while just about every CEO pays lip service to innovation, many do little beyond mouthing the words.

Why? Because the majority of top managers are just that—managers! They have made it to the top by being good at what they *did*— meeting sales objectives, supporting existing customers, acquiring new business, managing mergers and acquisitions, achieving quarterly sales goals, and so forth. Innovation, with its risk, uncertainty, and inherent right-brained imagination is just not part of their DNA.

As a result, many top managers can be indifferent or even hostile towards new ideas and this creates a major challenge. It's a good bet that if senior management stifles innovation, good, creative, imaginative people will get impatient and will go elsewhere—sometimes even taking an idea with them to either start their own venture or give to someone else.

Training

To successfully innovate, two skills must be present: Knowledge and imagination.

Knowledge comes from doing research and actual experience but it also comes from having the right technological training. As mentioned previously, America's devotion to the education of its students in high quality math, science, and engineering has dropped to levels lower than those of countries now competing with us. Signs are all over, from Finnish mobile phones, to superior Japanese hybrid cars to Indian tech support.

Imagination and creativity, openness, and wonder are all important talents and abilities for innovation, and yet society provides little encouragement to those who can perform this feat. Today's economy rewards the logic, analysis, and procedural parts of our brains. Standardized testing highlights procedure and analysis, not creativity or imagination. Salaries and job offers reward the technicians.

Success

Perhaps most ironically, many times a challenge to innovation results from a company being too successful. Successful companies can lack urgency. As Robert Herbold points out in *Seduced by Success*, when companies perceive a lack of urgency or concentrate on defending versus growing and attacking, they become vulnerable. Many successful innovators have trouble sustaining their desire to innovate simply because they begin to develop a desire to protect the success they now have from risk. Some call it the "play-not-to-lose" syndrome, versus playing to win!

Our economic landscape is littered by once-successful companies falling by the wayside because they failed to aggressively innovate. Kodak, once the king of photography, did not pay attention to the fact that digital photography was emerging. Sears, the first billion-dollar retailer lost out to Wal-Mart. General Motors, our first company to earn

$1 billion annually, lost to Toyota, a company constantly looking for improvement. The list goes on and on.

Myths

Bet you expected this one. But it is true! Many myths and "*myth*stakes" (truths that have been misapplied) held by today's businessmen and innovators have made the job of innovation even more difficult and riskier than it has to be. Myths about failure rates, finding opportunities, ideation, what is needed, how to get great performance, and so much more.

WHERE DO WE GO FROM HERE?

In the rest of this book we will help you to comprehend some of these myths and also to better understand some of the roadblocks and challenges presented in this chapter. Once these myths are exploded, the challenges of innovation are far more easily overcome. Once these myths are debunked, you will become a better innovator!

THE PLEDGE OF INNOVATION:

So what have we learned?

I promise to . . .

Not be scared.

To value execution as well as ideas.

To encourage and champion the change-makers.

To protect against silos and turfwars at all times.

To train my staff to be knowledgeable and imaginable.

To never, ever, rest on our laurels.

And to set myself straight on the myths of innovation!

#1

80 PERCENT OF ALL NEW PRODUCTS FAIL!

As STATED in the previous chapter, fear of failure is perhaps the biggest reason why employees never even begin to take those first steps toward innovation. Why all of the trepidation and recalcitrance? Well, to be fair, it can be daunting to set foot on the path to developing a new product or service with the expectation that it will probably fail. So, a quiet bravery is required. And despite the fact that today's consumers will tell you they want new and improved things, the fact is, only a small percentage (the "early adopters") will actually be dissatisfied enough with what they already have to break ranks and take the plunge.

As we'll see later, an awful lot of things must go right in order for a new product to make it successfully. And, considering all of the challenges you face in being able to successfully innovate, it seems logical that a relatively high likelihood of failure is a reality.

After all, most marketers grow up *knowing* that 80 percent of new products fail. Right? We saw this in many of our school's textbooks. We still continue to see this in many of today's books and articles about new product development.

Where does this number come from? We're reminded of the laugh-out-loud headline observed during the 2008 presidential election: "Eight-four Percent Say They'd Never Lie to a Pollster." Should we believe them—or the 16 percent who admit they lie? Or were the 16 percent lying when they said that? The mind boggles.

Certainly, when hoping to develop something new and different, failure is a distinct possibility. *But 80 percent?* Wow, that really is a

demoralizing number! This brings us to some major questions pertain-
ing to the 80 percent product failure statement.

First, what recent study does this come from?

Second, what truly defines the criteria for "failure"?

Will the Author of 80 Percent Please Stand Up

Actually, a lot of articles still state the 80 percent failure rate. BUT it
is a myth. And, it is a very harmful myth.

As a result of this myth, some companies and upper management
become *so worried* about failure that they will go to extraordinary
lengths to avoid it. Much of the research and testing that is done is
for the purpose of trying to de-risk innovation. And the big challenge
here is that so much attention can be placed on trying to take the risk
out of innovation, that the result becomes *not* avoiding failure, BUT
rather, failing not to succeed!

The 80 percent new product failure rate is a myth because it mis-
leads us to think that this is the failure rate among all types of companies in all types of industries. It's a myth because the articles state that
this rate is based on "some type of study." Whose? We can't find it! But
that doesn't stop people from continuing to repeat it. One of the hall-
marks of myths is that people perpetuate them. That's because myths
usually include more than a little truth, but mythmakers whittle and
polish the rough edges of reality in order to produce a fable that can
be easily learned and repeated. Inevitably, reality is further distorted
with every retelling until we are left with a simplistic morality play in
which virtuous Yankees defeat wicked Confederates, or high-minded
cowboys and frontiersman defend their women from murderous thiev-
ing savages—until this myth is then turned upside down, converting
the "murderous Indians" into peace-loving Native Americans, whose
superior civilization was destroyed by greedy and violent capitalist
exploiters. The same is true of the old saw about 80 percent. 'Tis a little
true, but mostly fable.

We call it a myth because, while some articles report studies that have shown new product failure rates in the 80 percent range, many others report far more favorable results. Recent studies by the Product Development Management Association (PDMA) claim new products have a **59 percent success rate!** And, according to Robert Cooper, author of the book *Winning at New Products*, most in-depth studies site **success rates at about 65 percent**. And for products that are superior, unique, and differentiated, the success rate is an exceptional **98 percent.**

Back in 1997, a major study conducted by Linton, Matysiak and Wilkes, Inc. on 1,935 new product introductions found that the top 20 U.S. companies enjoy a **76 percent success rate!** Simultaneously, they found that among small, non-professional, non-marketing oriented firms, the success rate was a paltry 11 percent.

Finally, how could the average failure rates of new product introductions be 80 percent when one of the largest concept-testing, laboratory test-marketing, new-product testing services, BASES, promises that 90 percent of the time, actual market results will vary no more than plus or minus 20 percent from their test findings.

Mathematically, let's assume that half of the time, actual results could be on the negative side. Let's also assume *very conservatively*, that in all of these cases we would call it a failure. Then, what they promise is no greater than a 45 percent failure rate (half of the 90 percent).

If the new product development effort is guided by smart strategic thinking and the market introduction is directed by intelligent targeting, positioning, pricing, and communication, we can state with certainty that the probability of failure is far less than the dreaded 80 percent rate we have grown up with. Yet, innovation is still riskier than it needs to be, largely because of inter-company politics and poor marketing efforts.

So the truth of the matter is, just as there were virtuous cowboys and reprobate cowboys, success and failure rates vary all over the place.

But, when using a solid innovation process, and applying solid strategy and good sound marketing, there is no reason to assume that you are more likely to fail than to succeed. But even with a lower failure rate, we still must ask ourselves, are the "failures" *really* failures?

WHAT DO WE MEAN BY "FAILURE?"

In the corridors of power, the other "F-Word" is Failure: To fall short. Achieving an unfavorable outcome. Yes, but versus what, exactly? And is it truly an abject failure, or is it, in fact, a hard-won lesson?

As we've stated, the innovation process is best described as a journey. It is not merely an event. Innovation is about exploring, discovering, inventing, developing, refining, launching, and perhaps even re-launching.

When we say that sometimes failure is not truly failure at all, but rather a true cost of learning, we mean that the knowledge gained from any and every initiative can lead to a significantly profitable and successful innovation down the line. We're reminded of something Malcolm Forbes is credited with saying:

"Failure is a success, as long as we learn from it."

Now, frankly, if we were to look at every new product idea that has gone forward for a little more learning, then perhaps we can say that, yes, there have been studies that about only one in seven *ideas* makes it to success. But ideas are learning steps. Hopefully, a company's innovation process learns from each idea and kills or modifies a bad one well before spending a great deal of time and money against it. In fact, to include an "idea" as part of a "failure" would have us re-think one's attempt to walk. We believe the average toddler fails to walk until he has tried and "failed" dozens if not hundreds of times. So do we deduce that, in total, there is a 99 percent failure rate to walking? No, there is a 99 percent success rate for humans to walk.

The sticking point for many here is how one accounts for the "cost" of learning from the failure. If the cost is applied solely to the failed attempt, then of course, it is seen as a financial failure (cha-ching!). Just add it to the ever-growing legend of the 80 percent number. If on the other hand, companies allocate this cost to a future innovation that winds up being born out of this process, then it's a different story. Sure, the eventual success may be seen as *a little* less profitable, but the cost of *the failure* goes away. It becomes a cost of *the success.*

Confused? Don't be. How many times do you talk to an individual who apparently has gone through a miserable time in their lives, only to be told by that same individual that they would not have changed a thing in retrospect? Why? Because wise people realize that they have come out of the experience better, smarter, and more successful precisely because of the "misfortune" they have endured. Have you ever heard of the "College of Hard Knocks?" Well folks, this holds true for companies and inventors as well as any other kind of survivor. If it doesn't kill you it makes you stronger.

All of this reminds us of the myth of the "overnight success." Seth Godin says, "It takes about six years of hard work to become an overnight success." We've never quantified the amount of time it takes to become successful, but agree that Seth makes a very good point. It's easy to look at companies and people and gush about how they made millions "overnight." Think of all the companies no one had ever heard of for years and then, boom! They are the talk of the town. Actor-comedian Jim Carrey was failing for years as a stand-up comic, playing seedy nightclubs and living in his car before he finally achieved his "overnight success" and his $20 million-per-movie pay rate.

The heart of the matter is, so many of today's blockbuster successes came about as a result of learning from failed attempts. In fact, speaking of heart, even the first implanted artificial heart didn't exactly prove to be all that successful. In 1982, Dr. Robert Jarvic implanted the Jarvic 7 artificial heart. The Jarvic 7 artificial heart was intended to last a lifetime. Unfortunately, it only kept its first recipient, Dr. Barney Clark alive for 112 days. Hey, that's a whole lot better than what could have happened to Dr. Clark had he not received the Jarvic 7! But, as his own journal attested, 112 days is not near the "lifetime" for which the device was intended. Success? Failure? You be the judge.

Fortunately, despite its shortcomings, the first Jarvic 7 was successful enough to lead to more development, and further testing. Now, the Cario-West temporary Artificial Heart (developed and evolved from the Jarvic 7) posts a 5-year survival rate of 64 percent. It looks a little bit more like a success now, doesn't it?

And, when it comes to some of our well known inventors, like Ford and Edison, we find here too, that some of their big successes had a lot of pre-testing, costs, and failures associated with them. To make his cars more affordable to the everyday consumer, Ford realized that he needed a far more efficient way of production. He looked at other industries (a suggestion we make elsewhere in this book as an excellent way in which to find insights), found some core principles, and then took 5 years to test, fail, refine, and develop the first moving assembly line.

Among Edison's 1,093 patents and many successful innovations (most notably the light bulb, phonograph, and motion picture camera), is probably one you haven't heard of: The Edison Cement Company. Like all cement stories, this one is "hard" to believe, but Edison really did begin his company to exploit the many uses of cement, such as building counters, slabs, and houses. The only trouble was, the cost and weight of concrete made this idea a loser. But here too, enough learning went into it that eventually his cement company was hired to build Yankee Stadium.

One of today's modern-day inventors, James Dyson, inventor of Dyson Cyclone Technology, stated that he went through some 5,000 failures before he finally successfully introduced the Dyson Cyclone Vacuum. As he encourages others: "Keep on failing . . . it works!"

One thing you can't fail at is running out of examples of perceived failures that led to eventual future successes. But there are additional questions when it comes to determining the criteria for failure.

Sometimes failure occurs because expectations are set too high. In reality, the innovation is profitable, sizable, but perhaps just not as big as expected. So is the innovation a failure. Or is there a failure to set appropriate objectives and realistic expectations?

Oftentimes companies test their concepts and eventual product launches against "norms." We have seen unbridled joy and cheering occur when an initial concept "beats the norm." Conversely, coming in "below the norm" not only causes sadness and frustration, but usually the cancellation of the innovation itself and maybe even a pink slip for someone.

Wait a minute! What is the "norm" based on? We have seen product concepts intended for one type of consumer or one particular category, tested against a "norm" for all types of consumers or categories, which is frankly, absurd. Would you test a new product designed for and marketed to children against the same "norms" used for products intended to appeal to female heads-of-household? Let us hazard a guess and say that we'll bet this type of product doesn't do as well against this norm because *not every woman has young children.*

We hate to break this to "Norm," but if the marketing effort is going be directed toward a target audience of children, most models will show that awareness and purchase by the mom will be too low, simply because the mom in question is not seeing the ad for the product in the first place. But wait, what about their children who will be seeing the ad and then later asking their moms to buy it? Doesn't that count for anything? Oddly enough, many testing models will say no.

Norms and objectives are so important with regard to determining success versus failure that, to be honest, one of our clients is seriously thinking of discontinuing one of its most successful and profitable new product launches in a decade, because it is not up to the original objective as stated.

In essence, how one treats objectives goes a long way in determining success versus failure. It is truly a glass-half-empty/glass-half-full scenario. Just because a new product fails to fully hit expectations, it should not be considered a failure. Unfortunately, many people would see it that way.

Many years ago, when one of our authors was getting his marketing training at Procter & Gamble, he had the opportunity to work on readying Era Detergent for a potential market launch. Era was one of two major new product initiatives of P&G's former Packaged Soap and Detergent Division. The other initiative was Dawn dishwashing liquid. Both were in their respective test markets.

Neither Era nor Dawn achieved 100 percent of their test market objectives. However, in virtually all of the test market progress reports issued by the Era Brand Team, it was stated, "We are pleased to report that we are *within* X percent of our volume objective." Simultaneously, while achieving virtually the same results, the Dawn Brand Team reported "unfortunately, we are X percent below objective." While, attitude and communication regarding performance versus objective was just part of the story, P&G decided to introduce Era detergent first, proving once and for all that it really is darkest before the Dawn.

Sometimes, one just has to have the courage to stay with a new product launch long enough for it to catch on and ultimately become a success. It's not that consumers are so dumb that they don't quickly catch on to great ideas. It is that adoption of new products sometimes takes quite a bit of time, especially if buying the new item requires consumers to throw away or replace something they now use. Also, adoption may take longer if the new offering involves a lot of learning. Think of the metric scale. It is superior to our inches and feet measurements but it had to be learned and old tools had to be thrown out. Instead we tossed the metrics, at least for now! The length of time it takes for consumers to accept a new product is so important to understand and plan around that we address this later in this book.

High definition television is a great example of planning for a long-term adoption rate before determining success or failure. In 1999, *The Tonight Show with Jay Leno* was the first regularly scheduled nightly program ever to be broadcast in HD. It begs the question: If a lame monologue joke is told in the forest and there's no one there to hear it, does it still bomb?

NBC understood that hardly anyone could even see the show in HD back then, (only 3 percent of households had HDTV sets), but it put its big toe in the water because someone had to be first. The Consumer Electronic Association tells us that the Peacock network's future-focused decision has paid off. That's because now the HDTV household penetration stands well over 50 percent, with estimates of 61 million HDTV sets sold and one-third of HD households owning multiple sets. A great example of "if-you-build-it-they-will-come."

What would have happened if NBC looked at consumer behavior instead? Keep in mind that about 97 percent of consumers were basically saying, "We think watching Jay Leno in standard definition is just fine, thank you very much. You really needn't bother with all the hassle and expense of broadcasting in high definition. We're satisfied with what we already have." But sure enough, as more people got a chance to see demonstrations of high-def, and word-of-mouth began to spread, standard definition was no longer good enough.

But who would buy an HDTV if there were nothing on TV being broadcast in HD? Once again, someone had to be first. Did you know that in the 1950s, many television shows were actually filmed in color despite the fact that 99.9 percent of the televisions available were black and white? Why bother then? Well, producers of the programs shot in color knew that the day when all TV sets would be color was going to arrive eventually, and they wanted their shows to be the first "re-runs" to be syndicated because they would be the only ones available in color. The investment proved to pay off handsomely as many staples of 1960's re-runs were drawn from shows shot in the 1950s with the prescience of being in color (*Wagon Train, Cisco Kid,* and *Sergeant Preston of the Yukon,* to name a few).

Those brave souls shot shows in color at a time when people could only view them in black and white.Or they broadcast shows in HDTV for a whopping 3 percent of the population, despite the fact that the chances of finding a real consumer need to fill was actually quite remote. And to this day, consumers are also pretty well satisfied with the products and services they now consume. So, if history teaches us anything, it's that to be successful, you have to literally wrench consumers away from something with which they are presently pretty comfortable. Several years ago, another new P&G product, Pringles (New Fangled Potato Crisps), was considered a dismal failure because after wonderful initial trial rates, longer-term repeat rates declined far more than anticipated. It did not help when a competing chip manufacturer ran full-page ads extolling the difference between their all-natural, wonderfully simple potato chip versus P&G's potato *cookie*! Good thing P&G stayed with it. Innovative marketing in the areas of communication, packaging, flavor, and size SKUs, and more has made the brand a blockbuster today.

Lastly, on the flip side, you must never be happy with 100 percent success! If you are too successful, you must question whether you are really playing "not to lose" rather than "to win." And true innovation is about winning. In fact, P&G, which claims a success rate in the range of 50 to 60 percent, states that this is as far as it wants to go because any more and it would be a sign of playing it too safe.

So, what are we talking about when we talk failure? Is it really learning? Is it performance versus some ill-conceived norm or objective? Is it a failure in test or concept stage? Is it a failure in market? If in market, how long did it take, and was it the fault of the innovation or the marketing behind it? Is it really part of a cost that should be allocated against the entire life of a product, not just the initial stages which served a learning purpose?

You decide, but remember:

It just means some failure isn't really failure at all . . . it is learning and learning generally has a cost. And over the course of a life, whether that of a corporation, or an individual, such cost must be placed against the entire life, not just the initial stages which might have been less than successful.

"You can't begin to succeed until you are not afraid to fail."

— COFFEY, SIEGEL, SMITH

MYTH **#2** THE ROI ON INNOVATION
IS TERRIBLE

As we mentioned in our first chapter, few CEOs are happy with the return on investment made in innovation. A variation on the "innovation-never-pays-out" theme that can sometimes be heard on the upper floors of downtown high rises through cigar-chomping clenched teeth.

As you will see later in this book, this unhappiness can be alleviated with a more productive, efficient process for innovation. But usually, the biggest reason for this discontent traces back to a lack of understanding of how to properly calculate the full return on investment that innovation actually brings.

MAXIMIZE RETURNS

Handled properly, innovation can provide a company with substantial market returns far in excess of the immediate earnings that result just from a product's launch. A study on the topic of "Stock Market Returns to Innovation," conducted by Ashish Sood and Gerard J. Tellis, professors at Emory University and USC, found that the market's appreciation of innovation could best be estimated by assessing the total market returns to the *entire* innovation project.

Sood and Tellis found that the stock market is likely to reward a company throughout the firm's research and development stages as well as for the actual introduction of a new product or service. For example, announcements regarding alliances, funding or expansions for the purpose of innovation could lead to positive market returns, because they may be perceived as deterrence to a competitor's entry, an enhancement of a company's competitive position, and an overall probability of increased sales and profits.

Notices regarding development activities such as working proto-types, demonstrations, patents, and future events could be seen by the market as a signal of confidence and optimism about the future. In fact, because they offer the greatest reduction of uncertainty in the marketplace, it was discovered that announcements of develop-ment activities generally secure the highest returns over any other announcements in the innovation project.

Fans of automobiles may recall this notion brought to life begin-ning in the 1950s with the advent of the "dream car." Following the wounds of war, the dream car was an explicit sign of optimism, a vision of a bright future, a sometimes naïve concession to provoca-tion and escapism—but a brilliant way to gin up the interest in a particular car company. By offering the public the auto company's vision of pure beauty, free of the restrictive standards demanded by the production chain, people would be more apt to buy the actual practical models for sale in the showroom. Today, the "dream" con-tinues to look to the future, and has matured and been translated into the "concept car," but the incentives to build optimism for the future remain.

There are often other "hidden" returns from an investment in innovation that might show up in areas not directly associated with the innovation itself. For example, we have talked before about how the introduction of a noteworthy new product can lift the morale of an entire organization. In these situations companies can sometimes enjoy greater efficiency in hiring and maintaining staff. Employees enjoy staying with a "winning" in-the-news com-pany and may forgo an offer by a competing company where the future may be in question. Further, top-performers generally want to work for top companies. All of this makes it easier for a firm to attract good people and do so with fewer marketing and advertis-ing dollars. Yet, firms never allocate these "returns" to the innova-tion itself.

There might also be additional "halo" returns from an innovation in the area of improved sales of a company's *existing* items. Retailers and other distributors may find themselves more willing to buy a firm's other, already existing items, in order to be able to purchase adequate supplies of a firm's new product. As a result, sales and returns on the firm's *other* products may improve without any additional investment on their part.

Further, if the innovation is an extension of an already existing brand, the advertising investment required to launch the new innovation may also benefit the sales of the existing brand. A classic example of this is when Aunt Jemima, a brand that once only offered pancake mix, introduced Aunt Jemima syrup. Not only did it sell a lot of the new Aunt Jemima syrup product, but the advertising behind its introduction also reportedly lifted sales of the pancake mix. How? Because consumers associate one item with the other and therefore will see an ad for Aunt Jemima syrup and immediately think, "Oh, Aunt Jemima pancakes now makes a syrup, too!"

Minimize the investment

When it comes to the other part of the equation, the "investment," good learning, experimentations, and due diligence up front can significantly help reduce wasteful dollar spending.

Management of innovation and new products is largely the *management of risk*. And, to reduce risk, you must be prepared to pay for relevant information—information that while somewhat costly, is miniscule relative to the heavy development, manufacturing, and marketing investment needed, as the new product is made ready, and finally launches into the marketplace.

It really boils down to knowing how many dollars to "bet" and when to bet them. A smart innovation process encourages spending more for up-front learning, where the costs are cheap. This allows you to delay having to ante up big dollars for actual development, manufacturing, and marketing *until* you have a lot more knowledge and a ton more confidence.

Let us illustrate this. Suppose, for $10,000, you had the opportunity to pick one card from a deck of 52 and if that one card is the ace of spades, you win $10 million. As enticing as the $10 million prize is, most of us would walk away. After all, there is a 98 percent chance of losing your investment.

But suppose that before you had to invest your full $10,000, you were able to buy down the deck, let's say, for an extra $100 you could cut the deck by one-quarter and then know if the remaining deck still held the ace of spades. Ooh, now it's a 1 in 39 chance. Okay let's go on. After passing that test, suppose that for another $400 you could buy and discard 19 of the remaining cards—enabling you to then learn if the ace is still in the last 20 cards. You've have spent a total of $500 and now if you gamble your $10,000 you have a 1 in 20 chance of making $10 million. Still chancy but getting better.

Okay, okay, we've learned a lot. Now, for a little more money we can learn even more. For another $500 you'll get to see every remaining card but the last two. Now you have whittled it down to just two cards and, if you are lucky, one is the ace of spades.

Sorry, that's all we're willing to give you. But look what you did! You did not have to ante up your $10,000 investment until the odds were 50/50. It probably gave you a lot more confidence. If you were unlucky, it cost you $1,000 or maybe as little as $100 (if you lost in the first bet). By paying upfront, in stages, you paid for knowledge. This knowledge put you in place to reduce your risk until you had much better odds.

Oh you might still lose. Just like in the real world, the failure rate of smart companies is far lower than those who just jump into the marketplace without proper testing. Remember from Myth #1 that successful companies (that have good processes and pay for information and testing up front) *succeed* almost 80 percent of the time. Others, who do not follow proper processes, failed almost 90 percent of the time. Finally, according to Robert Cooper, author of *Winning at New Products*, the average ROI for successful new products is 96.9 percent and pays out within 2.5 years. Fifty percent of successful new products achieve better than a 33 percent ROI.

It is no wonder then that smart companies will do what it takes to maximize their learning in order to minimize the likelihood of poor investments. Learning, through properly conducted concept tests, usage tests and even in-market tests, can greatly improve ROI. First, such research can help to uncover weaker ideas and encourage firms not to pursue what could be a costly mistake. Second, research results could provide guidance to help a company improve upon its original idea, thereby, maximizing consumer demand for the new product. This would result in more sales per dollar of marketing investment.

The key here is to do this research *carefully*. There are an amazing number of shortfalls and *mistakes* companies will make during this most important phase of the innovation process that can produce some horrendous results down the line. As you continue your journey through our book, you'll learn more about this.

While there is little argument that even a modest amount of learning and experimentation can save a lot of dollars, you must nevertheless accomplish this quickly due to the rapid speed in which innovations are now taking place. While admittedly not as thorough or accurate as broad-scale representative research, there is no reason that a firm can't at least use employees and friends to test or use potential new products and report as to their likes and dislikes. This can be a very efficient way in which to uncover potential red flags.

Involving your manufacturing organization and suppliers in the early stages of product development is another way to minimize wasteful investments, helping to ensure that the cost of the final product is as low as possible. Some product development experts state that 80 percent of the final cost of a new product is determined in the first 20 percent of the design cycle. Manufacturing and suppliers can suggest part substitutions, product adjustments, and more to help make the product assembly and final product cost as efficient and as low as possible. Conversely, when manufacturers and suppliers are brought in too late, you may find that the actual product tested in research could be unaffordable to ultimately manufacture and distribute.

WHAT'S UP PARTNER? SAVING MONEY!

Yet, an additional way to minimize the investment and risk is to share it with another company. Sharing risk with strategic partners is actually now becoming a more acceptable way in which to go to market. A good strategic partner can not only help share the financial commitment but also bring on a range of skills or assets that the original innovating company may lack—skills and assets that again, would cost more investment dollars.

Consider if one company has an extremely strong brand in one particular category, for example, cereals. Suppose it had solid research that its brand could do extremely well in an additional or different category, for example Frozen Novelties. However, to do business in this new category would require significant investment in manufacturing, and distribution, not to mention the need to perhaps hire additional sales help to approach the different buyers in this new category.

A prudent strategy might be to approach a strategic partner who is already currently marketing in the frozen novelty category and form a partnership. Each brings its particular strength to the partnership and greatly reduces the overall investment. The original innovating company does not have to invest in manufacturing, distribution, and sales costs. The new partner company will enjoy better efficiency from its existing manufacturing, distribution, and sales assets *and* will not have to invest in possible competitive actions that might be needed to thwart the efforts of a potentially strong new brand entering its category. The result? Overall, a far better return with far less additional investment.

There is a lot written lately about the term "Open Innovation." Change is happening so fast, and new products are coming to market so quickly that traditional "closed" innovation is being challenged in favor of a newly accepted strategy of Open Innovation. Open Innovation, was first promoted in 2003 by Henry Chesbrough, a professor and executive director at the Center for Open Innovation at Berkeley. The central idea behind open innovation is that in a world of widely distributed knowledge, it benefits a company not to be constrained by the use of its own internal knowledge. Instead a company could buy or license processes or inventions from other companies.

Open Innovation can be a significant tool in helping today's firms keep overall costs in line. Specifically, while internal R&D should remain an important aspect of product innovation, firms do not have to let the potential need for requiring heavy funding on equipment, space, and personnel severely limit their overall ability to grow. When a company opens its mind to more aggressively explore Open Innovation, it puts itself in a better position to develop new products with the help of *someone else's* budget, which spreads the risk and enables it to remain more flexible in leveraging its internal resources. Not a bad thing.

Using Open Innovation or at least some form of outside help is becoming so acceptable to some companies that they are actually *proud* of the fact that much of their innovation *is* "not invented here." One key finding in an IBM 2006 Global CEO Study of 765 CEOs and business leaders was that, in the minds of top executives, "external collaboration is indispensable." We again quote A.G. Lafley, CEO of P&G who says: "We want to be known as the company that collaborates—inside and out—better than any other company in the world."

Importantly, Open Innovation also encourages a company to generate funds from inventions that it has no intention of marketing. Specifically, internal inventions not being used in a firm's business could be licensed, joint-ventured, or spun off outside the company. This not only generates wealth from ideas that otherwise would have sat around and collected dust, but also provides a value to the marketplace and keeps a firm's entrepreneurial people motivated and loyal. Talk about a *great* return!

One of the key reasons that is often attributed to Procter & Gamble's dramatic turn around has been its version of Open Innovation called: "Connect and Develop." Through this practice, the company's R&D and other departments are strongly encouraged to connect with outsiders and work toward a company goal of having at least one-half of all new product introductions come from outside the company by 2010.

One particular example of success from Procter & Gamble's Open Innovation practice involved its Pringles brand. Specifically, P&G wished to place jokes and sayings on actual Pringles chips. As you might guess, trying to print on a potato chip is about as easy as dancing to talk-radio. Even the great minds of P&G couldn't figure that one out, at least not without spending a huge amount of time and dollars in the process. But, by openly soliciting help, an answer surfaced from a small bakery in Italy that had been printing edible images on desserts. Apparently you can read your cake and eat it too, when in Rome.

Glad ForceFlex, Swiffer Dusters, Olay Regenerist, and the Crest Spin-Brush are just four of more than 130 other P&G products developed through their "Connect and Develop" initiative over the past few years.

WHEN WILL DILIGENCE GET ITS DUE?

You've probably heard the expression "opportunity knocks," but did you know there is also a saying that "opportunity blinds!" It is amazing how many times we may wish for something so badly that we somehow ignore bad news. One of the authors of this book actually fell victim to this several years ago. He was presented with a novel idea for, of all things, a superior car washing operation. The author, wanting at that time to dramatically increase his income, wanted this opportunity so badly that "somehow" he failed to do the proper market-testing.

Oh, he studied national averages, did all of the right spending ratios, and consulted the national associations, but he never did a local market assessment. And, the local market he invested in wound up having dramatically different use patterns than the average market nationally. Oh, but he knew better than that! He knew that he should also look at the local market numbers. But, he did just "enough" research to help him feel good about his investment decision. As a result of his blindness, that "wonderful" opportunity cost him dearly. Things did not come out all right in the wash, and he was left high and dry instead.

You'd be surprised how often we have seen companies or other investors pursue what they think are highly innovative ideas when, with a little due diligence, they could have discovered that their "new" ideas already existed in the market.

One of our favorite examples occurred several years ago when DSI, a toy company (which no longer exists, hint, hint!) went to investment bankers/underwriters to raise money to go public. During DSI's pitch, the CEO unveiled the **next big thing** in toys that they were planning for the next year. It was a cool-looking, remote-controlled toy motorcycle.

To the delight and amazement of the bankers, DSI's CEO impressively took this "soon-to-be-hot-can't-miss" remote controlled motorcycle toy for a test drive up and down the bank's huge conference table. The bankers loved it. The investment dollars came hand-over-fist. The big oversight? Had they done just a little due diligence, the eager investors would have seen that the DSI toy was just like two others that were already on the market! Within two years, the company did an Evel Knievel-style crash and burn and was gone—and so was the investment.

Just look at all of the venture capitalists that invested so heavily in the Dot.Com Era of the late 1990s. Seriously. Did anyone stop to ask how in the world were those dotcoms going to actually earn money? We all should have realized that anything coming from a place called "Silicon Valley" was probably too good to be real.

More recently, how did the United States of America, the richest nation on earth, whose economy represents 30 percent of the global economy, arrive at the precipice of a financial panic and collapse? Had there not been a steady and constant infusion of "easy money" and credit into the U.S. economy by the Fed for years on end, a housing bubble of the magnitude of the one that exploded in 2008 could never have been created. Had the politicians of both parties not coerced and pressured banks, S&Ls, Fannie Mae, and Freddie Mac to make all those sub-prime mortgages, then to tie this rotten paper to good paper, convert it into securities, and sell to banks all over the world, there would have been no global financial crisis.

But that would have required due diligence. Instead, we were required as taxpayers to give 5 percent of our gross domestic product to buy up suspect securities backed by sub-prime mortgages.

Naturally, innovation requires an immediate investment in time and funding in return for *potential future* revenues and profits. We've also discussed elsewhere in this book that the possibility of failure, while not as high as the 80 percent rate that some have reported, is still a distinct possibility. But, as we hope to have persuaded you by now, it is a very necessary investment for long-term survival and growth.

All of the evidence suggests that, when a successful innovation is launched, its effects on company earnings can be enormous—if calculated properly. Most studies show that 35 percent of a firm's annual revenues are generated from products or services that were not in existence five years before.

After all, isn't it better to spend proactively on first-to-market innovation with the hope of growing the business, rather than be forced to use precious dollars in a reactionary way to defend from an attack by a new innovative *competitor?*

We have to agree with Peter Drucker when he says:

"The only way to predict the future is to create it!"

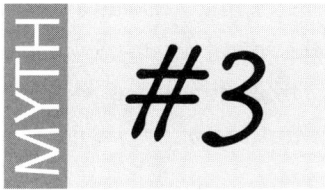

MYTH #3 — Don't Bother Unless it's Perfect

Oooh, this can be a deadly myth. Unfortunately, it is one of the most popular and enduring myths that we encounter because it is held by so many, including Art Directors. They tend to work and work just to get that "perfect" typeface on the new package. Then there are the Product Designers, looking for that bottle with the perfect feel and touch. Not to mention the R&D departments that can spend as much time as they are allowed, just to explore the newest technologies. Finally, there are even some executives who happen to feel that the new product is just not quite good enough for them. Beware of the old bromide: *"Keep fixing it until it's broken."*

We are also reminded of a story we like to tell, in which Henry Kissinger continued to ask Winston Lord "Is this the best you can do?" every time he handed him a draft policy paper. After nine attempts at revising the document the staffer finally replied in exasperation "Yes, this is the best I can do!" and Kissinger says "Good, now I'll read it." That's nice, and now he had a more perfect report, but what *significant* new learning did he get from that report versus what he would have obtained from the original? And how much added time did it take for Winston Lord to "polish and hone to perfection" just to give Kissinger the same basic information? More importantly, how many additional critical facts could have been reported and learned in other reports that Lord could have been working on instead of trying to make a single report "perfect?"

To be clear, we are not preaching laziness here. Far from it. And we would never advocate the marketing of "schlock" products. Quite frankly, we *are* demanding perfection, but what we are actually seeking is a perfection that *the consumer* has to perceive—not you! And that's simply because there is a law of diminishing returns at play here. Prudence and pragmatism should be the rule of the day. So, allow us to simply remind all you innovators, manufacturers, and marketers that you are always making products for *the consumer*—not for yourselves.

You recovering perfectionists out there are probably asking yourselves: *"What's the problem with taking the extra time and effort to make things perfect? So perfect in fact, that the end result is even better than what the consumer is expecting!"* What's so wrong about that, you ask? Plenty!

First of all, perfection always takes time and money. This means that the cost of developing the new product will be higher than it has to be and will negatively impact the ROI. It could also mean having to pass some of this extra cost on to the consumer, especially if it is in the use of better, more premium materials.

Speed to market can be especially important when trying to head off an emerging competitor or capitalize on a window of opportunity that might present itself, like perhaps some extra capacity opening up in the sales force at a certain month on the calendar. Speed is also important considering corporate goals and manpower availability. Then there is the sad fact that the marketplace changes so rapidly.

Take too long trying to perfect your innovation and any upfront consumer testing that was done to validate the idea in the first place may no longer be applicable. Even the best new product can fail if introduced too late. The companies that can respond to quickly changing needs will flourish and those that can't will be left behind. Speed to market is a crucial element in being successful in the global marketplace. As the brilliant General George S. Patton reminds us in a famous quote: *"A good plan implemented today, is better than a perfect plan implemented tomorrow."*

Placing too much attention on perfecting a new product also creates lost opportunities. People and staff who are spending too much time on perfecting one item cannot simultaneously be working on the development of another. Too much funding going to negligibly improve a new product means less money available to explore the development and launch of other products.

The truth of the matter is, companies should orient the new product or service to deliver "just enough" to satisfy the customer. **That is truly perfection.** No consumer will pay for "too much" or pay for "more than he needs." The only person that will pay for more than what is needed is you! As A.G. Lafley, CEO of Procter & Gamble likes to say: *"Perfection is the enemy of good enough."*

Of course Lafley is paraphrasing Voltaire. The original quote in French is *"Le mieux est l'ennemi du bien."* Literally translated, as *"The best is the enemy of good,"* but is more commonly cited as *"The perfect is the enemy of the good."* In other words, pursuing the "best" solution may end up doing less actual good than accepting a solution that, while not perfect, is effective. You could also infer that the best makes that which is good seem to be worth less, which would not be a great business practice to follow with regard to innovation or anything else, for that matter!

The bottom line is, when you or your company want a perceived upgrade in some manner, be it lifestyle, software, processes, or new product "refinements," be circumspect. Have you ever known someone who was considering moving across town for a slightly better house, only to lose a lot of money in realtor's commission and closing fees? It happens.

Our takeaway from Voltaire's original point about "perfection," specifically, rather than simply "better," is that to attain a perfect new product, whatever it may be, becomes infinitely more difficult as you near it. So, at some point, you have to cut your losses, and simply say, "Good enough." As we have said, this is not a justification for shoddy workmanship or laziness, because that would certainly not meet our standard for "Good enough." The point is more to know when to realize that any additional effort toward improvement will result in a trifling improvement, especially in comparison to the effort required.

You also have to consider the limits of human capacity, as even the great Einstein has warned. History has shown us time and again that those who wish to implement utopia go to murderous lengths to achieve it at the price of life and liberty. We also see it in those children who, stricken with the need for perfection (a solipsism in itself) ruin their lives in that futile pursuit. They simply cannot finish any project because it could be "improved."

We know of physicians and researchers who have found that fellow physicians, fellow researchers, and, most importantly, patients have used the promise of perfection (or the expectation of perfection) as a rationale for doing nothing, while rejecting actions that would have achieved beneficial, but not perfect results.

You'll never get anywhere with innovation or new product development when a "good" solution isn't pursued because its not "perfect," or when nothing at all is attempted, simply because perfection won't be attained.

Perfection is a mirage. You can't reach it, and the more time you try to get to it the more time you waste. Aiming for excellence is wonderful, but aiming for perfection is just bad business practice.

One of our favorite stories concerns the ceramics teacher who announced on opening day that she was dividing the class into two groups. All those on the left side of the studio, she said, would be graded solely on the quantity of the work they produced. All those on the right, would be graded solely on their quality of their work.

Her procedure was simple: On the final day of class she would bring in her bathroom scales and weigh the work of the quantity group; fifty pounds of ceramics rated an "A", forty pounds a "B," and so on. Those being graded on quality, however, needed to produce only one ceramic pot—albeit a "perfect one"—to get an A.

What do you think happened? Surprisingly, at grading time, the works with the highest quality were all produced by the group who was being graded for *quantity*.

It seems that while the quantity group was busily churning out piles of work—and learning from their mistakes—the quality group had sat theorizing about perfection, and in the end, had little more to show for their efforts than grandiose theories and a pile of clay.

What costs more money, the clay it took to learn, or the time spent thinking without any tangible results? Naturally, the time it took to produce inferior results costs more. By far. But be sure to ask yourself if the clay pots still worked, as clay pots should? And, importantly, did the knowledge gained from making better clay pots have any value?

The analogy for innovation and the development of new products is clear. By focusing on quantity that can be produced now and demonstrated now, you can learn more about your product or service than you will with a plan for what the product might be years from now with some open-ended quality bar. And since none of us would be willing to ship a poor-quality product, the experimentation will continue to occur. The only difference with this example is that experimenting with numerous "clay pots" in the short term is probably less expensive than making one at a time in the long term.

A *BusinessWeek* article suggested "imperfect technology greases innovation—and the whole marketplace." So, if you'll permit us to paraphrase Voltaire: "Perfection is the enemy of innovation." Why? Perfection is expensive, unattainable, time consuming and limits flexibility—all qualities needed for innovation.

It seems fitting to end this chapter with yet another quote, this time from H. Jackson Brown, Jr. (former ad agency creative director and the author of the *New York Times* bestseller *Life's Little Instruction Book*.)

"Some things need doing better than they've ever been done before. Some just need doing. Others don't need doing at all. Know which is which."

Amen to that, Brother Brown!

MYTH #4 — WHEN IT COMES TO INVESTMENT IN R&D, SIZE MATTERS!

OH, NO IT DOESN'T!

In the last five years, Hewlett-Packard invested 15 percent in R&D while Dell invested only 5 percent, yet still managed to clean HP's proverbial clock.

How?

Simple. Despite HP's corporate mantra ("We are the technology company that invents the useful and the significant"), Dell out-innovated them in process innovations led primarily by their operations folks. Innovation that leads to sustainable competitive advantage can be initiated and led by any organization in the company. R&D represents the engineering department's lead, and in general pays off well in double-digit growth markets and increasingly poorly in single-digit growth markets. If you ever want a good barometer of your company's lack of innovative thinking, the continuation of major investments in R&D during slow-growth markets may be as good an indicator as any.

General Motors, despite being the first U.S. company to enjoy annual revenues in excess of $1 billion and despite reportedly out-spending all of its competition on R&D, now continues to struggle with billions of dollars in losses. Toyota, by contrast, has been growing virtually everywhere it does business, with record profits in 2007. It ascended to #1 worldwide in 2008. Toyota, today's automotive monster, did not come close to outspending GM in R&D dollars, but found a way to develop its products and processes faster and more efficiently. In fact, Toyota is considered one of the top 10 percent of corporations in the world that get the most out of every R&D dollar.

Having swept by Chrysler and Ford, and topping GM in sales in the U.S. market in 2008, how is Toyota (which documents a million internal innovation submissions a year with the vast majority having nothing to do with product) succeeding? First, it makes fine cars, and it revolutionized the industry by getting out of "used" cars and instead selling "Certified Pre-Owned" cars. Second, Japan is showing some innovation of its own by manipulating its currency to keep it cheap against the dollar, to keep the price of Japanese autos below comparable U.S. models. Third, Tokyo strategically maintains a lock on its home market by imposing a value added tax on auto imports from America, and rebating that tax on autos and parts exported to America. This double-subsidy can give a Japanese car a 15 percent price advantage over a Ford or GM car in both markets.

It is even a genius of innovation that, in setting up plants here in the U.S., Japanese auto companies are free of the "legacy costs" of pensions and health insurance for retired U.S. workers. Japanese companies have almost no retired American workers. Legacy costs at GM, Ford, and Chrysler must be factored into the price of every car.

To stay competitive in their home market, U.S. manufacturers are closing down plants, laying off American workers, and building their cars outside the United States. Hardly a recipe for innovation.

A Booz Allen Hamilton global innovation study conducted among the top 1,000 public companies spending the most in R&D, found no simple relationship between R&D spending and corporate performance. While boosting R&D spending may increase the number of patents a firm controls, neither the number of patents, nor their quality was found to have any relationship with future corporate financial performance.

In fact, only two companies on the list of top 50 in R&D expenditure were actually on the list of the top 50 most innovative companies.

Unfortunately, part of the reason for the discrepancy in R&D spending and its results lie in the facts that many R&D labors are unfocused and waste money in duplicating efforts or reinventing items others have already examined. Good ideas often get stuck in bottlenecks and silos. Consumer understanding and appropriate market planning may also be lacking. But there is another side of this equation. Namely, that more results are being traced to better thinking and better overall innovation processes.

In its report "New Concepts in Innovation," the Business Council of Australia agrees with the authors of this book that a more 21st century view of innovation should include almost *any* strategic or operational business change that delivers new outcomes, and that the less contemporary, more traditional focus on R&D is flawed. As our Toyota example proves, it is precisely because business innovation does occur through a range of mechanisms such as business strategy, management practices, process adaptation, and capital investment in new plants and equipment that the R&D correlation is no longer a reliable indicator. In fact, many firms are rolling out new metrics to conduct measurements of "non-technological" innovation.

So if all of this is true, why do firms lagging in innovation continue to spend (waste?) more and more money on R&D? Because some of them still feel it is a measurement of commitment to innovation. They simply operate under the old school bromide that firms that pursue R&D are "valued more highly" and "perform more profitably" than firms that do not. This really isn't old school thinking. It's thinking from the school they tore down to build the old school.

So, even as you roll your eyes when watching your 401(k) fluctuate, don't panic when you see that U.S. companies are spending less on R&D (as a percentage of worldwide R&D from 43 percent in 1986 to 32 percent in 2006). Let's get in the Way Back Machine together and listen to what Steve Jobs said on November 9, 1998 in *Fortune* Magazine:

"Innovation has nothing to do with how many R&D dollars you have. When Apple came up with the Mac, IBM was spending at least 100 times more on R&D. It's not about money. It's about the people you have, how you're led, and whether you get it."

I don't know about you, but I feel better now. I feel better because what Jobs is saying is that the greatest innovators today aren't really *product* innovators, they're companies and people who build new business *models*. And you don't get there from here by simply increasing your R&D spending. On the contrary. Instead it comes from a change in the way an entire organization looks at opportunities to innovate itself and its markets.

There is no doubt that this takes big-time courage and leadership to buck the incumbent business models, no matter how well entrenched. But the fact of the matter is that it is always easier to stay the course than to set a new course.

One of the biggest innovation myths out there is that the iPod was a new product. Not. Every single piece of the iPod product already existed and in fact was sourced elsewhere by Apple. There was absolutely no innovation involved with the *product*. Ah, but the true innovation was the iTunes *business model*, which every competitor and analyst deemed insane, by the way. And it *was* completely starkers—until it changed the way we all behave. Apple's business model called for generating revenue not just through the sales of iPods, but also through convenient, relatively low-priced sales of downloadable content through iTunes! Now it seems like we were the crazy ones for not figuring it out sooner. Go ask some stakeholders at Sony and see if they would agree.

The most interesting thing about the ramp up to the iPod is that Apple's percent of R&D relative to sales was steadily *dropping* from 8 percent in 2001 all the way down to a measly 3 percent in 2007. But if you look at what Apple's stock price was doing during this same time frame, you would see that between 2001 and 2007, the stock price was *up* more than 2,400 percent. Do you see the deep set of values in play that are constantly emerging around innovation?

The authors of this book aren't saying that R&D is going to go away. Of course not. There is always a vital role for R&D to play in the investment of new ideas, but if you ask us what will be playing an even bigger role in creating value and wealth going forward, it isn't the products—it's the models. As our previous myth (The ROI on innovation is terrible) reminds us: innovation is about more than R&D, you just have to figure out how to measure the way you invest in and reward innovation beyond R&D. Because the fact is you *can* measure innovation outside R&D. It's not a black art. Believe us. It wasn't that long ago that folks were saying you couldn't be scientific about quality in manufacturing either; so don't believe everything you hear—especially the myths.

In short, it is not the money spent in R&D that guarantees the best overall performance in innovation, but rather a company's capabilities and that usually comes down to the genius of human capital.

MYTH #5   THE BEST INNOVATIONS COME FROM FOLLOWING TRENDS

MOST OF US TALK in terms of "following" the trend. And that's where the trouble begins when it comes to innovation. How can innovation "follow" anything? Aren't the two mutually exclusive?

Of course, for the die-hard innovator, "current trend" would be an oxymoron.

That's because we want to *capitalize* on a trend, not follow it. As demonstrated in our previous myth, our job is to uncover the "what-can-be" and the "why not?" versus rehashing the "what-is" or "what-has-been."

Just about every major innovation in the history of the planet actually cut against the grain. After all, a breakthrough by definition cannot be lockstep with history. And the best innovations are hard to imitate simply because they accelerate or contradict history in their quest to be new and different.

Naturally, there are two sides to every story, and one argument says that for every person that likes something, there is inevitably going to be a person who does not. You can put this to the test easily. Look at any major motion picture release. You'll find critics who rave that it's Oscar bait and you'll find critics who pan every minute of it while complaining that they lost two hours of their life that they'll never get back. Every election cycle we have Senate seats that come down to fewer than 100 votes out of millions cast to determine the winner. Essentially, you never see polls that show the public 100 percent in favor of anything. So, when you are busily running after something "trendy," not only are you shooting where the rabbit *was* (which is anathema to innovation), but you'll also ignore the opportunities that may exist if you run in the opposite direction.

For example, the conventional wisdom says that this country is in the midst of an obesity crisis, right? Then what in Heaven's name is Burger King doing? McDonald's put Ronald on a diet and began offering salads, but Burger King decided that calories and fat are the way to customers' hearts. Literally. Remember the "Enormous Omelet Sandwich" with 46 grams of fat and 1,950 milligrams of salt? It was everything people love in a breakfast sandwich, but twice the size and twice as satisfying, according to the sales pitch anyway. The strategy led to a 20 percent increase in breakfast sales by catering to hardcore fast-food addicts. Burger King discovered that although fast-food fans made up only 18 percent of the population, they accounted for almost half of their profits. The company's CEO said in a *Newsweek* article that these menu options were "democratic choices." So how did Burger King capitalize on a trend? They went against it, of course!

Our own client, Wendy's, did not launch a new low-cal diet burger, but rather, "The Baconator!"

Years ago, we were consulting for the Borden Company, working on their non-dairy creamer, Cremora. Back then the big trend was to reduce fats, so everyone was going fat-free, of course. It ignored the fact that coffee drinkers use creamers to make their java deliciously creamy, not deliciously fat free! While the top brass at Borden continued to insist that Cremora launch a fat-free version (that would predictably have some major taste shortcomings), our own hunch was to go counter-trend. We tested an Extra Rich and Creamy version of Cremora. The testing results were through the roof. In fact, they beat the scores for the original recipe version of Cremora that was on the shelf at the time. Oh, and if you're wondering why you don't remember "Extra Rich and Creamy Cremora," it's because it never launched. Upper management ignored the scores and continued to fret over media pressure and the trends. Did we neglect to mention that Borden is no longer in business?

Don't get us wrong, we love trends, and we are always looking at them. But we use them as stimulus, and we also use them outside the category of any given brand we're working with to ensure that the trends inform, but do not dictate any "happy hunting grounds" of opportunity.

THE END OF TREND?

Matt Mattus speculates in his book *Beyond Trend: How to Innovate in an Over-Designed World* that trends may have outlived their usefulness if you're counting on them to lead you toward innovation. Of course they will always have their place as a form of stimulus in adjacent or near categories, but in and of themselves, they are becoming homogenized.

Why?

Mattus explains that behind the doors of the world's most competitive businesses, intellectual property is quietly becoming the best new way to look at brands and their development, not trends. This radical shift in thinking is happening because intellectual property combines the ideas of meaning, story, and creativity to go much further than any original expression of a product's trend arc could possibly do. And tracking a particular brand's intellectual properties can lead into more surprising and effective experiences then pure trend following. As a marketer, you may prefer to call this notion more of the "emotional quotient" of a trend or say that it is the story of the brand's trend (the meaning of the brand's journey or "brand essence").

It's essentially a way of articulating the emotional connection and lasting impression that defines the qualities, personality, and uniqueness of a brand. That intellectual property characterizes what a brand stands for in the minds of customers and stakeholders. It embodies the brand's core competencies, advantages, culture, and values.

You can even think of it as the heart and soul of a product or service. And since it establishes a positive, powerful connection with everyone it touches, it's worth keeping an eye on. Because, let's face it, relationships change. Every innovator digging for gold should pay attention to everything that represents the relationship and intrinsic value a brand provides to the customer. It can be an invaluable source of inspiration.

If you view intellectual properties, or brand essence as a type of long-term positioning, you'll see how it can be reflected in the quality and evolution of a product, how it is communicated and marketed, the type of care and concern customers receive, and the way stakeholders support it; you'll find a rich source of material around which to ideate.

Hallmark is an interesting example. A few years ago it liked to use the phrase, "Enriching Lives" to capture its intellectual property and company culture. Enriching Lives represented the basis for how Hallmark served customers, innovated new products, communicated, marketed, and merchandised its stores. It permeated every aspect of the company and business all the way to the work environment. But if you were keeping an eye on how Enriching Lives continued to serve the brand over time, you would notice a shift. Now Hallmark prefers "Caring Shared." What went into that decision and what does it mean for the future with regard to broader areas of opportunity for innovation?

Keep in mind that an organization's intellectual property or brand essence may be summed up in a few words, but it is *not* the company's slogan or tagline. Hallmark's *essence* is now "Caring Shared," but its tagline is "What memory will you make?" Nike's tagline is "Just do it!" but Nike's essence is "authentic athletic performance."

The intellectual property of the Target brand might be described as "cheap chic"; the emotional benefit might be the ability to look stylish and hip, even on a budget. When doing innovation work for Target, you'd have to follow that gestalt to see where it would lead. We can see today how their iconic advertising, packaging, retail design, and stylish, but affordable, merchandise are staying true to its intellectual property.

Whatever you call this perspective, it explains why following brands could be more helpful than following trends in your search for inspiration. Just consider the explosion of brands in odd and unexpected places! Through the lens of brand expansion into storytelling and entertainment, Mattus believes the role of innovators in today's business environment is now forever changed. And we agree with him. It is generally accepted as an inevitable that it will no longer be enough to simply communicate an innovation with a consumer. If only it were that simple! Rather, our job will be more to move the end-user emotionally, in the deepest possible way. Mattus set out to quite literally travel the world to see what he could learn from marketing powerhouses and young upstarts alike. All in an effort to "follow the trends." Ah, but this turned out to be a *myth*stake as we would soon find out.

That's because from Tokyo to Milan, Los Angeles to London, he explored whatever he could find by way of "current trends" and instead of triumphantly discovering inspiration, he discovered a whole lot of . . . nothing. Around the world, nothing much was new! Sure there are some micro-trends (mid-century modernism in design, the Green Movement, and so forth), but Mattus already knew about those from the safety of his office before even setting foot on a plane. There is a global sameness that is pervasive. Beyond the obvious cultural differences in Japan or England, the McDonald's and Ikea stores there are pretty much the McDonald's and Ikea stores here, proving the myth behind following trends.

But uncovering emerging trends that might be bubbling under in specialty boutiques and one-off artist shops is another matter, as is applying your own discernment and imagination to existing trends as we explain in detail elsewhere in this book. Following the *trajectory* of a trend is a critical element.

That's because the Next Big Thing was invented decades ago. Did you know the Internet is 40 years old? Or that Dr. Martin Cooper invented the cell phone 36 years ago, but it took many, many years for the industry to approach "full bloom" status? In nearly every case, it takes more than a generation for a major innovation to gain a significant foothold in the marketplace.

In general it takes more than a generation for a major innovation to gain a significant foothold in the marketplace.

So as you ponder what the next great innovation will be (beyond the one you are personally working on, of course!), take a look around. It's probably already been invented, but you're not going to see it in McDonald's or Ikea, because they are home to current trends. You may, however, uncover them in that underground boutique. This is simply due to the fact that most great trends have a small, but growing base of fans and are being carefully watched by a few industry analysts like the authors of this book—and their loyal readers.

Naturally, trends aren't always "things," either. Time compression is one of largest of emerging trends that can be a wonderful catalyst for innovation if you follow the curves. Even though technology is the engine that propels it today, time compression actually began over 150 years ago with the introduction of time zones. It got another big shot in the arm during the 1940s with the introduction of fast food and the first microwave oven (not to mention instant photography and the commercial airliner). Computer technology was the next Great Leap Forward and raised the bar even further when Moore's Law and its 18-month cycles moved the product development needle from steady to a blur—until it has reached to point of drinking out of a fire hose.

But let's look at time compression more closely as an example. Now that every kid is growing up in a new gadget world, they have become, by necessity, multitaskers. It would have been unthinkable in the 1940s to drive a car while talking on the phone, eating a drive-thru hamburger and tuning the dial on your satellite radio. So let's not follow the trend, but let's follow the trend's accompanying *trajectory*.

In the 1920s, the average U.S. adult slept almost 9 hours each night. By 2008, that figure had declined into fewer than 7 hours. More than a third of all lunches are eaten "on the run." Almost three-quarters of people today watch TV while simultaneously surfing the web. See how understanding the trajectory of time compression could be one of the keys to unlocking future consumer behavior?

We will consistently demonstrate throughout this book that Innovation is both an art and a science. This is the perfect place to illustrate some of the science with little empirical evidence, most notably the hard, cold facts of the stock market.

Michael Covel wrote a blockbuster book a few years ago that is as invaluable today as it was then, *Trend Following: How Great Traders Make Millions in Up or Down Markets*. It's a classic and a must-read for anybody involved with the markets, even if you are just blindly plowing money into your retirement accounts. It is also a wonderful illustration of principles that apply to innovation. You might infer from the title that "following" trends is the way to go, but Covel explodes that myth beautifully. By "following," Covel means to understand, monitor, and track the trends—not pursue, go behind, tag along, or chase. The difference is key for the greatest innovators, and greatest traders in history.

One of the best who is profiled in Covel's book is John W. Henry, owner of the Boston Red Sox, who returned 21 times the S&P 500 from 1998 through 2003. Wouldn't that be a nice record for innovation?

Importantly, Covel takes no prisoners in showing why the understanding of trends (versus copying them) is the superior trading methodology. He lays waste to all other styles of investing/trading that have analogs to innovation (buy and hold, technical analysis, and so forth). Much in the same way Burger King increased sales by going the opposite of "trend" (indulgent vs. healthy), the same conviction allowed traders to make huge profits from some of the greatest financial disasters of modern times such as the Enron debacle, and the sub-prime bubble. It was precisely the trajectory of the trend—and understanding where the market was *going* before it went there—that allowed these traders to reap the benefits. Sound familiar? Just as with breakthrough ideas, the innovators that are literally ahead of the trend curve are already positioned to profit because they are not following trends, but forecasting them. It is not a magic formula, but it works like one.

TRANSCENDING THE TREND

In one way, trends (as we know them) are really just an expression of emerging consumer needs, desires, and values. In this sense, they are distinct from the latest "fad" or "craze" which we would all be loathe to follow. By capitalizing on trends, you can constantly influence and shape the products of tomorrow, some of which may forever change the marketplace.

Naturally, innovation goes hand in hand with trend. It was "trendy" to listen to music on vinyl records, until someone thought it would be great to make it portable, thus began 8-tracks, which became cassette tapes, which became compacts discs, which became iPod/iTunes and MP3s. All of which proves that in order to take advantage of a trend and build your business, it is important to spot the trend early. Food manufacturers who "went organic" early—not the chasers—reap the rewards (as the early death of Kellogg's Organic Raisin Bran will attest).

So, if you are to *win* in the marketplace with new products, you've got to use trends the right way. Here are our rules for **Trend-Scendence,** our proprietary application of art and science that takes a trend beyond the ordinary range of perception when developing preeminent new products:

- Capitalize on trends that fit with brand equity.
- Provide added value to the expanded target by addressing needs not previously met.
- Leverage new or transferred technology.

All of this naturally begs the question: which came first, the trend or the innovation?

Do consumer desires and trends spark the innovation of new products? Or, do innovative new products create the trends that wouldn't have existed otherwise? The answer is Yes. Capitalizing on trends can be an important stimulus for developing new products. Better yet, if possible, *start* a new trend all by yourself!

As fun and interesting as it is to gather trends, and more importantly, keep an eye on them, the practice is not an end in itself. The insights you gather are only useful as part of an innovation process that can be applied to the critical business decisions that you have to make in your ongoing search for breakthrough ideas with a competitive advantage.

By all means, continue to monitor underlying trends, uncover emerging trends, and do whatever you can to help understand the everyday lives and challenges of people from around the world. It's a great way to discover which features and benefits consumers may need from the innovative products and services (yet to be invented!) for which they will line up to spend their hard-earned cash. As your targeted consumer's lifestyle and values change, so do their needs. And it is the innovators who react the quickest that will usually reap the best rewards for their company. Just keep in mind a principle that every innovator from Edison to Einstein did so well: *Lead*, and never follow.

MYTH **#6**

To successfully innovate, you must deeply understand and listen to the consumer: a.k.a.

THE CONSUMER IS KING

How can anyone argue with that? Every marketing major learns in Consumer Behavior 101 that the holy grail of marketing and, innovation in particular, is to be "in touch" with the consumer, that the "consumer is king." And yet, Steve Jobs, one of the modern day heroes of innovation says, "You can't just ask customers what they want and then try to give that to them. By the time you get it built, they'll want something new."

The current CEO of Microsoft, Steve Ballmer says, "There's no substitute for innovation, of course, but innovation is no substitute for being in touch, either."

He seems to be riding the fence with this statement. In other comments, Ballmer reveals his true thoughts on the matter, which is that it, meaning Microsoft, knows best what the future holds for consumers. Is this right, or is it simply misguided arrogance?

A consumer marketing luminary, A.G. Lafley, CEO of Procter & Gamble, represents the common wisdom of "the consumer is king" more clearly and emphatically when he offers that at P&G one of the keys to their innovation success is to not only be in touch, but to "live it." Now that is not just "being in touch," it's downright fanatical! Indeed, we've been part of many projects where the client has requested that it be able to literally live with their consumer in hopes of finding the key to innovation success. Is this right, or is it over-zealous or even Pollyanna?

Or how about one of the legends of innovation, Thomas A. Edison? He once said, "I find out what the world needs, and then I go and try to invent it."

The entire consumer research industry, not surprisingly, promotes the idea that "consumers are king" and that by surveying them, observing them, psychoanalyzing them, or even hooking them up to brainwave monitors, we can find out what they need, and then, as Edison suggested, simply create a solution. There is every kind of research method—focus groups, dyads, triads, one-on-ones, shop-alongs, ethnographies, conjoint analyses, segmentations, need-state studies, and more. Plus there's a plethora of experts who claim to offer the secret pathway to consumers' hidden desires. My favorites are the social scientists, such as cultural anthropologists, psychologists, sociologists, semioticians, or even facial gesture coders. We've even worked with a cat behaviorist! These folks often claim to be able to help articulate the unarticulated needs and desires of consumers (or animals). You know, the deep, dark stuff that no one talks about, or is even aware of—needs and desires that are latent in our psyches until someone tweaks it with an innovation.

So, the secret to innovation, according to this point of view is to delve ever deeper. After all, if this is true, then they get paid lots of money to help innovators study the consumer. How can I be so cynical about this, given that my own firm generates millions of dollars per year in revenues helping our clients "stay in touch?"

I can't tell you how many times we have been hired to help a company innovate shortly after it has spent a million dollars or so with a prestigious management consulting firm such as McKinsey & Company or Cambridge Group to do a large and comprehensive segmentation study based on behavioral and attitudinal measures, producing reams of data, and clever ethereal segment names, and almost no real insight regarding innovation. Nonetheless, these studies are treated with near biblical reverence.

If this *myth*stake had a theme song it would be Dave Matthews' "I Let You Down":

I have no lid upon my head
But if I did
You could look inside and see what's on my mind
You could look inside and see what's on my mind
I let you down
How could I be such a fool like me
I let you down

The problem with all of this is that it is a *myth*stake, well intentioned, but misunderstood and often horribly misapplied, and, it seems, the consumer is always letting us down. The truth is that most innovations do not come from consumer research, no matter how creative or powerfully sub-conscious it may be. This is blasphemy you say!

Yes, I know it's hard to believe, but studying the consumer, in and of itself, almost never results in true, disruptive innovation.

We've learned that what is missing in "the consumer is king" mentality is imagination. True disruptive innovations come from a future-focused vision of *what can be.* Thus, the problem with most traditional consumer research is that it only deals with *what is.*

Perhaps Einstein said it best:

> *"Imagination is more important than knowledge."*

So where does that leave us? Is Microsoft's "we know best" right after all? Start with some good technology and figure out how to sell it? As I write this sentence, I sense the microchips in my MacBook Air groaning with righteous Orwellian indignation. Cool down my incredibly light and thin friend.

Microsoft is neither right nor righteous, but it is not completely wrong either. Many disruptive innovations do come from a new technology that did not exist before.

Which came first? The microchip or the PC? I am going with microchip. Indeed, the microchip did come well before the PC. Two engineers, Robert Noyce and Jack Kilby, hold patents for the integrated electronic circuit, granted in 1958. Of course, this may be the single most significant invention or technology since the wheel. The applications of this technology came after, such as the PC (Apple II), and millions of others ranging from cell phones, to putting a man on the moon, to pacemakers. None of these innovations would have been possible without the microchip. And, the important point here is that few if any would have even been *imagined*.

So, in the above case of the microchip, the technology actually inspired and to some extent revealed possibilities that simply conducting direct consumer research never could have done. Wait a minute, you say, aren't there countless examples of meaningless technologies that have no value in the marketplace whatsoever? I recall many examples of this from my days with P&G. I remember visiting with our vaunted Miami Valley Labs group for a presentation of upstream technologies they were pursuing in the juice products category. In that presentation I met a scientist who had been working for a number of years on technology to produce the perfect tasting apple juice. He had built a not-so-small pilot plant to produce this pristine juice. It was a miniature factory. The only problem is that there was no significant unmet consumer need or desire for this perfect tasting apple juice. The category was and is very price sensitive, so the profit potential was negligible. The pilot plant was shut down. Years of work by an extraordinarily talented and intelligent scientist down the drain.

So understanding the needs and desires of the consumer are paramount after all! But, if I knew then what I know now I would have approached that meeting differently. I would have asked for a presentation of the technology behind the apple juice and then facilitated an application imagination session. Who knows what we might have come up with?

You see, what we have learned at **LaunchForce**™ is that innovation is really an evolution of Einstein's philosophy that "imagination is more important than knowledge." We look at innovation as follows:

$$(KNOWLEDGE + IMAGINATION) \times FOCUS \times SOLUTIONS = INNOVATION$$

Einstein had it right when he opined that all of the mathematical or scientific knowledge in the world does not lead to great discovery without the application of imagination. That is, envisioning what is not articulated. In our world the equation is modified as follows:

$$(KNOWLEDGE + IMAGINATION) \times FOCUS = INSIGHT, THEN$$
$$INSIGHT \times SOLUTIONS = INNOVATION$$

Okay, enough of the pseudo math lesson for the day. What does this mean for marketers and researchers? It means that what often is heralded as "consumer insight," is simply consumer knowledge—data, facts, description, trends, and so forth. True consumer insight transforms consumer knowledge via imagination into an unfulfilled consumer desire or unmet need, with a focus on the particular needs or objectives of a business, and that represents an opportunity. And opportunities beg for potential solutions, which is where innovation comes from. The additional factor of **focus** is critical, as knowledge and imagination are only useful to the degree that they meet the needs or strengths of the particular business or brand. A true insight represents new territory, a discovery, an "aha!" experience, it fundamentally asks the question "what if?" and it is grounded in the relevance and focus on a particular business or brand. The problem is that you don't get this kind of insight by collecting data; you must apply imagination and vision to find the breakthrough.

Now that we have defined what is and is not true insight, the door swings wide open regarding ways to obtain it. Of course, there are all of the traditional and known consumer research methods, any and all of which can, in the right situation, be transformed via imagination and focus, into statements of genuine opportunity.

The truth is that there is more knowledge available that is not considered typical consumer research, but can also be transformed into valuable insight, and often is more inspirational to opportunity identification than consumer research alone.

FUTURECASTING OPPORTUNITIES FOR INNOVATION

At LaunchForce, we use a process called **FutureCaster**™ to discover dynamic, and robust areas of *true insight* and *opportunity* for brands. For years I have been preaching to anyone who would listen that this is the most exciting and creative part of any innovation process. It is the small nugget of gold found by sifting through tons of sand and rocks; it is the profound holy grail of innovation. It is, in fact, what Thomas Edison was referring to in his oft quoted "1 percent inspiration, and 99 percent perspiration" view of innovation. To be clear, the "1 percent inspiration" is the identification of a genuine insight—what we have described as the fusion of knowledge, plus imagination, together with focus on the objectives of the brand. Once that is complete, then, and only then, does the "99 percent perspiration" in the form of time and effort begin to develop and ultimately launch solutions.

I was recently reminded of the validity of this view when at Walt Disney World with a client. The story of Walt Disney is the embodiment of "dreamers and doers" coming together to achieve great things. In Walt Disney's case, he was the "dreamer" and his brother Roy Disney was the "doer." Each brought a unique set of skills to the table, which was necessary to realize the dream. The problem is that all too often corporations are filled with doers, with the dreamers being cast out as unproductive, well, dreamers.

The FutureCaster process takes a somewhat different approach to the identification of opportunities than what is standard operating procedure in the consumer products industry by re-uniting the dreamers and the doers in all of us. It embraces the idea that inspiration and imagination are required to discover and conceive of future-focused opportunities rather than descriptive knowledge of "what is." Of course, given that our clients hire us to help them with this work, we also need an approach that is consistent and systematic in its ability to produce results. We can't rely on the chance. The key to the process is the way in which we force ourselves, and our clients, to view the world with new eyes, from multiple new perspectives. We do this by thinking of the world of knowledge as **The Three Worlds of Insight:**

1. **Interior World;**

2. **Consumer/CustomerWorld; and**

3. **Visionary World.**

Each World of Insight begins as an examination of knowledge from different perspectives, and through a process we call **CIFAdeation,**™ a fusion of Consumer Insight Focus Area and Ideation, we apply imagination to generate hypotheses of unmet consumer desires or needs. This process yields hundreds of potential opportunity areas or CIFAs. The final step of the **FutureCaster** process is to prioritize the areas of opportunity. We accomplish this with a quantitative study among target consumers that is referred to as a **FutureCaster** Mapping Study. With the findings from this study we are able to identify the most compelling opportunity areas and then proceed with confidence to the solution ideation process.

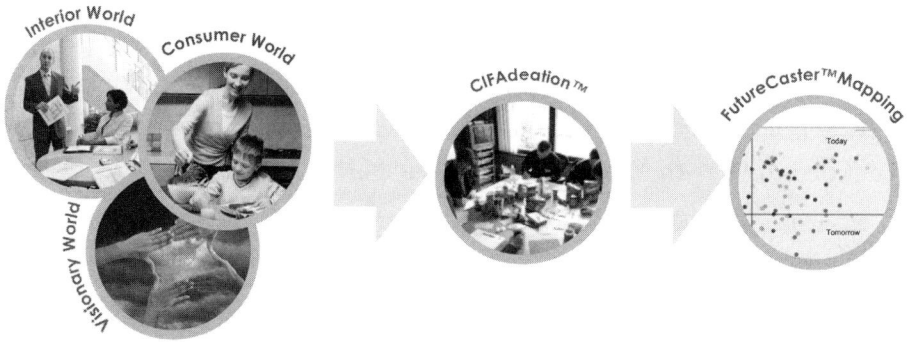

Interior World of Insight

The **Interior World of Insight** is the realm of current knowledge or research that is already owned by our client, together with the strategic focus that makes sense for that business. When we begin an assignment with a company it very often has reams of research, into which it has invested hundreds of thousands of dollars. Just as often, the current players in the business do not have any real understanding of this research or even interest in it. I understand this sentiment, as marketers and researchers do not have any incentive to go back and leverage research conducted by a previous team. We, however, have no such bias, and have found a way to use the "trash heap" of existing research and current knowledge to inspire new insights and give new life to the tremendous investment in knowledge that our clients own. Also included in the interior world is a thorough dive into current capabilities, often focusing on manufacturing methods or proprietary technology. Below is a list of many of the knowledge sources we consider part of the Interior World:

- Trend reports
- Usage and attitude studies

- Brand equity studies
- Habits and practices studies
- Satisfaction tracking studies
- Segmentation studies
- Need state studies
- Ethnographies
- Historical new product concepts and screening studies
- Product tests
- Historical advertising reel (both the client's and competitors)
- Blogs
- Consumer advocate magazines
- Factory tours
- R&D presentations
- 800-number reports
- Technology presentations from R&D
- Off-label or alternative use of products
- Sales reps (especially reports of successful and unsuccessful sales)

The real key to making this part of the process productive is to create a roadmap of where a brand or business can or should go, a vision statement that includes broad strategic areas of opportunity or potential competitive advantage. We use a format we call **Trajectory Illumination**™ to accomplish this objective.

Trajectory Illumination

Trajectory Illumination (or TI) is simply a process to systematically assess the current direction and inertia of a brand's innovation and assets and to hypothesize alternative directions or "trajectories" that could yield growth opportunities. The figure below illustrates the various dimensions of TI. It is comprised of six angles of innovation, surrounded by a wide variety of trends or innovation styles that could impact the brand or frame of reference. Each angle is intended to be a potential key to unlock new ways of thinking about a brand or category that lead to true insights. The components are explained below:

Frame of Reference or Brand

While this is typically brand focused, sometimes we look at an area of interest or frame of reference such as "luxury foods" or "heart health." Using a topical approach to TI can be very informative, as it allows clients to understand their area of interest from a broader perspective than their own world or category. For example, if I am a marketer of a spaghetti sauce looking to add nutritional benefits to my product, it is helpful to understand how other products and services address the issue, and thus learn what they have learned. **Some of our most compelling insights have come from examining examples from outside the product category at hand.** The Frame of Reference or Brand simply defines the lens we will look through to assess the six angles of innovation.

1. First-Need™

This angle of innovation assesses the functional and emotional needs that a brand satisfies at the most fundamental level. We have found that it is enlightening to go back to basics when identifying the needs that a particular brand satisfies for its customers. To do this, we use Maslow's well-known Hierarchy of Needs as seen below. In a nutshell, Maslow's theory states that human beings are motivated to satisfy their needs beginning with those at the bottom of the pyramid. The needs in the lower half of the pyramid are considered "homeostatic deficiency" needs, meaning that we are compelled to meet these needs when there is a deficiency and they are never quelled. For instance, breathing is something we all need all the time. The upper half of the pyramid represent "being" needs, that are positive when met, but not motivating when deficient. We pay particular attention to the lower level deficiency needs, as these often reveal the most provocative insights.

Maslow's Hierarchy of Needs

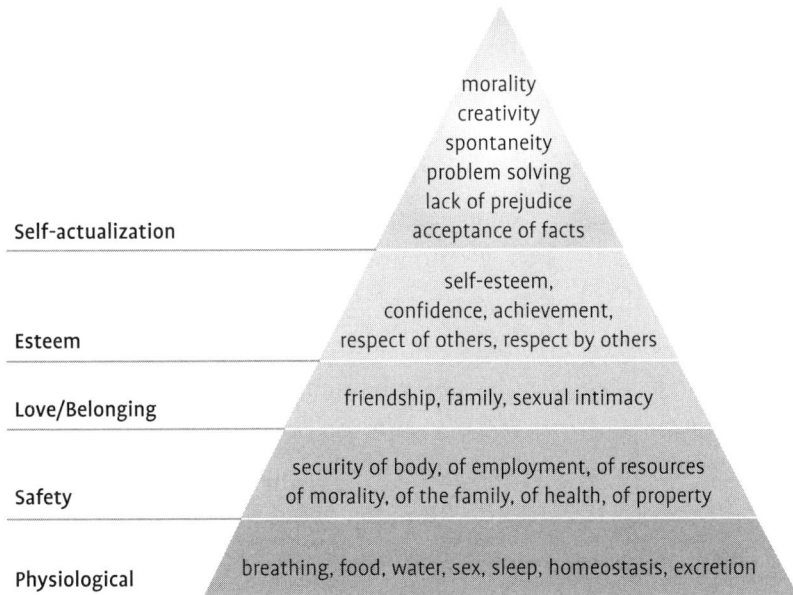

Self-actualization — morality, creativity, spontaneity, problem solving, lack of prejudice, acceptance of facts

Esteem — self-esteem, confidence, achievement, respect of others, respect by others

Love/Belonging — friendship, family, sexual intimacy

Safety — security of body, of employment, of resources of morality, of the family, of health, of property

Physiological — breathing, food, water, sex, sleep, homeostasis, excretion

Let's take, for example, the ubiquitous invention of Thomas Edison, the light bulb. What needs does the light bulb satisfy? The light bulb satisfies our need for security or safety from things that go bump in the night. In the caveman days this might have been a saber-tooth tiger looking for dinner. Once you understand the basic need behind the light bulb, you soon realize that this was simply a specific solution to the need of the security and safety from things in the dark. And then you may explore or consider that there are alternatives. What if we invented contact lenses that allowed you to see at night? What if everything you needed to see glowed with light? Your mind begins to open up to alternatives, albeit sometimes wild ones. Nonetheless, this fresh perspective is the starting point of all innovation.

2. Re-visioning™

This angle explores the positioning and equities of a brand from the standpoint of the nature of innovations that positioning suggests or

supports. Another way of looking at this angle is to ask, what is the brand's vision? The way in which a brand formulates its vision can have dramatic impact on the path of innovation or trajectory it will follow. As an example, let's consider the tale of two brands: Hunt's Tomatoes and Bertolli Olive Oil.

Examining Hunt's track record of innovation, you see that it has stayed very close to home, offering tomato-based products that are used as ingredients in cooking, and catsup. In fact, the brand's website offers that the Hunt's difference is, "A natural beginning for your great meals . . . perfectly natural, perfectly delicious . . . fresh tomatoes."

A lot can be learned from thinking about the innovation implications of the above statement. It clearly suggests that the vision of Hunt's is to be an ingredient brand, primarily tomatoes. So, its innovation trajectory is clear and narrow. If you look at its current product line-up, you understand it has been nothing if not slavish to this narrow positioning. Their line includes tomatoes offered as:

Diced

Original

Roasted Garlic

Sweet Onions

Balsamic Vinegar, Basil, and Oil

In Sauce

Basil, Garlic, and Oregano

Green Pepper, Celery, and Onions

Petite

Petite with Mild Green Chilies

Organic

Diced

Whole

Crushed

Pasta Sauce

Pasta Sauce with Garlic

Diced Tomatoes with Basil, Garlic, and Oregano

Whole

Original

No Salt Added

Stewed

Original

No Salt Added

Crushed

Puree

Sauce

Original

No Salt Added

Roasted Garlic

Basil, Garlic, and Oregano

Paste

I don't know about you, but it looks to me that Hunt's has pretty much tapped out the trajectory of tomato innovation based on its current positioning. The point is, what if they considered alternate positionings that could suggest new opportunities? The problem with this brand is that currently there is "not much there" from the standpoint of an extendable, portable platform. Without giving it all away, what if Hunt's considered an alternative positioning or vision statement, something like "The perfectly natural ingredients to perfectly delicious meals." This positioning would suggest other natural ingredients and meal-starter ideas beyond tomatoes, and is just a small degree different than the current statement. To further make the point that a brand's positioning or vision has dramatic impact on its ability to innovate, let's take a look at another brand that took a different angle of trajectory, Bertolli.

According to the brand's website, Bertolli olive oil is the world's leading brand, created some 140 years ago by Francecso Bertolli in Lucca, Italy. If Bertolli had followed a similarly narrow trajectory as Hunt's, it would likely offer olive oil in many flavors and sizes. Instead, its positioning appears to be something along the lines of, "Authentic Italian cuisine you can make at home."

This positioning has yielded a wide range of products including olive oil, pasta sauces, and frozen meals. A listing of their products is below.

Classic Dinners

Pollo
Chicken alla Vodka & Farfalle
Chicken Parmigiana & Penne
Roasted Chicken & Linguine
Chicken Florentine & Farfalle
Grilled Chicken Alfredo

Carne
Roasted Pork & Cavatappi Pasta
Italian Sausage & Rigatoni

Frutti De Mare
Shrimp Scampi & Linguine
Shrimp, Asparagus & Penne

Pasta & Sauce
Spinach & Ricotta Cheese Manicotti in a Tomato Sauce
Cheese Tortelloni in a Tomato Cream Sauce
Mushroom Ravioli in a Mushroom Cream Sauce
Four Cheese Ravioli in a Tomato Basil Sauce

Mediterranean Style Frozen Dinners
Steak, Rigatoni & Portobello Mushrooms
Chicken, Rigatoni & Broccoli
Garlic Shrimp, Penne & Cherry Tomatoes
Rosemary Chicken, Linguine & Cherry Tomatoes
Shrimp & Penne Primavera

Oven Baked Meals
Meat Lasagna Rustica
Stuffed Shells in Scampi Sauce
Chicken Parmigiana & Penne
Tri-color Four Cheese Ravioli

Premium Pasta Sauce
Champagne & Portobello Mushroom
Summer Crushed Tomato & Basil
Sun Ripened Tomato & Olive

Olive Oil
Extra Virgin
Classico
Extra Light Tasting

Pasta Sauce
Red Sauce
Organic Sauce
White Sauce
Vineyard Premium Collection Pasta Sauce

As you can see, this line-up is far more extensive than that of Hunt's. Both use lots of tomatoes. But one brand had a bigger and richer vision that served as a launching pad for a wide range of products. Bertolli's positioning makes me hungry, Hunt's does not. Part of the art of dreaming or re-visioning a brand is to create positionings that are rich with substance and appeal, perhaps even a bit of romance. I would argue that if Bertolli wanted to sell authentic, high quality canned tomatoes, it would offer formidable competition to Hunt's. I doubt that it would go there, however, given the commodity nature of the category, but the point is that it could. Each of its product categories will likely continue to innovate along the lines of recipe variety, but its positioning suggests it could also enter new categories where "authentic Italian cuisine you can make at home" is significantly relevant. Some possibilities include: salad dressings that use olive oil, fresh pasta, frozen or refrigerated pizza, desserts, appetizers, and more.

3. Slicing and Dicing™

The third angle of TI considers the nature of segmentation in a category and explores alternative schema as a way of unearthing insights, thus the title slicing and dicing. Brands tend to have a static view of the structure of their category, as though that is the only way a category could be organized. So we slice and dice by dreaming of alternative segmentations or structures to bring into focus new needs that were not visible before. We like to think of this exercise as using a kaleidoscope to look at the world, with each turn creating a whole new beautiful vision. Let's take the yogurt category as an example.

The yogurt category initially evolved, from a segmentation point of view, primarily along the lines of age, with yogurts for adult women and children. The next phase of segmentation or slicing and dicing has been more need-based, with yogurts offering products positioned as follows:

- Low-calorie for help in weight management

- Sensory preference (thick, whipped, fizzy, etc.)
- Nutritional needs (fiber and calcium)
- Disease management (digestive health, blood pressure)

Each of these segmentation schemas represents platforms of innovation opportunity. For instance, weight management yogurts deliver their promise by offering low-calorie food that satisfies a craving for sweets. What if they went further to offer the benefit of satiety, helping you feel more satisfied and full so you don't consume as many calories, or what if they offered metabolic management products that actually help you burn more calories. On the contrarian's side, what if they also considered that some people actually want to gain weight or muscle and created special products for them? Each of these "what ifs?" present potential areas of opportunity that are within the current trajectory of the category.

We can also imagine potential new areas of need for this category. What if yogurt could help provide energy in the morning as a healthier alternative to coffee? What about mental focus and acuity, what about sports performance or recovery, what about skin care? You can see how the "what if?" kaleidoscope begins to reveal exciting and uncharted territory. Of course, these new areas of opportunity are simply hypotheses until they are validated with the target consumer via research, but as you can see, the thinking process begins to open up worlds of potential white space.

4. Occasioning™

Every brand or category has a dominant occasion of use. When we think of food this is pretty straightforward with certain foods being used for breakfast, lunch, dinner, dessert, and so on. The power of this angle, however, is to think more deeply about occasion than time of day. The key to this angle is to explore the context in which a product or service is used. What is going on with customers in their world at the time? This view of the world often reveals new needs that are unmet. Also, considering alternative occasions can be a powerful tool to unlock opportunity. If I am a food that is primarily eaten at breakfast, then what could be done to create offerings for lunch or afternoon snacks? A good example of "occasion" innovation thinking is found in Walt Disney World.

We all think of Walt Disney World as the quintessential family summer vacation destination. This is the occasion. Disney, however, began to see it differently, as more than just a family summer vacation destination. It reframed the occasion as a destination where dreams come true, a place for all kinds of "celebrations to remember." This thinking opens up quite a bit more opportunity than family vacations, to include weddings, anniversaries, birthdays, retirement, and, importantly for Disney, it is an incremental idea that gives a reason to visit the park throughout the year.

5. Senspiration™

This angle takes a close look at the physical interface and experience a consumer has with a product or service and the emotions attached to that experience from a multi-sensory point of view. It can be very insightful to breakdown the experience consumers or customers have with a product by systematically considering how each of the senses is impacted by the offering. We understand that products and services that offer a multi-sensory impact are easier to remember and more distinctive. This is because our senses directly connect with our right brain and nervous system in a hardwired way, unmediated by language or symbols, offering a clear path to creative thinking. Let's take a look at each sense:

Touch How does a product or service feel? Is it rough, smooth, slippery, clean, fuzzy, moist, dry, hot, or cold? Whatever it is, considering the alternatives can often reveal potential opportunity. This seems pretty straightforward if you are talking about consumer products, but you may be wondering how this applies to a service. Let me tell you about a retail establishment we discovered as part of a trend walk in New York City. The store was a skin care spa. When you walked into the store all of the products were displayed in water, flowing like a small serene river around the store. It was as if you were picking each moisturizing product from a small stream. Not only was this visually appealing and distinctive, but the water feature added considerable moisture to the air. You felt more moisturized and relaxed the moment you walked in. Just imagine what the products could do for you?

Smell Again, when thinking about food, we understand that smell is an important and powerful part of our enjoyment and memory. Our brains store the vivid memory of smells attached to the complete memory of people, places, and events in our lives, and the emotions associated with them. During my P&G days, we used the sense of smell to create emotions and memories for our brands, adding the smell of fresh roasted coffee to instant Folgers, the aroma of fresh-peeled oranges to Citrus Hill, and so on. The key to this angle is to consider the smells, good and bad, associated with your product or service, considering the potent emotions attached to them. Now, for those of you now wondering what this has to do with non-food, or services, I challenge you to walk into a Hollister store. Hollister fills its store with a fragrance that is its signature. One of our female associates offered that it smells like men, and in a good way. That's a pretty powerful reaction simply by infusing the air with perfume. What is your brand's fragrance?

Taste If I am a bank, what is my taste? Most of you probably imagined a Dum-Dum lollipop based on a childhood memory of having received one from the drive-through teller. What if a bank offered its customers an elegant chocolate mint instead? Would that create an impression? I think so. Food products obviously spend a lot of time and energy assessing and refining taste. In Trajectory Illumination, we look at taste primarily from the point of view of generating alternatives or new possibilities. For example, if the taste profile of a product is sweet-fruity, we wonder if it could be sweet-fruity-salty, and so on.

Sight The sense of sight is often our first perception of the world around us, and as such, it influences and shapes how the rest of our senses respond. Chefs understand that we taste with our eyes, so the presentation of food is the first moment of truth that sets the tone for the taste and smell. Football coaches regularly say that they see better than they hear. And we all say that we will believe it when we see it. I discovered firsthand the power of sight on the perception of a product while at P&G working on Citrus Hill orange juice. I conducted experiments where I varied the color of the juice using a small amount of red food dye and then conducted *taste* tests, obviously not blind ones, with employees. The results were striking. The juice with a slightly darker orange color was perceived to taste better by a margin of 2-to-1 than regular (un-dyed) orange juice. By changing the color, the juice tasted better. Only a crazy marketing guy like me (a.k.a. *dreamer*) would have done such an experiment. My R&D counterparts were chemical engineers, so this was somewhat like voodoo for them. Nonetheless, they proceeded to explore ways to create a darker colored orange juice through the addition of varieties such as Italian blood oranges! How can you vary the sight of your brand to create a new perception?

Sound I've always been intrigued with the way in which a simple sound can become recognizable as a complete entity. I worked at Tupperware, and everyone knows the sound of that brand— *"burp"*—an ingenious demonstration of the product's famously effective seals. Start-up an Apple computer and you hear a strong chord, or "chime" as it is known by Apple users. It was a C Major chord developed by a sound engineer named Jim Reekes. The chord is now an F# Major, but I am not sure why. In discussing the purpose of the startup chime, Reekes revealed that he wanted a "fat" sound that would be different from the sound that Mac users would hear after a crash of the system, thus creating a positive emotion. We are all familiar with Pavlov's dog experiments with bells. What is your brand's Pavlovian response? Is there a sound that defines your brand?

6. Re-Placing™

The last angle of innovation asks the unthinkable question of how to replace the brand or category in question, how to make yourself obsolete, how to deliver the brand or category benefits in a completely new and different way that could smash current performance standards? Developing answers to this question leads to potentially revolutionary concepts. I imagine that this type of thought process could have led to the development of P&G's Swiffer Duster. Product developers looking the dust-cleaning category could have gone down the path or current trajectory of making an incrementally better dust cleaning spray. Maybe they could have come up with a spray that was 10 or 20 percent more effective, but that probably would not have been enough to overcome Pledge's consumer brand equity and loyalty. Instead, they created a completely new approach to dusting:

> *"Swiffer uses electrostatic action and Lift & Lock Pockets™ to capture and remove dust, hair, crumbs and common allergens from floors, appliances, furniture and other surfaces in the home."*
>
> —from P&G press release

The Consumer World

The Consumer World is where we use direct observation and query of consumers (or customers if B2B) to understand their needs, wants, emotions, and stereotypes, a kind of consumer-insight compass if you will. These terms are defined as follows:

Needs What are the fundamental needs the product or service fulfills? For example, thinking about infant car seats, the needs are for my child to be safe in the event of a car accident and, perhaps, for my child to be contained so that I can focus on driving.

Wants The wants are the ways in which I desire my needs to be fulfilled. Again, using the infant car seat, I want a car seat that is easy to use, that is comfortable for my child, has a sound reputation for safety, matches the upholstery in my car, helps occupy my child, keeps him quiet, and so forth.

Stereotypes These are the beliefs about the product or service. For infant car seats, I believe they are hard to install, my child does not like being in them, they are hard to clean, I don't really know if my child would be safe in an accident.

Emotions These are the feelings about the product or service. Thinking about infant car seats I may be feeling a variety of somewhat negative emotions such as stress, hurry, guilt about confining my child, as well as positive emotions such as satisfaction of protecting my child, and love.

By looking at the consumer through this multi-faceted lens, we are able to discover far more insights than if we take a more straightforward approach.

While there are many research methodologies that can be used to accomplish this goal, we have found that when it comes to inspiring innovation, it is best to directly immerse our team and our clients into the world of the target audience. It is important to gain a view of the consumer that sees a broader context than the transaction represented by the given product or category. So often as researchers, we tend to look at the consumer through a microscope, and in doing so, miss the truly big opportunities.

To do this we use a method called **Consumer Vérité**.™

Consumer Vérité

Stated simply, **Consumer Vérité** is patent-pending observational methodology that seeks the "truth" of a situation by allowing the respondents to develop their own stories and narrations about a subject of
interest without the mediation (or interference) of an interviewer. We
do this by sending digital video cameras to recruited respondents with
a detailed activity workbook that has been developed with the project's
learning objectives in mind. The workbook contains specific activities
we want the respondents to complete during a specified period time
and is developed to help us ferret out the needs, wants, stereotypes and
emotions of the subject. The key to the method is having the respondents narrate the video so that we are hearing what they are thinking
and seeing what they are seeing at the moment of truth. Traditional
research is confined to asking consumers to remember what they were
thinking about an event that happens in the past. As a result, critical
details are lost. An activity as simple as "tell us what is in your pantry"
becomes fascinating as the respondent narrates what's and why's of
the pantry contents.

Recently we were working with a client who was interested in
understanding the subject of *mother and child bonding and connection.*
We could have asked our panel of moms to tell us about the subject,
but that would have missed the golden nuggets we learned by using
Consumer Vérité. What we were able to see was a variety of scenes of
moms and kids interacting in ways that would have not been possible
if we were physically present. For instance, one family filmed for us
their nightly reading and prayer time. This is a time that is private and
intimate, yet we were able to "be there" through the video. Listening
to this family's prayers was powerful, as they revealed the things they
are thankful for, their fears, and their aspirations. The insights for our
client were profound.

I recall another assignment where we were interested in understanding the situation of "feeding cats." While I cannot share with

you the specific insights gained here due to confidentiality, I can tell you that it would not have been possible to gain them with any other methodology. Why? Two reasons really. Firstly, people feed their cats early in the morning in the midst of getting ready for their day. It is a time of hustle and bustle, and multi-tasking, and clearly not a time when you can show up with a team of interviewers at the front door. Secondly, there were some consumer and cat behaviors that, with the presence of "guests" in the house, likely would have been squelched due to their social acceptability. I know your interest is piqued now, but the point is that we saw things that would not be seen or heard with other methods.

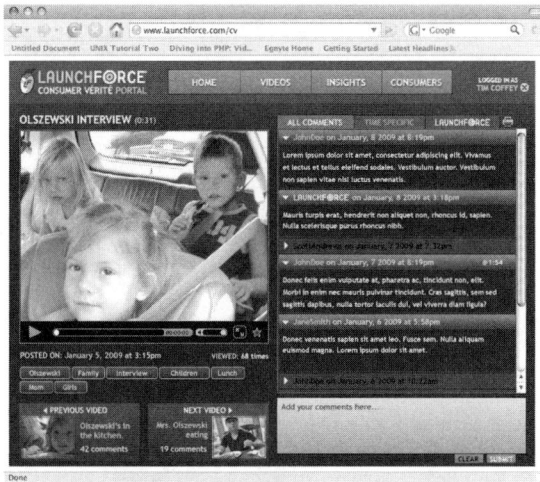

In addition to this method being more intimate and un-censored than traditional research, the way in which we engage our client in the process also adds to its value. As we discussed earlier, it is important to design the process to add imagination to the knowledge we are gaining. To do this, we post videos edited by our team to focus on rich insights (as shown above). This website allows multiple members of the client team to view the videos on their own time and to provide their own observations, insights, and inspirations. The video becomes the stimulus to their imaginations. This consumer video helps generate conversation and build ideas within the organization. When was the last time you talked about market research at the water cooler? Having viewed the videos as a team, we then follow-up with the respondents either by phone or in-person to probe about issues or questions that have come up. Again, our client team member will join us for these follow-ups, deepening their relationship with the consumer in a way that is not possible with other kinds of research.

Net, net, the admonition of A.G. Lafley of P&G to "live it" and even live with your consumer is indeed key to finding new insights, but there is a right way and a wrong way to do it. Further, the process must include the opportunity for team members to dream with the intimate view of consumers as the stimulus. We prefer the idea of not just living it, but also, giving life to the observation of consumers.

The Visionary World

The Visionary World seeks to expose the team to a more future-focused perspective than the Interior or Consumer Worlds of Insight. This final world of insight is the most important of all as it forces the consideration of where things are going or could go, rather than where things are. Honestly, this is the fun stuff! I mentioned earlier how the development of the microchip preceded the explosion of innovations that were made possible by it. The point of this step is to explicitly seek to expose innovators to the knowledge of leading technology, trends, and lateral thinking as a way to inspire the discovery of opportunities. Given the highly creative nature of this step, there are many ways to attack it. At LaunchForce, we have found it helpful to focus our thinking with three basic process tools:

1. Expertspectives™

We engage appropriate "experts" to join the innovation and insight team to bring their unique perspectives to the discussion. We ask these experts to make presentations to our team about the area of interest or subject matter, and then lead a discussion regarding the implications of what was learned or inspired. Some examples of interesting experts we have used are:

- Master Chef
- Nutritionist
- Psychologist
- Animal Behaviorist
- Consumer researchers from relevant but non-competitive companies
- Sensory Scientist
- Public Health Ph.D.
- R&D Managers/Scientists

2. Inspirience™

We create inspirational experiences for our clients that transport them into a completely new perspective. One favorite Inspirience is to take clients on a very specifically designed tour of Walt Disney World. It is a venue that provides a vast variety of experiences that are relevant to our clients. As an example, we were working with a food company that wanted to learn more about sensory discovery for their products. We designed a learning tour to help them learn first-hand how Walt Disney World manipulates the senses of its guests to create a memorable and exciting brand experience. A memorable activity was the 3D *Bug's Life Show* that gave our clients an inspirational education in using all the senses in a dramatic way. I can still remember the fear and excitement of the bees flying around me, and "stinging" my back. It gets me every time. Every moment of our time at Disney was a planned learning experience that generated insights that are not possible by simply hearing about them. If you are not up for a trip to Walt Disney World, there are many other ways to create inspirational experiences. One interesting activity we created recently for a skin care company to discover new opportunities with women was to pull a montage of video from popular movies and TV shows featuring stereotypes of the target audience. Watching *Sex and the City* was an unusual, but highly inspirational way to discover insights. What makes Inspirience work is that your brain has to process the information you are receiving in a completely different way than the typical analytical approach to research.

3. Trendscendence™

It is important and meaningful to explicitly explore trends by focusing on the potential implications and insights they present for your product or category. Again, this exercise forces you to consider a multitude of different perspectives that often will lead to the discovery of new insights, or, as you will read later, to imagine new ideas. We use the trend wheel shown below as our template, but you can use any trend presentation to drive this activity. As an example, if I were a bank, what are the implications of the locovore/organic foods trend? Follow me here. Locovores are people who desire to buy and consume foods that are sourced from local/nearby and typically small suppliers. This is because there is a sense of trust and safety and freshness and civic support or pride and environmental responsibility. Now I start to diagram the connections or implications for the bank. What if we (the bank) emphasized our local commitment by creating programs that support the community? What if we offered a more environmentally friendly approach to banking? Could we be the "green" bank? So you can see that even a trend that on the surface has no apparent connection to the product or category is potentially meaningful. This works because consumers or customers are not just consumers or customers of the particular product or service, they are people with diverse of concerns, and we are always marketing to people.

Throughout the process of insight discovery via the Three Worlds of Insight, we are developing a long list of potential consumer or customer desires that we believe are unmet or not met as well as they could be. The next step is to test our hypotheses with the intended target audience so that we can prioritize our solution-generation efforts. Going back to Thomas Edison, we have spent all our energies so far to identify potential consumer needs or desires (his one percent inspiration). At this point we have a lot of inspiration. So that we know which path to pursue with our "perspiration," it is helpful to find the areas of opportunity that are potentially most opportunistic. We do this using a quantitative research methodology we call FutureCaster Mapping.

FUTURECASTER MAPPING

FutureCaster Mapping asks consumers or customers to evaluate the list of potential *wants* that emanate from the *needs* we have identified throughout our discovery process. The mechanics of this study are very straightforward. However, it is the list of wants that makes it unique and valuable. The respondents in the study rate each want statement with two scales: 1) How desirable is the statement? and, 2) How well is the statement of want currently met by existing products or services? Using the results from these two questions we create an opportunity matrix, as shown below.

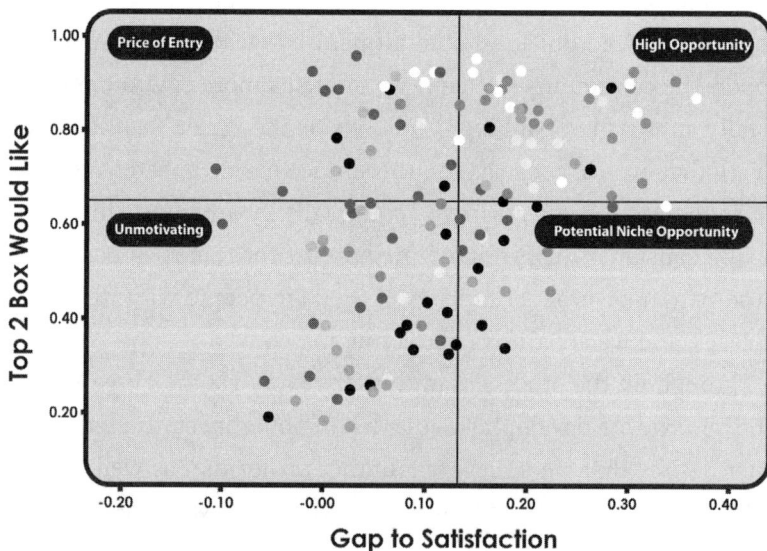

The attributes that fall into the upper right quadrant are those that represent the greatest opportunities, as they are wants that are highly desired *and* they are perceived to be unmet by current products or services. These are the areas we will now focus on to generate potential solutions. Considering the other quadrants, the upper left quadrant represents attributes that are highly desirable, but already well satisfied. Unless your brand or business is deficient in these areas, innovation focus here will not be as productive. The lower right quadrant represents statements that are not desired by a large percentage of the market, and are not well satisfied. These may represent niche or emerging opportunities. And, last and least, the lower left quadrant are wants that are not wanted that much and are perceived to be well satisfied. No man's land for sure when it comes to innovation.

With a focused perspective of the wants that are wanted and not well satisfied, we are now ready to invent solutions. We are ready for Edison's 99 percent perspiration.

So, is the consumer king? The answer is clearly yes and no! The problem is that the king cannot tell us what he wants. We must imagine our way to the discovery of true and new opportunities.

MYTH #7   THERE IS A SECRET OF HOW TO BE CREATIVE

ONE OF MY favorite stories occurred over 20 years ago when I was in advertising. During a meeting with a client and our creative director, the client, out-of-the blue, became irate and began to threaten us to tell him the *secret of creativity!* Granted, this guy was very strange, but he was quite serious. He totally believed that there was some "secret" formula that we used to come up with creative advertising ideas. (Well, there really is, but we're sworn to secrecy.)

Having remembered this story, and in practicing what we preach, we felt that we too, should look outside *our* category, Innovation Consulting, and ask other creative types how they come up with ideas. What's their "secret" for inspiration? You know, maybe it will help all of us to learn new ways in which to find creative inspiration. So here's what we learned:

JIMMY GERARDI, MASTER CHEF, FWMCS, CMC

Chef Gerardi has been a consultant, and chef for such companies as P&G and Smuckers. He has been an advisor to the Food Network. We regularly call upon him to add expert opinion to new food ideation. Jimmy tells us:

The stimulus for the inspiration comes from everything I experience and or observe. It really is not conscious. Examples: watching what people have in their shopping carts while I shop, walking through a restaurant and seeing what people have on their plate and their behavior, seeing someone do something unusual while driving (like reading a newspaper placed on the steering wheel or trying to eat a large slice of pizza), watching the clouds at the beach, or smelling a new aroma.

Watching others create is also inspiring. I saw a flight attendant mix white and red wine together in the galley. As I was exiting I asked her if the passenger requested that. She replied, "No. They asked for rosé and we are out of it, so I made it." Brilliant! Working with other "creative" experts gives inspiration that lasts long after the project is over, sometimes forever.

I love playing "what if?" Examples: What if instead of cooking a Peking duck I cooked a Peking turkey? What if I add merlot to the chocolate brownies? What if we order the wine first and then choose the food? What if there was a knife that sharpened itself?

What if we grow garlic that does not have to be peeled? The list goes on and on and not just food related.

I will look at completed creations and will make changes right up to the last possible minute and maybe after that. Disney Imagineer Training reinforced this. I learned, "when you have the answer, turn it upside down and look at it every three degrees." Speaking of change, I love and embrace it. The ability to change is paramount in the food industry; food is very much like fashion. But there are the classics, which can always be updated.

Lots of trend watching. Not just in food, but music, fashion, entertainment—everything you can get your hands on. Not just nationally, but everywhere you can get it from.

Having fun. I never feel like I am working because I enjoy what I do so much. I think it also contributes to the amount of energy one has when you love what you are doing.

Nature and Concept Cars by Kristina Dryza

In looking at automotive design and creation we came about an interesting essay on how Mazda uses nature for inspiration for its ideas.

Mazda's "flow" (*Nagare*) design concept was introduced two years ago, and for the design team in Yokohama, it felt very natural to be inspired by nature.

As Atsuhiko Yamada, Chief Designer at the Yokohama Design Center told *Car Design News*, "It felt natural then, as it does now, as fundamentally we are all a part of nature."

Joe Reeve, a designer at Mazda's Yokohama studio added, "We wanted to stop being inspired by the 'normal' stuff. It's usually pictures of planes, anything mechanical, or other design disciplines that are a primary source of inspiration. It's traditionally been car design being inspired by other forms of design."

Most car designers are trained solely to design cars, and the field is seen as an isolated discipline of design. When wider spheres of influence are referenced—lifestyle, societal values, the environment—the ideation process blossoms. It opens up to be more reflective, and much less fragmented. The design process is then seen (and understood) as part of the inter-related whole.

MATT FISCHER, CHIEF CREATIVE OFFICER

Matt is an award winning, highly recognized Creative Director. He has served as SVP, Creative Director for FCB, NY among other top agencies, including WonderGroup. He is winner of eight Clios and has been credited with creating one of the highest scoring Super Bowl TV ads.

What do I do to get inspiration? Stimulus, stimulus, and more stimulus. First, I am a voracious reader. I read two to three books a month. Topics are varied, but center around my personal interests in business, social media, history, and on the recommendations of others. I also read three newspapers everyday. I scan for articles that interest me and satisfy my innate curiosity but I also look for pertinent articles on the advertising/media industry, technology, my client's industries, and social trends.

Next, I go to lots of museums (all types) and movies to feed my need for historical context. Today's creative is so much more about the changing landscape of distribution than the art itself that I try to be as immersed as possible.

Last but not least, I'm a big believer in human nature. I observe people as they navigate their daily lives and I look for the universal truths that reflect those behaviors—funny, sad, ridiculous, and authentic. When creative taps into core truths about people it is extremely powerful.

Truth is, inspiration requires doing your homework everyday so when the moment comes, it is grounded in knowledge and experience.

DUNCAN BILLINGS, VP, CHIEF DEVELOPMENT OFFICER, HASBRO INC.

Duncan manages the entire Hasbro Global innovation process from up-front ideation, through design and engineering and all of the way through development to manufacturing in both the U.S. and the Far East.

"Big ideas" drive brands and business. They change companies and they change categories.

Ideas come from everywhere. I personally often observe my own kids and their friends and always try to immerse myself with the consumer. Observation is critical. Going into the stores, watching how people react at retail. As an example, during the 2007 New York Toy Fair, I was in a major store looking around. Webkinz had just hit big in the year before and we, of course, had the Littlest Pet Shop. I saw a mom and a daughter, about 10 years old. The girl said that she wanted a Littlest Pet Shop, but mom suggested Webkinz because of the Internet tie in. The kid agreed. I was on the phone immediately to ask my team to take Littlest Pet Shop online to counter Webkinz. And we did, within a few months.

Ideas can come from anywhere in the world . . . but the world is a very big place. We view the world as one ideation entity, there are great ideas all over the world, but you must be systematic. We often use outside resources, the inventor community. The toy industry has long been open to, and inspired by outside inventors. Our inventor community extends internationally and we get a lot of ideas from other countries. We are now building a worldwide system to have "boots on the ground" in different countries like Japan and the UK.

The biggest thing is not being afraid. The biggest ideas can make people uncomfortable. We have a culture here at Hasbro that recognizes that ideas drive our business. We nurture this because in a new-ideas business you can't punish failure.

I love ideas. That's what makes a difference and that's why I love the business.

IN SUMMARY

No one seems to just look at the "numbers," the data, or just "ask" the customer. Each *explores* many different areas in their own ways. All seem to be adventurous in their own ways. Each has his or her own journey. And they all *observe!*

MYTH **#8**	WHEN LOOKING FOR INSIGHTS, FOCUS GROUPS ARE BEST STAFFED BY "FRESH" CONSUMERS

YOU HEAR this one all the time. All the energy is spent scrambling for respondents that have had "no past participation" in focus groups.

To our way of thinking as screeners, this is one of the strangest pre-requisites that we see. For some reason, it is felt that to ensure unbiased consumer responses, potential respondents for focus groups should be screened out "for priors." Sounds like an old episode of *Dragnet*, doesn't it?

But here are just the facts, ma'am: Getting a fresh batch of consumers for each qualitative project means that you have to start from scratch with every single group!

It is no wonder that qualitative research has the reputation of just finding more of the same learning that has been heard before? In fact, you'll often get the same top-of-mind insights from every two-hour session.

To be reasonable, it's not really all that fair to expect that consumers can give you everything worth knowing about them in a single two-hour session. After all, at least half of them aren't even sure they should say what they actually think. We call them the "Pleasers." That's because they feel as if their role is to give you what you're looking for. They don't want to disappoint you, so they literally are there to please.

Then you get some folks that we like to call the "Riffers." They just start "riffing" on a subject—making it up as they go along—looking for the moderator to nod in approval at some point. You can tell they have never thought all that much about the topic before and won't figure out how to articulate their true feeling until they are home later that night making dinner. *Then*, it suddenly strikes them. Too late for us, though.

Charlotte Horseman, Director of Consumer Insights at Launch-Force, and a 15-year market research professional suggests that good research should enable the researcher and consumer to get to know each other more deeply and to work collaboratively to uncover the real motivations and influences that drive consumer behavior. So, she asks: "Why not engage a set of consumers to take a longer journey with you? Why not use the same consumers for up-front focus groups, follow up in-homes, and then have subsequent discussions?"

The real objective is not just to see if you can learn something new from focus groups. It's much more important than that. The goal is to find consumers to engage in a more-engaging **process.** Focus groups are an excellent vehicle to screen for and select a few great respondents—the ones who are creative, articulate, and represent various interesting aspects of the consumer base. So why not invite them to stay with the next steps of your insight process, such as in-home ethnographies, diaries, and other qualitative methods?

By using initial focus groups to screen for those to engage in the next phase of the process, you'll enjoy the benefit of reducing much of the risk of having "duds" involved in the more expensive and complex qualitative techniques. You will have seen these people, heard them speak, and gotten some sense for how they think and how engaged they are in the research process. You will already have heard how they talk about your category and whether or not they are truly qualified.

This is lost if one merely recruits consumers straight to in-homes or ethnographies.

Now you can engage this select, truly qualified set of consumers in more in-depth exploration. You won't have to spend precious time re-hashing basic ideas because you got those out in the first focus groups. Both you and the participants will know what has already been covered. As you match up what the respondent said in the focus group to what you see at the in-home visit, a clearer picture will begin to emerge.

By engaging these same consumers after in-home observations (or other tasks), you're bound to uncover more. You'll also have the advantage of being able to recall observations from the focus groups and tie them to what you saw in the at-home ethnography. In this way you can let participants explain and expound at length.

The key is to keep it going. You can do this by taking new concepts back to that same set of consumers, as well as fresh ones, to see how the two sets of consumers respond. You may discover that one set has thought a lot about the category and their own relationships to it, while the other is completely green.

Another option to think about is gathering together your in-depth participants in another group discussion. But this time, because of the steps they've taken with you along the way, they will be a small, highly engaged and enlightened team capable of having an expert consumer panel discussion on your topic. It is true in life (as well as focus groups) that the more comfortable and "at home" someone feels, the more he or she will feel like sharing.

It's really this simple. If you give consumers the time and opportunity to show you their true insights and breathe new life into your qualitative research, they'll do all the heavy lifting for you.

MYTH #9   ONLY "RIGHT-BRAINERS" ARE CREATIVE

BACK IN THE 1970s it became popular in marketing circles to inquire if someone was a "left brain" person or a "right brain." Kind of an agency version of "what's your sign?" If you were a "lefty," you were thought to be logical, methodical, and rational. "Righties" were the soulful, sensitive, creative types.

Or so legend would have it.

Like all great myths, they are rooted in a half-truth of sorts. Ah, but *which* half?

To this day, popular psychology still tends to make broad and sometimes pseudoscientific generalizations about certain functions (e.g., logic, creativity) being lateral—that is, located in either the right or left side of the brain.

Let's start with some facts: The human brain does indeed have two distinct hemispheres and the sides do resemble each other. In fact, the other side generally mirrors each hemisphere's structure. Yet despite the strong similarities, the functions of each hemisphere are different. However, did you know that the extent of specialized brain function by area is anything *but* a "no-brainer?"

Oh sure, functions are lateralized left and right but those are more like functional trends, really, and not applicable in every case. Let's be clear: No person is a "left-brain" or "right-brain" only.

There's a brilliant new "brain test" floating around online at *www. launchforce.com* that shows a spinning cup and spoon and asks whether you see the image rotating clockwise or counterclockwise. Unlike other tests online that say if it spins clockwise, you supposedly use more of your right brain (and if it is spinning counterclockwise for you, then you are supposedly more of a left-brain person), this test isn't as cut and dried.

That's because you probably know someone who has taken similar tests only to complain later that the test "told" him he was a left-brain person, even though he knew himself not to be into left-brain associations such as "math and science."

The LaunchForce.com test is smart enough to know that you can't use spinning cups and spoons to characterize someone's brain strengths. That would be too crude a view of the lateralization of brain function, or the concept that each side of the human brain specializes in certain mental activities.

The whole notion began, after all, in the 1960s, when Roger Sperry studied epilepsy patients who had a nerve connection between their hemispheres surgically cut. He found that the left brain hemisphere seemed to possess "speech and a rational, intellectual style," while the right side was "inarticulate, but blessed with special spatial abilities."

Modern neuroscience studies using brain-imaging technology such as MRIs, which show the active areas of the brain while a person is trying to perform a task, have further suggested that language ability tends to be localized in the left hemisphere, while spatial ability tends to be in the right hemisphere.

The launchforce.com spinning cup and spoon exercise points out, however, that doing any complex mental activity requires cooperation from *both* sides of the brain (although certain processing tasks required for that activity may be concentrated on one side or the other).

In other words, saying that creativity and imagination are strictly right brain functions is an over-generalized statement, or what we like to call around here, a *myth*. It's not as if you have a special creativity module somewhere in your brain. It's an all-or-nothing proposition.

Michael O'Boyle, a psychologist at the University of Melbourne, Australia, conducted a study that found mathematically gifted students did better than average students on tests that required *both* halves of the brain to cooperate.

This demonstrated that, while the typical person might lean more heavily on one hemisphere or the other to do mental tasks necessary for math calculation, the most innovative and creative among us more fully integrate both hemispheres of our brains.

The idea that emotion processing only occurs in the right brain hemisphere and fact processing in the left is also *myth*leading. Brain-imaging studies have shown that people process emotion using small parts of both brain hemispheres.

The popular notion of an "emotional" right hemisphere that contrasts sharply with a "rational" left hemisphere is like what the *Scientific American Mind* called a "crude pencil sketch made before a full-color painting."

To prove this point, neurologist Dirk Wildgruber of the University of Tübingen designed tests that relied on the intonation of language rather than on its plain content, because how a person says something often transmits more emotional information than what he or she is saying.

Imagine saying, "I love your new haircut" with a smile in your voice to someone. Now imagine shouting "I LOVE YOUR NEW HAIRCUT" with an angry tone in your voice. The phrase is a compliment, but it will either be graciously accepted or rejected depending on the tone. That's because the difference in the intensity of the emotional expression has everything to do with how it is received. Experiments like the one above have proven that the emotional coloration inherent in tone stimulates two brain regions, one in the frontal lobe and one in each of the parietal lobes. Differentiating intonation is the result of numerous small contributions from both hemispheres. This conclusion gave Tübingen and his researchers much to ponder. Suddenly, the question of whether the right hemisphere is primarily responsible for emotions could not be answered clearly. Which hemisphere takes the leading role seems to depend not just on which sense is stimulated (vision or hearing) but also on the nature of the stimulus (tone versus words).

An analogue to this is a widely circulated test that shows the words for certain colors printed in different colored ink. Reading the word "pink" in purple type and the word "orange" in yellow type actually causes the brain to ping-pong while deciphering the meaning from the tone (or color in this case). Either way, it takes the entire brain to do anything meaningfully, whether it's innovation or playing chess.

Continuing to insist that there are only left-brain or right-brain people also fails to account for the human brain's mysterious flexibility and plasticity. Someone who has had half of his brain removed encounters some problems such as not being able to move or see from one side of his body—but largely retain or relearn mental abilities such as language in the remaining brain hemisphere. All this research clearly points out that while Nobel winner Sperry was onto something with his right-brain/left-brain theories, trying to fully compartmentalize mental activity by brain hemisphere is a *myth*stake. It may account however, for the old saying that it only takes "half a brain" to do something.

So what do those inferior left-brain/right-brain tests like the

"spinning ballerina" (http://www.news.com.au/heraldsun/story/
0,21985,22556281-661,00.html) tell us, if anything? It's really more
of just an optical illusion. When our brains process visual images to
make some order or sense of the world, they have to make assumptions. The "dancer" example is just a two-dimensional image switch-
ing back and forth, but our brains process it as a three-dimensional
spinning object.

Depending on the assumptions made and visual cues picked up,
your brain can make the dancer spin either way. What that can tell you
about your personality and mental abilities is actually hard to say.

Two Rights Don't Make a Brain

Elsewhere in this book, you've seen Albert Einstein's famous quote that
"Imagination is more important than knowledge." Well, an interviewer
also once asked Einstein how he developed his complex scientific theories. "With a pencil and a piece of paper," he answered while pointing
to his head. Oh. I see. How simple.

But Einstein's reply clearly demonstrates the perfect union of ana-
lytics and creativity in innovation. Out of Einstein's working process
came many famous scientific theories, including the Theory of Rela-
tivity. Nothing could better illustrate the integration of the left brain
and the right brain: logic and reasoning coupled with imagination and
creativity, perhaps better described as "whole-brained" thinking.

Leave it to Einstein to help point the way to a current, fundamental
shift in innovation. It's not all about right-brain creativity and it's not
all about left-brain logistics. In fact, business leaders are embracing,
with great impact, the concept of integrating analytical abilities and
creativity together into a true *whole-brained* innovation model.

Remember *BusinessWeek's* christening of the "Creative Economy?"
How's that one for a whole-brainer. Of course it sounds like a buzzword,
but as *BusinessWeek* pointed out, companies that have embraced the
concept are gaining a bottom-line edge over those who haven't. . . .

Innovation and design point the way out of a lot of the difficulties U.S. companies face as high-paying jobs in tech and manufacturing shift overseas. But the smartest U.S. companies are learning that they can still lead the way if they listen closely to their customers and rethink product design. That's how Starbucks can charge so much for a cappuccino and how the Swiffer made the mop kick the bucket.

While innovation and creative design in products and services seem to point the way to future business success, there is more work to do. Innovation and whole-brained thinking should be employed to revamp companies' entire organizational structures—not merely their R&D, sales, and marketing departments—as they endeavor to bring successful new products and services to market.

Today's business leaders are faced with Herculean challenges and the complexities of doing business in a global environment. Competition is at a fever pitch and will continue to increase at unprecedented levels as emerging economic powerhouses China and India market their products and services on a global stage. Instilling an entire company with a whole-brained culture can make a profound difference in the way companies meet these new challenges.

After all, if business executives (who by reputation were cast as "left-brained") are expected to become creative thinkers, problem solvers, and innovators to keep their companies ahead of ever-intensifying global competition, won't the basic premises of whole-brained thinking serve them well? You could call this a move to integrate right-brain (creative, innovative and design) and left-brain (analytical, management) thinking in the highest circles of business.

RIGHT, YOU ARE

The entire corporate structure of Procter & Gamble could fairly be said to be left-brain leaning. But since taking over as CEO at P&G, A.G. Lafley has steadily worked to incorporate the right side as well. He brought P&G marketing veteran Claudia Kotchka into the new role of "VP for Design Innovation and Strategy" to turn P&G into what she calls a "design-centric culture." When the CEO of such a gargantuan CPG company embraces the integration of right-brain elements of design into the left-brain elements of strategy and its implications for developing meaningful customer experiences at this level, it signals that powerful changes are underway.

Companies such as Dell, Apple, Starbucks, Nokia, Samsung, and BMW have all embraced a whole-brained philosophy, as evidenced by the numerous articles and case studies referencing this trend and cataloging their successes. These companies have become leaders in their respective sectors. To be effective, this thinking has to pervade the entire corporate structure, from the CEO on down.

Just why are so many companies left-brain leaning to begin with? We think it is pretty obvious that our educational systems teaches courses, especially at the undergraduate collegiate and MBA levels, (where our business leaders are made), very much in a left-brain mode. Very few courses within school curricula embrace right-brain thinking, except the arts, it seems.

Speaker, author, and former White House speech writer Daniel Pink has boldly stated in leadership conferences, "The era of 'left-brain' dominance, and the Information Age that it engendered, are now giving way to a new world in which 'right brain' qualities—inventiveness, empathy, meaning—predominate. Indeed, we are moving from an era when the MBA was the most treasured recruit to the MFA (Master of Fine Arts) graduate who can provide a broadened approach."

And that broadened approach today is whole-brained. Otherwise known as an "integrative brain" model. A quick online peek at several of the nation's leading business school courses (Harvard, Georgetown, and Northwestern) show that they are now all offering to their MBA candidates courses in product design, product innovation, or the management of the design process. Although all are just single elective courses. Stanford University has established a new Institute of Design to make design strategy a "cardinal virtue" to both business and design students. The trend will most certainly continue.

The authors of this book believe that the current business leaders will embrace this new "creativity economy" as it unfolds. They must in order to survive. We predict that the corporate and design sectors will integrate their analytical and creative problem-solving strengths as never before. The dividends this will yield are better, more meaningful innovations and customer experiences. And that is where companies will ultimately realize the full potential of brand loyalty and brand equity.

Despite our crusade, we recognize that the shorthand use of these labels (left and right brain) are entrenched in business jargon and like most myths, aren't going to go away over night. So, practically speaking, how do you get folks who are more analytical, logical and linear to play in the innovation sandbox? It's critical to do so, because you simply can't champion breakthrough thinking if the team around you isn't buying in.

The unhappy task in converting innovation team members to using their "whole brain" can be turning the lines in the sand that some are forever drawing into more open-ended "how-can-we" questions. What makes it difficult is that it requires people to forget the past to some degree. But unless they do so, they will be blocking off large areas of their brain with a "No Access" sign.

We've found that when you're surrounded by people chewing on their pencils, it's probably because they can't stand some of the ambiguity and open-ended processes involved with innovation. If you just make it a point to clarify the process, and continuously remind them of where they are at in that process, you'll see them gradually relax. Of course, if you want to get really innovative, you will need to *increase* chaos. Not everyone wants to get aboard that train. Picasso said it best," The act of creation is first of all an act of destruction." Tom Peters perhaps said it second best," Innovation is a messy business."

In our chapter about BASES testing elsewhere in this book, we make the point that no innovation is truly "risk-free." If you can remind risk-averse analytical people of times in their lives when they've had a really great idea and how it came to them and how they felt about it, you'll be amazed to learn that even these kind of folks can stretch out and think big. Just remember that for years most corporations actually tried to increase predictability. Not exactly the best environment for innovation.

In the 1950s, the cure for polio was discovered at the University of Cincinnati by Dr. Linus Pauling. He was once asked: "How do you get a good idea?" He responded by saying "The best way to get a good idea is to get *lots* of ideas and throw the bad ones away." Concentrating on getting a lot of ideas is one way to short-circuit the perfectionists and self-censoring types. They'll be whole-brained in no time with a little innovation fluency.

As this book (and its title) hopefully has been demonstrating, the right use of humor is also a great way to help people use their whole brain. Is it any wonder when it comes to innovation that "ha-ha" and "aha" are so closely related? Isn't humor basically a surprise ending to a story? Don't you laugh when your expectations are challenged in a delightful way? Perhaps, when it comes to innovation, being playful is just as helpful as being funny.

Creative thinking exercises alternating between cerebral activity and a more physical, hands-on approach also tend to yield much success in getting the "whole brain" working. For a much deeper understanding as to ways in which to help analytical, logical, linear thinkers become whole brainers, read our next Myth on Brainstorming.

In summary, rather than the old bromide that you have to be right-brained to be creative, we believe that great innovative thinking occurs at that point when logic and emotion begin to fuse into a cohesive unit. And that's why we heartily endorse the education and training of our future innovation, business management, and marketing leaders, (while perhaps retraining current ones) with this "whole brain" integrative approach, effectively using both sides of the brain as Einstein did. It can only lead to some stunning new business successes and innovation that we've naturally never seen before. Perhaps not at the speed of light—but relatively soon.

MYTH #10   BRAINSTORMING WORKS!

I could wile away the hours
Conferring with the flowers
Consulting with the rain
And my head I'd be scratching
While my thoughts were busy hatching
If I only had a brain
—HARBURG AND ARLEN, FROM *THE WIZARD OF OZ*, 1939

The best and only way to turn Oz into "ahhhs!" is by forgetting everything you've ever heard about "brainstorming."

Because brainstorming simply doesn't work.

That is, if by working, you mean yielding new, breakthrough, never-before-seen ideas and concepts.

New research proves that brainstorming, as you know it, produces fewer ideas than if you just sat by yourself in a cornfield, like our friend the Scarecrow, and pondered ideas for a spell.

These days you hear the word "brainstorming" in popular speech about as often as you hear trademarked brand names like Kleenex, Band-Aid, and Jell-O.

But did you know "brainstorming" is a brand name, too?

Back in 1957, Alex Osborn is credited with coining the word to refer to the approach he developed for idea generation. Now the term is used so generically, its specific meaning is often lost. But be aware: contrary to popular belief, brainstorming is an inferior method of generating ideas!

As a reader of this book, you're probably a decision-maker frequently facing the task of generating new ideas, sometimes called "ideation."

Whether the ideas you're charged to come up with represent solutions to a manufacturing problem or novel ways to add new yogurt technology in a snack form, idea generation is an important group task, and brainstorming is often used in a generic sense to describe groups who generate ideas.

Taking a quick look back at history (so we can learn from it), when Osborn, who was a founding partner of the Batten, Barton, Durstine, and Osborn advertising firm, expressed frustration at employees' lack of creativity in problem solving and idea generation, he was convinced the problem was that they were evaluating and judging ideas to the point that all originality would be smothered. The tendency was for folks in the room to "clam up" if they had something truly original to say for fear of being shouted down as pie-in-the-sky dreamers. Not a great atmosphere for creativity, is it?

Osborn diagnosed the problem expertly; he just couldn't succeed at developing exercises that would truly free the imaginations of the participants. And if you've been in a brainstorming exercise within your corporation lately, you know this is true.

Why Brainstorming Is Mostly a Drizzle

Let me guess. You shuffle into a room, pressed for time. Most participants bring their laptops and lovingly cradle their "crackberry" at all times. Imposing easels of crisp, blank white paper stare back at the assembled group. The same staff members that are always invited to these things are there. No one could be called a pacesetter with a demonstrated ability in creative problem solving.

There isn't anyone clearly leading things, either. When the group's well begins to run dry, there is no one to point them in a new direction. There is no one to move them to a previously considered, but not fully explored, set of ideas when they are spending too much time discussing one particular category of ideas. Appreciable periods of silence begin to appear between responses.

Ugh. Can I go home now?

Finally, someone is brave enough to shout out the same idea he or she had last year. (These are what are known as "pet ideas," and they make frequent appearances). As soon as an idea or two are floated, inexorably, someone (R&D methinks) shouts it down as unworkable, impossible, and perhaps even unpatriotic! The repeated killing of ideas acts so much like a rolled up newspaper to the brainstormer's cold, wet nose. Okay, okay, we get it! No new ideas need apply.

After a tedious afternoon, where someone with decent penmanship is recruited to write down all of the "ideas" that were already in the participant's heads before they even walked into the room, the brainstorm is mercifully concluded.

You could have conducted the whole thing via e-mail—and it might have gone better since there would be no "Grim Idea Reapers" in the room to shout folks down.

Why does this happen over and over again?

It happens because brainstorming is putting too many opposing forces at war with each other. Logic vs. creativity. Blue sky vs. rain clouds. The spirit against the flesh. Arts vs. science. Mets vs. Yankees. And most importantly, the left side of your brain against the right side of your brain.

Suspending judgment is so difficult because the left side of your brain is, in effect, judgmental while the right side of your brain is "creative." The two are at odds. Creative juices cannot flow optimally when the blinding supernova of logic is drying them all up. It's almost downright unnatural. Kind of like a jazz musician who can balance a checkbook.

As discussed in our previous myth, experimentation has shown that the two sides (or hemispheres) of the brain are responsible for different manners of thinking and that each of us prefers one mode to the other.

The left side of the brain is logical, sequential, rational, analytical, objective, and looks at parts. The right side of the brain is random, intuitive, holistic, synthesizing, subjective, and looks at wholes.

It's not surprising that brainstorming doesn't work when you consider that most schools tend to favor left-brain modes of thinking, while downplaying right-brain ones.

Consider Mozart and his piano. There he is in Vienna, over 300 years ago sitting in front of those 88 keys playing a lovely concerto that can move you to tears. Sheer genius. Conversely, there is Travis, just last week sitting in front of his own set of 88 keys in Walla-Walla. Travis is playing the same concerto note-for-note. And you're crying as you listen, but not because he has touched your heart.

What happened? They're both playing the same notes. Yes, but Mozart is gracefully putting his wholebrained heart and soul into it, while alas, poor Travis is plunking along with left brain like he is typing on a keyboard, or solving a math problem. You can't just go through the motions and expect success. Hence the phrase: "One more time, with *feeling!*"

It's Not Whether You Win or Lose (actually, it kinda is)

As the name *BrainGaming* implies, the game is afoot.

The authors made a conscious decision to create teams or sides as with any game. Why? Because rivalry acts like a stimulant. Competition is a good thing when it puts pride on the line. Think of it as an ideational advantage.

By introducing a spirit of friendly rivalry into BrainGaming, you definitely ratchet up the motivation to get your brain in gear. You'll never be creative if you don't try, and playing for something is a way to get a room of people trying. Big time.

Of course we're not talking about smash-mouth football here. Although rivalry is created, it is important that the overall BrainGaming environment be relaxed, like a camping trip, because a laissez-faire mood is conducive to great ideas. The best part of BrainGaming is that it focuses everyone's attention on the positive. It's a fact that our brains are incapable of thinking of two things at the same time. So if we're concentrating on winning, we can't be thinking about losing. If we're staying positive, we can't venture into the dark side of negativity. And that's a good thing. So is a room full of people in which every single one of them is concentrating on trying to come up with the best ideas. When this happens, no one can be thinking about why a certain idea may be "stupid," or unworkable. Just like that, we've taken the potential idea-killer out of the room and found the Rosetta Stone Osborn could not: a way to truly free the minds (and more importantly the *imaginations*) of the participants.

ENTER BRAINGAMING

One of great fallacies of brainstorming is the notion of recruiting plenty of "right-brain thinkers" and "left-brain thinkers" and putting them in the same room so they can mix it up. The result is generally chaos.

BrainGaming was invented, not to pit one style against another, but rather to get everyone in the room more *whole-brained* and equally adept at both modes. Gently pushing the left brainers to become more right-brained for a while, and vice-versa.

The authors of this book figured out that in order to be more "whole-brained" in our ideation techniques, we had to give equal weight to the arts, creativity, and the skills of imagination and synthesis. Up until then, logic was the rule of the day.

To foster a more whole-brained experience, we use ideation techniques that connect both sides of the brain. By adding the "gaming" side to the equation, we incorporate patterning, metaphors, analogies, role-playing, visuals, and movement into what can otherwise be a more calculated analytical activity.

The other element that is critical with the introduction of games is the all-important reduction of fear. If you call a bunch of people into a room and ask them a direct question such as, "What form do you think our new cereal should take?" you might as well have a bright light in their face and a rubber hose at the ready. You won't get a breakthrough that contradicts history, but you may get them to confess to a crime they didn't commit!

Why? You can't be creative and simply unlock the better angels of your brain if you are intimidated, frightened, and have flop-sweat running down your brow. Even if the leader (if there is one) *tells* you "no idea is a bad idea, don't worry." It's sort of like when you are worrying about an upcoming task, like having to give a speech, or having an approaching physical, and your friend tells you "not to worry." That sure makes you stop worrying right? Not.

But what if you were having fun? What if you were relaxed, and laughing, and (gasp!) enjoying yourself? What if the meeting wasn't drudgery, but the time was actually flying by?

It's a scientifically proven fact that the more you are laughing, the greater the quantity *and* quality of your ideas. For the good of your customers, your own jobs, the shareholders, and each other, have a good time. Think, joke, and be merry for today we ideate!

That's why the person who is leading the ideation session really needs to be a pro. The fish rots from the head down and a most unholy stench can emerge from a room if the leader is not properly trained. Inexperienced leaders can let the room get out of control. They are incapable of recognizing when a horse has been beaten into the glue jar. They play favorites, and allow bullying and have no sense of clock management. As my grandmother would say, "God love 'em, they mean well." But they can mean the difference between success and failure.

Remember, by definition, a breakthrough idea cannot be lockstep with history. It either needs to accelerate it or completely cut against the grain. The best session leaders understand that and constantly push for breakthrough ideas.

This does not mean there is no such thing as a bad idea. And the best leaders will recognize them. A bad idea is something we did last year. Or something your competitors did two years ago. Or something that's currently on the shelf at your local grocer's. Leaders don't need to respect those ideas; they are not new.

Professional leaders *do* need to show respect for those ideas that haven't yet seen the light of day. It often happens that a particular idea will hit someone's subjective filter in the wrong way. When this happens, a great leader has two choices: Shut up, or make it better. Help the room to bend it, twist it, stand it on its head, but help that never-before-seen idea to live!

LET THE GAMES BEGIN

First the Focus: The simple truth of the matter is, any ideation without a focus will result in pure chaos. Sure, there may be lots of ideas in lots of areas, but most will be useless or infeasible. So, before beginning any ideation, there must be agreement as to what exactly the respondents are to focus on. For example, is it a product that helps moms and kids connect? Is it a product that makes it easy to take medicine? The greater the focus, the richer the ideas. It is far more productive to have 20 ideas focused in one needed area than hundreds of ideas all over the place!

In fact, it is far more productive to think of an ideation session as being a "problem solving" session. Once the "problem" is clearly understood by all participants, the "ideas" or answers, while still being creative, will be much more on target.

This is why we recommend that early on in the innovation process, you first identify potential consumer or marketplace "insights." Once the insights have been uncovered and agreed upon (as we teach you in the previous myth "consumer is king"), they become *the* "problem" to solve! In other words, they give you a "target" to hit with your ideas.

As an example, let's say we have uncovered an insight regarding consumers and breakfast. Specifically, we have uncovered an insight that people really could use a breakfast food that keeps them feeling full until lunch. Now think about how much more productive an ideation session would be if instead of being challenged to brainstorm a new type of breakfast food, we ideate around a new type of breakfast food *that keeps you full until lunch!*

Next the homework assignment: I know, I know. It sounds boring. It's supposed to. The idea here is to "drain the swamp" and release all of the pet ideas already in everyone's head *before* the day of the session. A review of everyone's homework at the beginning of the actual Brain-Gaming not only ensures a fast, targeted start for the session but also provides a nice springboard stimulus for the creation of fresh new ideas by others.

And don't forget to form the teams: For the actual BrainGaming session, get the participants into teams. As we have mentioned, teams help provide that extra incentive to be creative and it creates a focus on the positive. Even more important, we have found that smaller groups tend to create far better than large masses. For those unfamiliar with how most advertising agencies work, ads and other creative concepts usually come *not* from the Creative *Department*, but rather from creative *teams* within the department. Generally, it is a writer teaming up with an art director that is charged with coming up with multiple creative concepts targeted against a specific strategy.

We find that breaking a group into smaller teams, having the teams ideate independently from one another and *then* letting the entire group build on each team's ideas is the best of everything!

NOW BRING ON THE FUN!

Below are a few examples of BrainGames that do two things:

- Help people forget they are under the gun and eliminate the fear factor that would otherwise make them keep to themselves some of the ideas that come to mind.

- Create stimulus to get the room's collective brain in a space where new ideas are possible.

Earth Day

A kissin' cousin to Homework Assignment, this game shows old concepts that did not make it for one reason or another and the object is for the room to choose one at a time and recycle-to-refine. Or relegate it to the dustbin of history.

Dream-it

A true stimulus for ideation is to change people's perspectives and make them think of things in ways they wouldn't normally think of. For example, think of your particular product and come up with 20 new ideas for it. Kind of hard isn't it? Now, let's add some perspectives. What if your product were spiritual? What if your product were trying to be emotional? What if your product were trying to be different physically? We'll bet you can come up with probably 20 ideas for each perspective. In BrainGaming, give teams different perspectives to ideate around and watch the sparks fly!

Word Score

Teams are given a stack of words from the dictionary that are not typically used to describe the product. These are used as inspiration to create the germ of a breakthrough idea.

Occasions/Locations

Each person is given a blank sheet of paper and has a short period of time to list 15 times/occasions/locations where the new product in question would be used. Lists are passed to a neighbor who circles the most unusual or far-out entry on the list. The list is passed to another person to develop idea-starters against the circled entry.

Nine Iron Chef

Each person or team selects 9 items from a store visit (or a pre-selected stock of store items). These are used to create a new product idea. Ideas are captured on idea or starter sheets. Dial up the fun by inviting an actual chef to the activity.

Grocery Safari

Take the team on a quick tour of a grocery store to observe the unique ingredients, flavors, and food offerings. Thoughts and observations are captured on cards. Teams are given a stack of these cards afterward to help generate idea-starters.

Subscription Prescription

Each team is given a stack of magazines in and outside the category you are ideating against. The object is to cut out images and paste them to cards to be used to spark ideas.

Wheel of Fusion

Take BrainGaming to its literal extreme and create two wheels with six to eight "landing areas" from disparate places (e.g. forms & textures; places & things; macro trends & micro trends) and have two people spin the wheels simultaneously. The object is to *fuse* the two areas together when ideating. This can take you to some new places you'd otherwise never dream of. Make it more fun and have a place the wheel could land on that would obligate the person doing the spinning to have to do a silly trick or sing a song *a cappella*. Keeps the energy in the room bristling.

This leads us to a game that's a little more progressive than some of the others. What if you fused *ideation* and *karaoke*?

Ideoke

An inventive and fun way to provide insight into market needs, Ideoke is specifically designed for identifying unmet or idealized market needs, which can then be used as input to strategic planning and the identification of new business opportunities. As we're fond of saying, an innovation consultancy had better have innovative ideation methods. But never innovative for innovation's sake. No sir. It has to be effective.

Why Ideoke works

Most customers have a hard time articulating breakthrough ideas. Ideoke solves the problem by stimulating ideas and exploring needs and wants that they can't clearly state by engaging both the left and right side of the brain simultaneously.

It can be difficult (in a business meeting) to escape the left-brain focus on analysis, accuracy, and sequence. This style of thinking needs a creative, holistic boost and tapping into the more intuitive side is achieved with the demand to sing and think at the same time!

How Ideoke works

To insure 100 percent focus and participation, Ideoke features a win/loss risk and a team dynamic.

A Master Concepter (M.C.) acts as the host and helps select the teams. Once teams are selected, the lights dim, the glitter ball begins to spin and a DJ's beat-box starts to pound out the rhythm.

A Development Junkie (D.J.) mans an easel to record the ideas as each "contestant" takes the microphone and is pressured on the spot to answer a series of prompts under pressure and by singing the "answer."

EVERYBODY DANCE NOW

By forcing both left and right brainers to become "wholebrainers," criticism is ruled out and adverse judgment of ideas must be withheld until later.

Because it is always easier to tame down than to think up, Brain-Gaming activities like Ideoke welcome freewheeling ideas. The wilder the better.

With ideation of any sort, quantity is crucial. The greater the number of ideas, the greater the likelihood of a winner being buried in there somewhere. More needles and fewer haystacks, I always say.

Since "treeing off" and "popcorning" (the combination and improvement of ideas) is always sought, BrainGaming activities include a group dynamic that guides participants into suggesting how someone else's idea can be turned into a better idea—or how two or more ideas can be joined into still another idea.

Ideoke, like every other tactic in our BrainGaming arsenal, proves that the nature of group ideation allows for idea generation through the power of association, with "creative sparks" as a byproduct.

In other words, when Jane presents an idea to a group of Brain-Gamers, the power of association implies that her original idea might "spark" novel ideas both in Jane and in other BrainGamers.

BrainGaming's life force is the free expression of ideas.

CHECK YOUR JUDGMENT, NOT YOUR BRAIN, AT THE DOOR

Some of the best ideas are the ones currently stranded in your subconscious mind. Typical brainstorming sessions will never root them out because of the inherent social inhibition at play.

And that would be a pity. The fact is, an idea that appears strange or bizarre to some may actually be the creative spark the room has been looking for.

How do you break this cycle of evaluation apprehension and fear of explicit or implicit criticism?

You gotta go under.

Not Australia, but out of your mind.

HYPNOIMAGING

As a matter of transparent disclosure, the authors of this book are all trained hypnotists. We share Pavlov's view that it is possible for people to become less identified with sensory information and their own conscious minds—that in a state of "partial sleep," the lower brain stem allows an enhancing of the activity of the nervous system.

In the last decade, brain-scanning technology has made it possible to observe hypnosis' effect in the brain. EEG coherence measures have shown that hypnotic hallucinations can elicit the same brain activity as real experiences.

Each of us has experienced great success harnessing this mystical roadmap into the subconscious with an activity we call *HypnoImaging*—a powerful, guided visualization exercise that helps participants reinvent the familiar into the extraordinary by tapping into the most fertile areas of their minds.

The stage is set by creating a harmonious environment with a darkened room, scented candles, relaxing music, and yoga mats, sleep masks, and cushioned socks.

By getting the group members out of their physical routine, we can then begin to get them out of their mental routine as well.

Leading the group by lowering our voices and speaking in calm, measured, resonant tones, we mellifluously begin. Slowly and quietly, the group members relax through breathing exercises and leave their conscious minds behind. As they uncover and discover sights, sounds, smells, and tastes, they are instructed to remember everything and bring it back with them as they return from this hypnotic state.

See the sidebar in this chapter for a transcript of a HypnoImaging session held in the summer of 2008 for Purina.

One of the great advantages to HypnoImaging is that it allows the entire group to subconsciously "speak" at the same time (which would be impossible in the conscious state). In this way, there are no inhibitions in the total number of ideas that can be discovered and "brought back."

By immediately (and quietly) writing down everything uncovered after the session, ideas are captured simultaneously and nothing is forgotten. Judgment is avoided because ideas are captured in a relatively anonymous environment—all of which leads to a greater number of ideas.

HypnoImaging

Reproduced transcript of an actual HypnoImaging session held on June 9, 2008, for Purina

We're going to go on a little journey.
But we're going to *clear our minds,* first.
Feel yourself breathe.
Take a deep breath in . . . (pause)
. . . out.
Deep breath in . . . (pause)
. . . out.
When we breathe in next, HOLD your breath.
Deep in . . . *hold.*
Blow out your breath.
Deep breath in . . . (pause)
. . . out.
Become *aware* of your breathing.
(pause :10 seconds)
Relax.
Feel the muscles in your forehead.
Tighten the muscles in your forehead.
Let them *relax.*
Tighten the muscles in your face.

Relax.

Tighten the muscles in your shoulders.

Relax.

Tighten the muscles in your arms.

Relax.

Let your muscles *relax.*

Begin to feel energy flowing into your arms.

Out of your fingers.

Into the air.

Leave all worries behind.

Tighten the muscles in your legs.

Let them go.

Tighten the muscles in your feet.

Relax.

You begin to feel the floor beneath you.

You begin to feel heavier.

As you enter a deep state of relaxation, *let yourself go.*

Clear your mind.

Feel the gravity of the Earth holding you onto the planet.

Sense the movement of the Earth . . . *spinning.*

You're as heavy as lead.

Roll your eyes up towards your forehead—until you see a flash of light.

Relax.

You begin to get *lighter.*

Imagine you begin to rise and float above your body.

Lighter than air.

Floating through the air like a *feather* with no direction and no cares or worries.

You rise up as the wind takes you *higher.*

You look down upon the Earth.

You take in its *beauty.*

You begin to move forward.

It becomes completely dark as you begin to move faster and faster.

Feel the wind against your face.

You're moving at the *speed of light*.

As you begin to slow down—you're suspended in space and you can see *nothing*.

- CUSTOMIZED SECTION BEGINS

    You begin to think of your childhood.

    It becomes light.

    You start to see yourself—images of your childhood.

    You go back.

    You start to smell the aromas of food cooking.

    What do you smell?

    You realize you're looking at yourself—and you've been transformed into a cat.

    Walking through your home.

    What do you see?

    What do you smell?

    What do you crave?

    What are your thoughts?

    What are your feelings?

    Etc., etc., etc.

- CUSTOMIZED SECTION ENDS

You begin to rise in the air.

Looking down on the entire scene.

In your mind, remember everything.

Every detail.

Every feeling.

Moving further away.

Further up in the sky.

Everything becomes *smaller* . . .

. . . *darker*.

You begin to move through the air.

Returning . . . returning . . .

As you move through the air, you feel energy flowing into your body . . .

. . . into your mind.

The faster you go . . .

You feel you are *bursting* with energy.

With *power.*

With *courage.*

You are *emboldened.*

You'll be able to offer new, creative, bold thoughts with no fear.

You will remember everything.

You sense the light.

The glow of the sunrise over the horizon of the Earth.

Closer to the Earth . . . you return.

You see yourself.

You float above for moments.

You are *changed.*

Forever.

On the count of three, you will awaken *refreshed*, *energized*, creative.

And you will remember *everything.*

One . . .

Two . . .

Three.

Slowly remove your masks and make your way back to your tables.

CLOSING CEREMONY

Mere brainstorming groups are inferior to BrainGaming sessions in the production of the quantity and quality of ideas. The spirit, structure, and functioning of BrainGaming and the way in which groups are formed, trained, and expected to generate ideas is vastly superior. And the friendly competition engenders peak performance and a dropping of the guard.

In reality, continuous innovation is hard work. And continuously innovating the right products, features, and capabilities is even harder. But there is a better way to ensure you get what you want, and some of it *is* all fun and games. Most of all, BrainGaming gets you to think in unique and unusual ways, which leads to better innovation. And that, is no *myth*stake.

MYTH #11 CROWDSOURCING DELIVERS GREAT IDEAS ON THE CHEAP

ONE OF THE biggest trends in business today is a trend unto itself: Crowdsourcing. *Wired* magazine's Jeff Howe first coined the term in 2006. You may have heard it referred to as fansourcing, crowdcasting, open sourcing, open innovation, crowdfunding, mass collaboration, collective customer commitment, or wikinomics. But you probably haven't heard anyone point out the inherent and potential pitfalls. And that's a *myth*stake.

No matter what you call it, the basic premise is about tapping into the "collective intelligence" of John Q. Public. Companies from Procter & Gamble to Chipotle, Amazon, Eli Lilly, Twitter, Google, Facebook, and Yahoo are using e-mail, blogs, wikis, and YouTube to follow the trends and get in on the Great American GroupThink. Procter & Gamble created a democratic marketplace for innovation (an "Ideagora") to tap into the brains of 90,000 chemists in a forum designed for scientists to collaborate with P&G to solve R&D problems in return for cash prizes. It's the ultimate pay-to-play in which if you don't like the ideas, you don't have to pay for them.

It is true that a great idea can come from just about anyone, so crowdsourcing to some extent, makes sense. In fact, years ago my son who was eight years old at the time, gave me a great idea for what eventually became one of the hottest Super Soaker toys ever, the Super Soaker MDS (a multiple spraying water gun that could shoot in different directions). He also gave me a wonderful idea for a new type of cheese. It went from his mouth to my ear to my client's ear to a national launch within just six months. And, my wife recently gave me a potentially huge banking idea that we are just now presenting to clients.

But as much as anyone has the potential of providing you with a possibly great idea, it would be foolish, considering the importance of innovation, to rely solely on the "crowd." Not because the *hoi polloi* isn't increasingly more sophisticated and intelligent, but because the great masses (washed or unwashed) can really only know where you've been. They can't possibly know where you're going or where you'd like to go. The very notion of turning to the roar of the crowd to perform a professional service that you (or a third-party provider) would normally do is fraught with peril—even if it is free. Or maybe precisely because it is free. You generally get what you pay for in this great country of ours.

Elsewhere in this book, we have covered at length why it's a myth to think that you can really depend on consumers-in-a-vacuum to help you gain deeper insight into what they really want. And yet the "trend" is toward crowdsourcing to tell you what consumers want on an ever-larger scale.

The line is blurring between the producer of media and the consumer of media, to be sure. It wasn't that long ago (2006), that *Time* chose the collective "YOU" as the magazine's "Person of the Year." And we all champion the explosion of productivity and innovation as millions of minds that would otherwise have drowned in obscurity get backhauled into the *zeitgeist* of a global intellectual economy of scale.

But let's be honest about the limitations as it pertains to intellectual capital vs. intellectual economy. The idea of simply soliciting customer input is hardly new, of course, and the open-source software movement has long since proven that it can be done with exponentially larger and larger numbers of people.

And, just as there are unending sources of people who want to lose weight, starve themselves, race across the globe, or find a husband in front of millions on national television, there are equal numbers who want to help your business (qualifications be damned). Years ago, Doritos asked the public to make its Super Bowl commercial for them. The trend continues. But is that new? Of course not.

We've been hearing a lot about how Crowdsourcing can improve productivity and creativity while minimizing labor and research expenses. True enough, using the Internet to solicit feedback from an active and passionate community of customers can reduce the amount of time and money spent collecting data through formal focus groups or trend research. But there are some hidden *myths* here to be aware of.

Crowds are not employees. Don't think for a minute that just because you are an executive, you'll be able to control them, because you can't. And while it's true the masses often don't ask for cash or in-kind products, participants *will* seek compensation in the form of satisfaction, recognition, and freedom. They will also certainly demand time, attention, patience, good listening skills, transparency, and honesty. For traditional top-down organizations, this shift in management culture may prove difficult, if not impossible.

As an aside, "employee" sourcing of ideas has its limitations too. Many companies have tried setting up inter-office websites, wikis, and other tools to encourage all employees to offer new innovative ideas. Unfortunately, most companies that have done this report that almost all of the ideas that they received are pretty bad. So, it's not surprising that over a little time, management spends less and less time reviewing these ideas and even less time offering any constructive criticism. As a result, employees see little encouragement to continue offering ideas, and their participation goes down.

This happens because these companies are asking their people to do something for which they have absolutely no training. What should the ideas focus on? How do they know how to understand or look for customer needs? How do they know how to develop insights? How do they know how to understand a big, winning idea? And how do they know how to properly communicate the idea so that management "gets it?"

But even if all of these weak spots were removed, the main issue is that while crowdsourcing might be a great way for Netflix (the online video rental service) to offer customer movie recommendations, it is limited in its ability to offer valuable, breakthrough ideas no matter how cheap it is.

We're reminded of a quote from the brilliant Timothy Chou: "If you outsource to someone who is cheaper but not as smart as you, you have to spend a great deal of time managing them and you have to look over everything down to the tiniest detail."

Sound like fun?

It's also true that if you spend too much time managing, you'll lose most of the economic advantage you had for hiring "free" labor in the first place.

But notice what happens if you ignore the crowds and you end up hiring someone who is *smarter* than you (maybe an expert with a PhD, for example). In this case, you can let him run wild—unsupervised—and let him flourish on his own. That's when the real magic of breakthrough ideas and innovation happens.

How many of us, if we had the opportunity to hire an executive master chef, would tell him how to cook! It's the exact opposite. You tell him or her that you want a vegetarian dish that's savory, and perhaps a little sweet, and then you let the chef go to work.

If you go to the doctor with a pain in your shoulder, you want the doctor to make the pain go away, but you don't tell her how to go about it.

When it comes to innovation, rather than running to where the warm bodies are cheapest, run toward partners who are free—free to demonstrate their expertise. You'll find very little duplication of effort, if any. And most importantly, innovation can thrive.

It mostly comes down to whether you're more comfortable pushing or pulling. Would you rather use everyday people to help you innovate as a collective, or would you rather go out to the collective, but specifically seek out the best and the brightest to help you advance the common goal of breakthrough ideas?

Ideally, since good ideas *can* come from just about anyone, firms should try to elicit help and ideas from everyone and everywhere *as long as they can provide* the proper training and management. However, companies should not rely solely on these crowds for their next big ideas. A little professional help can go a long way to ensure innovation success.

MYTH #12 THERE IS NO SUCH THING AS A BAD IDEA

WHAT? You've never heard of "New Coke" or the "Ford Pinto?" Not to mention VH1's *Scott Baio Is 45 and Single* reality TV show. Of course there are bad ideas! Look no further than the courthouse: One out of every two marriages ends up in divorce. Now that's what we call bad ideas (even if it seemed like a great idea at the time)! We all know that lots of new products and other innovations don't pan out so well either, and at least some of these were due to the idea, itself.

We have mentioned that in Brainstorming or BrainGaming you must try to apply the "No idea is a bad idea" rule in order to free the imagination of participants and get as many good ideas to surface as possible, but this certainly does not mean that corporate funding and time should continue to go to every idea that comes out.

There are plenty of bad ideas to go around, so we must naturally do our best to try to weed out the bad ones before allocating too much time and money to them. The challenging part is to do this while keeping the potentially great ideas alive.

Indeed, many executives report that they have no shortage of ideas in their company "hopper." Rather, their challenge is determining *which* ideas to invest in. The weirder and more unusual an idea is, the harder it is to pick the winner from the loser.

How do you go about telling a good idea apart from a bad idea—choosing the cherry and leaving the pit?

If the innovation in question is *your* idea, chances are you've lost so much objectivity you might as well be trying to decide if your kid is the smartest one in school. That's why we need some guardrails to help us through.

The guardrails can come in all shapes and sizes, but basically, every company needs to set up meaningful criteria by which to judge ideas. The ideas should be consistent with objectives and within the capabilities, timing, and budgets of the company. Then, you should have a thorough understanding as to the potential costs it would take to successfully launch the idea into the marketplace, including true long-term revenue possibilities. Last, further risk/reward possibilities should be determined via research. Let's first, examine some suggested criteria.

DETERMINE OBJECTIVES

What are the objectives that the innovation must achieve? Each company will have its own, but it is important to first establish and agree upon them. This will not only help determine which ideas to go forward with, but will also minimize the waste of time and money right from the start by providing needed focus for all ideation participants. Objectives could include:

- **Growth** Are we looking for major growth? Do we want to enter new categories, capture share, or protect current volume?

- **Timing** Do we need to have this in the market by a certain date? Do we need products in our sights for the next 2 to 3 years?

- **Feasibility** Are we looking to get more out of existing capacity? Do we have the right distribution model in place? Are we dealing with the same corporate buyers? Must we make this ourselves or can we partner?

- **Risk Tolerance** Are we limited as to what we would be willing to spend? Are we looking for several relatively safer moves or a big game-changer? Are there certain things our company just won't do?

- **Revenue** Do we have a minimum revenue goal? Do we expect pay-out within a certain time frame?

Revenue is a particularly tough objective and question to ask early on in an ideas stage, and one must be careful not to kill a potentially great idea because of underestimating what customers might be willing to spend on it, especially if it is a very different idea.

Most of the time we suggest delaying the potential revenue question to the very end. But you don't have to be a Harvard Business School graduate to know that the more new and different an idea is, the greater its chances for both wonderful success or miserable, abject failure. It's a package deal, folks! It's certainly okay to include closer-in sustaining innovations within your overall innovation portfolios, but you also need to innovate game-changers, or you'll be in the Land of Commodities. And trust me, you don't want to be there. Why? Simply because commodities have the nagging habit of selling for commodity prices, which means margins are compressed and imitation is easy. Push yourself and each other to include the Land of New and Different in your innovation plans.

Some firms actually go through a formal idea screening process whereby various members of different departments rate each proposed idea in a variety of areas for the purpose of choosing the best candidates for further development. For example, first they would agree upon all key criteria on which the ideas will be judged. Then, they would assign a percentage weight to each criteria depending upon the relative importance of each criteria (so that all criteria add to 100 percent). For example, if anticipated cost of bringing the innovation to market is going to be considered three times as important as overall speed to market, then the percentage weight assigned to cost will be twice that given to speed (see below). Then every member scores how well each idea meets each criteria (usually on a 1 to 5 basis, with 5 being a very close fit and 1 being a very poor fit). Then a simple mathematical exercise is done whereby the importance weight multiplied by the degree of fit gives a total. The total of all of the totals yields a final weighted score for the idea. Each new idea's weighted score is placed against each other to determine which new product ideas seem to be best for moving forward.

RELATIVE IMPORTANCE X FIT (1–5)* = SCORE

Key criteria's relative importance *(in percent)*			Fit		Score
Cost to Market	15%	X	3	=	0.45
Speed to Market	5%	X	2	=	0.10
Easy to Develop	10%	X	3	=	0.30
Potential Profits	15%	X	4	=	0.60
ROI	15%	X	3	=	0.45
Potential Growth	5%	X	2	=	0.10
Sustainability	10%	X	3	=	0.30
Company Fit	10%	X	5	=	0.50
Capacity Utilization	10%	X	1	=	0.10
Passion for Idea	5%	X	3	=	0.15
TOTAL SCORE	**100%**				**3.05**

* Fit is determined as 1 being a poor fit and 5 being a great fit. Each criterion might have its own guidelines. For example: *Speed to Market*, 1 might be 36+ months, 5 might be 6 months or less.

Naturally firms should establish their own meaningful criteria. The above will just get you going.

Basically, it comes down to three important questions to consider:

1. Just how big of an idea could this be?

2. How feasible is this?

3. Can we make and sustain a profit?

Ultimate Costs

Assuming your ideas are consistent with the agreed upon objectives, it is also important to get a reasonable understanding of what the ultimate cost would look like to successfully bring each promising idea to market. You must determine if these costs are within your budget, or, if not, will partnership make sense?

- Are there significant technology, manufacturing and/or personnel hurdles that you must come to grips with?

- Is the new revenue expected from this idea going to be all incremental revenue or will it come from the expense of cannibalizing some of your original business?

- How difficult will it be for consumers to adopt this? Are new skills required? Will consumers easily understand the offering? How long will it take to truly make the item or service available to your entire customer base? (Distribution can be much slower than anticipated—and if customers can't find your item, they certainly cannot buy it!)

All of this and more should be considered to help shed light on potential marketing spend that will be needed.

Competitor Reaction

Sadly, firms in the early assessment of ideas often overlook potential reaction of their competitors and in reality, competitive reaction could be *the* most important determining factor of an innovation's ultimate success or failure. For example, if the innovation is not a game-changer but rather a relatively easy build on offerings already in the market-place, there is little stopping other brands from following you. Not only will this eat into your expected revenues *but*, if other brands are bigger than yours, their copy-cat innovation will automatically get more out of your innovation than you will. Many years ago, while directing the marketing of the #1 colored toilet bowl cleaner brand, Vanish, a toilet cleanser that also turned the toilet water a pleasing blue color, a far distant #2 brand, Tidy Bowl, out-innovated us and launched a *second* color—green. Tidy Bowl immediately gained extra volume and revenue with its additional color. It took significant share from Vanish since many bathrooms' color schemes fit better with green than blue. Well, guess what Vanish did?

Within the year, Vanish launched a copycat green-colored toilet cleaner. But, because the Vanish brand franchise was 4 times the size of the Tidy Bowl brand, Vanish Green outsold Tidy Bowl Green by 4 to 1. However, even more importantly, since retailers did not consider the colored-toilet-bowl-cleaner category large enough to carry that many SKUs, they decided to carry only the market leader—namely, Vanish! Tidy Bowl wound up watching virtually all of its Green distribution go down the crapper by the second year. The result? Tidy Bowl, the original innovator, received *zero* extra revenue from its effort while Vanish, the copycat, got *all* of the revenue. Some even said they were flush with cash. Some said that. We didn't.

As yet another wonderful example, several years ago we did quite a bit of innovation work with Borden Cheese. It didn't take us long to realize that no matter what we created in the sliced-cheese category, in a manner of months, Kraft would copy it, outspend Borden and wind up "owning" the idea themselves. With the significant volume advantage of the Kraft brand over the Borden brand, it was Kraft that would ultimately enjoy the greatest sales and profits from the new item, not Borden. In fact, just like the Vanish versus the Tidy Bowl example, many times Borden would lose all of the distribution it had on its own innovation, leaving Kraft to enjoy *all* of the revenue generated by the new idea, leaving poor Borden to wonder who moved its cheese.

We'll further address the importance of understanding category and competitor reactions later in this book.

Research

It goes without saying that consumer research is essential for helping to determine an idea's true potential. But we're going to say it anyway—just to be sure you're asking yourself these important questions:

Does the consumer intend to buy your new item? If not, does research indicate something that can be done to make your new offering more attractive? If yes, what are the most compelling reason consumers give for their interest? The latter point is truly critical for two reasons. First, there is a need for knowing what must be communicated to the consumer when the product is actually introduced into the marketplace. Second, to also make 100 percent certain that the number one preferred attribute or benefit the consumer gives for her purchase intent isn't accidentally cut out as a cost saving measure prior to launch. That can be the unkindest cut of all.

Your Final Warning

In trying to determine which ideas might have merit, avoid the group-think mentality along the "Road to Abilene." Too often, once an idea gets going and picks up steam within an organization, it is very difficult for someone to stand up and say, "Wait a minute!"

The expression "Road to Abilene" comes to us from the arduous journey of those early cattlemen on the frontier of the American West. And it's a wonderfully instructive cautionary tale today. Many times, due to a strong manager, or CEO, your innovation team could feel that it is simply better for their overall job security to recommend only those ideas that they believe their manager will like. Other times, it is amazing just how "smart" the CEO is. That is, everyone in the innovation group immediately recognizes that whatever the CEO suggests is a "great idea." Why? Because these managers let their team take the Road to Abilene.

The great paradox with the Road to Abilene is that everyone in the group just goes along and does everything that not a single member in the group *really* wants to do or even thinks is a good idea in the first place! If, on the other hand, just one person would actually speak her mind, she would find that perhaps many others and maybe even *everyone* else feels the same way. And then there really would be a better decision, and a better place to be than finding yourself "all hat and no cattle."

THE ROAD TO ABILENE

A story by Jerry Harvey as told by the Reverend John H. Nichols

They were sitting around on the porch in Coleman, Texas. The temperature was 104 degrees, but the porch was shaded, and everyone was comfortable.

Then, Jerry Harvey's father-in-law said, "Let's get in the car and go to Abilene and have dinner at the cafeteria." In the back of Jerry's mind a little voice said, "This is nuts. I don't want to travel 53 miles in the heat of summer in a 1958 Buick to have dinner in a lousy cafeteria."

But Jerry's wife said, "It sounds like a great idea." And Jerry heard himself saying, "Sounds good to me. I hope your mother wants to go." And Jerry's mother said, "Of course I want to go." Four hours and 106 miles later, they returned. The heat had been brutal. Perspiration and dust stuck to their clothing and bodies. The food, as Jerry guessed, had been awful.

Later that evening Jerry said, quite dishonestly, "It was a great trip wasn't it?"

Nobody spoke.

Finally, his mother-in-law said, "To tell the truth, I really didn't enjoy it much. I would rather have stayed home, and I wouldn't have gone at all if you hadn't pressured me into it." To which Jerry responded, "I didn't pressure you. I was happy here. I only went to make the rest of you happy." His wife said, "You and Dad and Mamma were the ones who wanted to go. I just wanted to make you happy." And his father-in-law said, "I never wanted to go to Abilene. I just thought you might be bored sitting at home with the rest of us."

So, they all made a 106 mile round trip in the God-forsaken desert under furnace-like conditions to eat unpalatable food in a dingy cafeteria, a trip nobody even wanted to make.

In summary, there are definitely some bad ideas floating around many companies. There are also some potentially great ideas. And most importantly, with proper care, it is possible to weed out the good from the bad before committing too much time and money to the bad ones.

MYTH #13 GREAT IDEAS WILL MAKE YOU RICH!

How MANY TIMES have you seen someone's new product in the marketplace and thought to yourself: "Damn, *I* thought of that a year ago. I could have been rich!" Well, here's the sad reality. *Who cares? Ideas are cheap!*

One of our favorite bumper stickers reads, "Ideas Are Easy. Innovation is Hard."

That's because most folks confuse mere "ideation" with actual innovation. To be clear, coming up with smart, creative "ideas" is a critically important part of the innovation process, and the part usually considered to be the most fun and praise-worthy, but it is the rest of the innovation process that carries the big costs and risks. Before an idea gets to become a real live product, someone first has to pay for the salaries and fees, designs, up-front inventory, research, marketing, lease hold improvements, and whatever else is necessary just to get it ready for the market. Income, *if it occurs at all,* does not happen *until* you have spent all the money necessary to get the item actually introduced and successfully distributed into the marketplace—and that assumes it even gets there in the first place!

Generating ideas is *not* innovation. The generation of good ideas is **Creativity. Innovation** is the *application* of the ideas. Those of us who have tried to do innovate on our own have learned the hard way that the high costs are in the flawless and expert execution of those great ideas. That is why the big riches, as they should, go to those who take the big risks—those that *pay* for the man hours, testing, development, manufacturing, and marketing of the idea.

If this book can impart any one particular piece of advice to would-be innovators and entrepreneurs, it is to be willing to take a *smaller* piece of the pie in return for someone else's money. After all, a small piece of the pie will be worth more to you than a big piece of nothing.

What about sweat-equity, all of that hard work you will be doing to bring your idea to the market? Well, certainly there is a value in it, but sadly, when was the last time you tried to pay for a mortgage with sweat? Realize that money talks, and sweat—well, sweat just smells bad. Sorry.

Many years ago, I decided to leave my nice safe position at P&G to start a new venture. I had come up with the idea of fast-food pizza. At that time, there were fast food hamburgers (McDonald's, Burger King, and Wendy's), roast beef (Arby's and Roy Rogers), chicken (KFC) and even fish (Long John Silver's and Captain D's). But one of America's favorite foods, the one kids consistently vote for as their *most favorite* (pizza), took about 30 minutes or more to make and bake.

The inspiration that occurred to me though, was that it would be very possible to actually do fast food pizza and there was certainly a need for it. I recalled my days as a native New Yorker walking around the city and passing by one pizza-by-the-slice store after another. They were everywhere, and they were fast. But, virtually no one outside of New York City had ever even heard of them. Plus, there was certainly no *chain* of fast food pizza-by-the-slice stores. So, I had the great idea, and all that remained for me to do was open a few stores and eventually become the next Ray Kroc.

Well, obviously that didn't happen because if it did, I would be co-writing this book from the friendly confines of my own private island (instead of hunched over the desk in my office). But for all my trouble pursuing big dough through pizza, I did learn a valuable lesson. After spending months learning the art of pizza making and going without a salary, I spent a significant amount of savings and opened Cincinnati's very first pizza-by-the-slice store in a well-trafficked strip mall. It was like being the first Sbarro's on the planet. Business was great. There was a line of people out the door and believe me, I was providing "sweat" equity, because *I* was the one working the pizza ovens, which could get as high as 700 degrees on a good day.

On just the second day of operations, the mall owner, a very wealthy real estate mogul, came in and was so impressed with what he saw that he wanted to invest on the spot. He was willing to fund the opening of my stores in *25 of his malls*. All he wanted was 50 percent of the business. It wouldn't cost me a dime more. Of course I said, "No thank you." Why give up any of my business?

As with any new business, mistakes were made, and those mistakes cost money—money from *me*. And in order to fund the opening of my next four locations I had to take out an extremely expensive loan. There was no financial room for "testing" and certainly no room for eventual *myth*stakes, and as for marketing, well that was totally unaffordable. To make a painful story short, any way you slice it, I wound up almost going broke and leaving the business within two years. Oh yeah, and the realtor who wanted to help me get going—in 1975, he eventually funded the start of Chi-Chi's.

Keep in mind that great ideas are born everyday but those who think them up usually don't do anything with them. In fact, way back in 1931, today's mobile phone was created. It just wasn't executed. Chester Gould, a veteran cartoonist began drawing a comic strip featuring Dick Tracy, the daring and dashing police detective. One of the innovative crime-fighting technological tools Gould armed Tracy with was a wonderfully conceived two-way wrist radio/TV. Miraculously, Tracy was able to converse with (and see) his team from just about anywhere. He didn't have to find one of those scarce payphones that were in only a few places at the time. Obviously, Gould did make some good money on his comic strips, but it was Motorola and others that claimed the riches for the mobile phone. It was they who spent the time and money to actually develop it. We're sure that iChat owes some debt of gratitude to Chester Gould's feverish imagination as well.

We could probably devote an entire book to the history of comics and their impact on inventions, technology and innovation, but at least one more example must be mentioned because it is the opposite of Chester Gould's introduce-it-in-the-comics-and-invention-will-follow formula.

It is the curious case of William Moulton Marston and the polygraph (Lie-Detector). Marston created Wonder Woman, but in the period after World War I when he was a doctoral student in the psychology department at Harvard University, he also worked on the systolic blood-pressure test used to detect deception. It was the first polygraph test, and it was Marston's wife, Elizabeth, who should be credited as a collaborator. That's because she was the one who originally brought to Marston's attention that when she got mad or excited, her blood pressure seemed to climb. That's all he needed to hear to begin his research and ultimate invention.

About 20 years later, Marston was quoted in a published interview as saying that he saw the great educational potential of comic books.

The article caught the eye of the publishers of National Periodicals and All-American Publications (two of the companies that would merge to form DC Comics) and hired Marston as an "educational consultant."

In the early 1940s, super-powered male characters such as the Green Lantern, Batman, and its flagship character, Superman, dominated the DC line. Once again, Marston's wife served as his inspiration; she told him he should create a *female* superhero.

Now keep in mind that Marston was a noted psychologist and already famous for inventing the polygraph, so he created a pseudonym, Charles Moulton, before bringing his new superhero idea to DC Comics. He was quoted as saying "Not even girls want to be girls so long as our feminine archetype lacks force, strength, and power. The obvious remedy is to create a feminine character with all the strength of Superman plus all the allure of a good and beautiful woman."

Like any great innovation, there were fits and starts. His first name for this character from an all-female utopia who became a crime-fighting U.S. government agent was "Suprema."

Okay, the name needed some work and was changed to "Wonder Woman" in the second draft, but beyond her superhuman strength and agility, Marston needed a "hook" to distinguish her powers from all the other superheroes. After giving her heavy silver bracelets that could deflect bullets, Marston (in a Chester Gould reversal) used the very lie detector he invented as inspiration for his newly minted heroine. "The Magic Lasso" was the missing piece to her costume and ability. Sometimes also referred to as "The Golden Lasso," with it Wonder Woman was able to bind villains, forcing them to tell the truth. Anyone caught in the lasso found it impossible to lie.

The editors loved the idea, and Wonder Woman made her debut in *All Star Comics* #8 in December 1941, just after Pearl Harbor was bombed. The character next appeared in *Sensation Comics* #1 in January 1942, and six months later, *Wonder Woman* #1 hit the stands. Wonder Woman has been continuously published by DC Comics ever since, and is one of only three characters to share in that distinction.

As we've learned in our journey to understand innovation, once a problem or opportunity (or CIFA) is uncovered, there are many ways to ideate around it. The Golden Lasso was of course nothing less than a lie detector, like the lie detector upon which Marston modeled it. It was just a new and different idea that solved the originally uncovered problem or opportunity of detecting lies.

An "invisible plane" was added to her arsenal later, but we'll probably have to wait awhile before that innovation becomes reality (unless you count the stealth bomber).

Now if only I had created a Pizza-Man character that produced truth—and by implication, justice and freedom too—through pizza-by-the-slice, I might have been famous. Or at least I might have had the chance to meet Lynda Carter.

Either way, you can see throughout history how pop culture can influence innovation, and how innovation can influence pop culture. We fully support both.

And as it applies to ideas versus execution? Ideas are just ideas until they find someone to execute them. And, as we learned from Wonder Woman, a great idea can be executed in many ways.

Elsewhere in this book we will talk at length about the importance of process, execution, and marketing and the key roles that they play in innovation.

MYTH #14   A GREAT IDEA SPEAKS FOR ITSELF

OH, SURE. A great idea speaks—but in what language and to whom? The myth is that a great idea speaks in the perfect way to every person who encounters it. That it *sells* itself. Nice thought, but believe this and you have just discredited the jobs of everybody in marketing, sales, advertising, and packaging. And, if you fall victim to this myth, you may never see your "great idea" reach the marketplace, let alone fail in it.

That's because everyone's ears are different. They hear things in different ways. If you've ever played "The Telephone Game," then you already know this. You can blame your brain and how it processes information if you feel the need to play "The Blame Game" instead.

YOUR BRAIN: FILTERED OR NON-FILTERED

In most organizations, there are three major types of "ears," and they all flow through the particular brain filters of the individual.

MovEARS and ShakEARS: Most corporate managers have this style of listening. They hear the idea and wonder aloud how it will get done, and where the realistic hurdles are. They are left-brained dominant.

SynthesizEARS: Neither in one extreme or the other, this type of listeners try to strike compromises and harmony with the new idea upon hearing about it. These are smallest percentage, the duel-dominant (right and left brained).

EntreprenEARS: These listeners have never heard an idea they didn't love and embrace unconditionally upon first hearing about it. Anything's possible as it flows through their ears and into their brains. Unadulterated right-brainers.

In light of these various styles of listening and brain-filtrations, an extremely important, but often overlooked, part of the innovation process is communication. Any communication oversight, whether it is how the idea is conveyed from one team member to the next, from one department or division to the other, from the innovation team to upper management, from the company to the consumer being tested, or from the final test result to the actual consumer marketplace, can cause a great idea to crater.

INSIDE THE ORGANIZATION

Different people within an organization have diverse objectives. Make sure you understand how the idea you are proposing satisfies *their* objectives, not just yours. Is their objective risk-avoidance, speed to market, capturing shelf space, status, or overall profit growth?

Remember, there is a significant difference in how left-brained people see the world versus how right-brained people see things. Is it a left-brained manager to whom you are presenting the idea? If so, you better provide a significant amount of detail and specifics for him or her to grasp what you are trying to propose. Do what it takes from deductive to reductive reasoning to reach this West-of-the-Pecos style of brain. Too often we have seen upper-level managers kill a potentially great idea because they just didn't get it, or they just couldn't picture it. Whose fault is that? Yours! That's right. The buck stops here and so do the great ideas.

THE BATTLE BETWEEN ENTREPRENEARS AND MOVEARS/SHAKEARS

It would almost be impossible to overstate the challenges posed between right-brained and left-brained communication. In one of many instances we remember from our advertising days, we had to present a storyboard of a proposed TV spot to a particular client. Like most storyboards, it provided the client with about 8 example frames of what would go on in the proposed 30-second spot. Each frame consisted of an artist's illustration of what various scenes might look like. As was typical of most advertising types, we were card-carrying right-brainers, and like most creative advertising people, we had no trouble fully understanding the flow of the spot. Having been in the industry for decades, we could easily look at a stick figure and *imagine* how it would look as a real person, how it would move, and so forth.

However, the client, being a very tactical left-brain business manager, first had an issue with the spot being only :08 seconds long. After all, there were only eight frames on the storyboard, doesn't that mean the commercial is :08 seconds long? Thirty-second spots should have 30 frames on a storyboard, right? Uh-oh. We knew we were in trouble. It got worse. The client also had no idea what the stick figures in the storyboard illustrations would look like as real people, moving around. He just could *not imagine* it. The final point came when he said, "I just don't like the commercial because the characters in it are not smiling!" When we assured him that in the *real* 30-second spot it would feature *real* people smiling—not grim-faced stick figures—again he just couldn't imagine it.

Separately, different individuals in various departments or functions probably will have unique experiences from those of the innovation team. After all, senior managers, by definition, generally have an "advantage" over most workers in their number of years of experience alone.

Unfortunately, the confidence and heavy experience of managers makes them, by nature, the greatest resistors to change. It can threaten their power (why didn't I think of that?). It can affect their jobs, their specific brands, factories, or system that they are working on. It can create an entrenched bias in them to the point where they begin feeling they know better than anyone (especially younger, less experienced innovators) what can and cannot be done. You must be prudent to spell out the "imaginative" what-ifs of the big idea and why the times, needs, and opportunities are different today versus the past.

When communicating the potential idea to other departments or functions, be especially careful to present it in a way that it makes sense to them. Like a consumer, do not expect that they will easily understand how the new idea will benefit them. Equally as important, realize that other departments usually feel that they have enough on their plates without having to entertain something new. As Helen Tarvor, Head of Brand Development for Boots the Chemist, UK, warns, "Until someone makes a great new idea easy for your part of the business to implement, it will be like pushing water up hill for many."

Remember too, that when an innovator or innovation team believes it has a great idea, it is usually is the result of having spent quite some time and money uncovering keen insight and understanding that lead to this idea. As a result, the innovation team is in possession of all of the background knowledge and decisions that caused it to exist in the form it is in. Sadly, many times the key corporate decision maker is put in the position of having to decide whether or not to pursue a suggested innovation without being apprised of the valuable insight and understanding that led to the idea in the first place. As a result, without knowing the rationale behind the idea, he just may not get it.

In one particular case we were working with a pharmaceutical company's innovation team to develop a line of products for teenagers. One particular insight came through to the group loud and clear— color was an important trigger as to age acceptance of the product. If the color was more along the lines of a Mountain Dew, the product would be seen by teens as being far more appropriate for them than if it were colored red, a color typically associated with kid formulas.

The product concept was drawn up. The product was to be green. The innovation team presented it to the brand team and the brand team loved the basic idea but changed the product color to, you guessed it, red! Why? That's the color that *they* were used to in their life experience. They were not a part of the innovation process and they were not in possession of the original insights that led to the concept in the first place. Fortunately, in this particular instance, we were able to intervene and "remind" everyone why the color was not supposed to be red.

Naturally, much of this communication challenge can be mitigated if more departments, people, and even management are involved in the innovation process sooner rather than later.

TESTING: WHAT A CONCEPT!

Concept testing is a well-accepted practice in many organizations. It is the process whereby firms secure initial consumer reaction to the basic idea in order to help them assess whether further company attention is warranted prior to having to spend additional time, money, and other valuable resources.

Importantly, if one is to try to ascertain initial consumer reaction to the idea, it stands to reason that the idea better be communicated to consumers in a way in which they can adequately understand it. It seems obvious, right? But it is in this simple phase that we see huge mistakes being made—mistakes that can kill what could be the makings of a huge idea, or conversely, mistakes that way oversell the possibility of success.

We will address this and other *myth*stakes regarding concept testing later in this book.

THIS LITTLE PRODUCT WENT TO MARKET

Would you believe that the single biggest reason that actual products introduced into the marketplace perform differently than how they tested is that, when introduced, the *communication of the idea* is different than what was tested? Ahhh, thank you advertising agencies! It is the job of a good creative agency to create an interesting ad campaign behind the new product or service being launched. While many are very good at crafting entertaining, enjoyable ads, too many times the ad has little, if anything to do with the idea that was tested—no matter how many awards the ad may have won! The same holds true in the final package design. Did the package designer create a package that clearly communicates the main important idea that was tested in research?

One bitter lesson that we learned years ago involved a new product for Borden Cheese. The concept was for a pizza-flavored cheese slice. The concept test carefully explained the product, its flavor (in this case, cheese pizza and pepperoni), its look, and, importantly, how to use it to make grilled cheese sandwiches taste like a fresh pizza, pizza burgers, zesty Italian salads, and more. The concept scored very strongly among both adults and kids. The in-home taste tests scored very well. The product was launched and after huge initial trial, it was an abject failure. We knew the flavor was fine and the trial was solid. What happened? In going back, we realized that the ads and promotions designed to launch the brand never delivered one important element of the concept. Namely, how in the world you actually go about using the product. Left to their own devices, consumers didn't care much for pizza-flavored cheese on a salami sandwich, or other less exciting uses.

Another sad situation involved working with a major consumer packaged goods food company that had a horrendous new-product failure rate. We began working with them, developed some new innovative product concepts, thoroughly and carefully tested these concepts, and then introduced the actual products into test markets, where they all fell on their collective faces in failure. The reason? Whereas the marketing plan clearly showed that there would be reasonable advertising communication when the new products were launched nationally, economically, the brand teams could not afford advertising in the test markets. Whoops!

Nationally, the brand would deliver enough sales and profits to fund the development of a high-priced TV commercial (half a million dollars or more, according to their ad agency) and the high price of other collateral. But in test markets, there would only be a fraction of the total sales and profits that were to be expected nationally, and therefore it could not afford the high-priced commercial and local media costs. *So this company would typically launch its new products into a test market without advertising to communicate the actual concept to the consumer.* Couldn't it just do a simple, far less expensive test commercial to at least get the communication into the test market? It should have. It didn't. And it failed in every test market over and over.

In closing, we believe communication is such an important, overlooked part of the innovation process that we strongly recommend that the innovation group *stop* before taking its idea out to anyone and first determine, agree, and write what the *key selling ideas* are for the CEO, brand group, retailer, consumer, and any others in the decision chain. As with any *key* idea, it must be communicated in a way that it is simple, meaningful and *brief.*

- **CEO?** What is the way in which you will describe the idea to the CEO so that he is interested—i.e., sales potential, cost, profits?

- **Brand Group?** If going to an existing brand team, how, will this help their business and how can it fit easily into what they are doing?

- **Retailers or distributors?** Why should they carry this new item? How will it build their category sales?

- **Consumers?** What is the core idea, the one-sentence selling message critical to the consumer?

MYTH #15 IT IS MORE IMPORTANT TO BE LIKED THAN TO BE UNIQUE

HERE'S A QUIZ: What do all of these brands have in common?

Fresh & Easy	Archer Farms
INC	W Products
Eating Right	Sunny Meadow
Kirkland	Spring Valley
Durabrand	Mary Kate & Ashley
Great Value	Kid Connections
Metro 7	Sams Choice
Equate	Disney Magic Selections
Private Selection	Active Lifestyle
Ozark Trail	Full Circle

Did you get it? No?

How about:

Craftsman	Ol' Roy

The last two are the dead giveaways. Craftsman is, of course, Sears. Ol' Roy, America's #1 dog food, is Wal-Mart. All of the above are just examples of the many retailer-owned private-label brands.

Why are we talking about private-label brands in a book on innovation? In our previous myth, "No Such Thing as a Bad Idea," we caution about trying to think about how the competition is likely to react to your innovation. Sometimes the best innovation isn't necessarily the one with the best consumer interest. Rather, sometimes the best innovation is one to which your competitor may not be able to aggressively react. Well, here is where we present perhaps the fiercest potential competitor.

Over the past several years, a major shift has occurred that has created a most formidable, new type of competition. It is competition not just from other manufacturers or suppliers, but rather competition from the retailer—from the very party one needs to distribute your products.

Retailers have long since had their own private-label products on the exact same shelves and display racks where they stock major national brands. But now things have changed. Retailers have become far more marketing savvy. No longer are they packaging their own brands in boring yellow or white, sterile-looking packages that scream "generic" from across the aisle. No longer are they just going after the cheap side of the marketplace. Now they are aggressively launching their own creative brand names and they are using sophisticated, stylish packaging and logo treatments. Some have even installed their own innovation departments. It is no longer the case that most private-label brands look like only a cheap alternative to the national brands. Disney Magic Selections? That's Kroger! Archer Farms? That's Target! Ozark Mountain? That's Wal-Mart!

Concurrent with the move towards marketing sophistication on the part of retailers, has been the birth of a far more educated, savvy consumer. Today's consumers have come to realize that in many cases, the store brand (even if they know it is a *store* brand) offers the same quality as the national brand. When today's consumers find a particular value such as a store brand whose quality perceptually matches the national brand, many will actually spread the word through their social networks and other connections. And tomorrow's consumers (today's kids) are indicating that they will be even more savvy when it comes to bargain shopping. Even kids find it "smart" and cool to shop for their clothing at Wal-Mart.

A recent fact that further attests to the power that private-label brands are accruing is that the prices of these brands seem to be getting closer and closer to those of their national competitors. Therefore, retailers no longer have to offer significantly lower prices on their brands in order to entice consumers to purchase them over the national ones. They can offer almost similar prices—meaning they get even more profits and have even more incentive to continue copying other's innovations.

Today, store brands have grown to represent a major part of many categories from food, to clothing, to hardware, and more. They already represent an estimate of almost 20 percent of total U.S. grocery dollar sales and in some categories store brands make up the majority of volume. Further, because today's consumers and retailers are so savvy and well informed, we can expect store brands to continue to grow in importance.

If this isn't alarming enough to today's manufacturers, take a look at Kroger's published statement on its corporate brands:

CORPORATE BRANDS

Corporate-brand products play a central role in the Company's merchandising strategy and provide a key competitive advantage to Kroger. We are using our corporate brands to build and solidify customer loyalty. Our vision is to inspire customers to choose our stores because of their exclusive, preferred brands. Corporate brands such as Private Selection and Naturally Preferred, plus our new Active Lifestyle and Private Selection (PS) Organic brands are Kroger's ultimate loyalty program because customers can buy these brands only in our stores.

Our supermarket divisions typically stock approximately 11,000 private-label items. Kroger's private label grocery items, in terms of dollars, represent approximately 24 percent of the Company's grocery sales. Our share in terms of units is approximately 32 percent. High-velocity items, such as milk and canned vegetables, explain a substantial portion of the difference between these two figures.

And, Kroger has stated to many marketers that its goal is to have as much as 75 percent of its sales eventually come from its own corporate brands.

As you can well imagine, there are two sides to the retailer phenomenon. On one side, retailers have been a big boon to the innovation industry because many times it is they who demand that today's marketers innovate and create new, exciting products to help grow their categories (and with it, the retailers' sales). However, on the other side, if the innovation is not different enough, if it is not well protected, and if it is large enough to draw big volume, then there is little standing in the way for the retailer to copy the innovation with a brand of its own.

So, what does this mean for innovation?

Most importantly, today's retailers are becoming less accepting of new product offerings from manufacturers. The fact is they are filling some of the opportunities for new-product needs all by themselves. Further, they are now more reluctant to give up valuable shelf space just to any run-of-the-mill, new offering that is nothing more than simply another variety of a product already on their shelves. Unless it is going to build new sales for them, why bother?

One way in which to help create and protect a perceived uniqueness between your new brand and an existing brand or a store brand is through aggressive marketing and brand building. In fact, this is just one of the many reasons why licensing has become such an important marketing tool for manufacturers. Retailers and other competitors can come close to copying a manufacturer's new kids' food introduction, but not if that new food item carries the name of "Sponge Bob!"

Another way in which to better ensure that retailers will see an innovation as being meaningful and worthy of their shelf space is to actually involve them in the upfront development of the product itself. However, considering the competitiveness of retailers, there is always the possibility of each retailer demanding that you develop a "custom" product just for them. However, overall, the plusses of involving the right retailer will certainly outweigh the negative of having them refuse to stock your new item once it is ready to launch. Manufacturers now work with key retailers to develop custom marketing efforts and special product assortments. Perhaps they should involve them more in the product development area as well.

In fact, the toy industry has for many years, closely involved retailers early in their product development processes. Years ago, toy manufacturers previewed their ideas, proposed packaging, and even their proposed advertising to retailers *before* ever deciding to actually go to market.

THE BIGGEST IMPLICATION OF GROWING STORE BRANDS

Perhaps the most important suggestion that store-brand power has on manufacturers' innovation is the emphasis that must be placed on a new product's "uniqueness." While many companies will take the important step of testing their ideas with consumers before taking them to market, oftentimes, almost all of the attention is placed on determining the consumers' intention to buy.

As we discuss elsewhere in this book, manufacturers that test their concepts with consumers may look at several factors like purchase intent, value, purchase frequency, and uniqueness. But, most of the attention (and sometimes *all* of the attention) is placed on what is called the "top-two box score." That is, when consumers are asked how likely they are to purchase the new product—definitely will buy, probably will buy, may or may not buy, probably will not buy, definitely will not buy—those that state that they definitely will or probably will buy are considered top-two box. For most companies, the "Go" or "No Go" decisions simply require that 60 percent or more of all respondents fall into the top two boxes.

The big problem with emphasizing the top-two box, "definitely/ probably will buy" score, without strongly considering product uniqueness, is that it can mislead you terribly as to the overall potential of the new product.

Specifically, if the new product being tested is not very different from a product consumers are now using, then of course, consumers would see very little risk in trying the new item, thereby giving the tested product a high "definitely/probably" purchase intent. However, if the new item is not significantly better than the consumer's current brand or if the current brand defends itself with price reductions, couponing, and so forth, then you can bet that in the real world, consumers would switch back to their current brand in a heart-beat, leaving the new item to languish on the shelf and die.

Without factoring in the importance of how "unique" consumers perceive a new product idea to be, you run the huge risk of not only developing, manufacturing, and inventorying a product that consumers would not be loyal to but also a product that retailers will refuse to stock! No matter how much consumers say that they would buy a new product, unless it is different enough from existing offerings, retailers realize that their customers will readily substitute an already existing product if they cannot find yours. Therefore retailers have no compelling reason to give up valuable shelf-space just to carry your new item.

In fact, sometimes it is even better to have a product that scores modestly in the top-two box area but strongly in uniqueness. This is the sign of an attractive niche brand opportunity. This would be an item that would have "just enough" consumer interest to warrant its distribution. *But* because of its uniqueness, retailers could be more open to stocking it. Why? The sales of this item would likely be totally incremental to the store, *and* because of its modest sales volume, it will be too small to warrant a retailer, or anyone for that matter, copying it.

The best path to success begins by focusing on innovations that retailers cannot easily refuse to stock or follow with their own private label version, because they cannot make it or copy it, or won't make it because it costs too much or will take too much time. If the innovation is truly unique, retailers not only will be more compelled to stock the item but they will probably have difficulty in copying it, or at least copying it quickly. And that's what we like to call "a good thing."

Always remember, the answer to your new product idea's potential success is *not* whether a significant percentage of consumers like your new product. Rather, it is that *enough* consumers will want to buy your new product because they find it to be unique.

MYTH #16 — BUILD A BETTER MOUSETRAP AND THE WORLD WILL BEAT A PATH TO YOUR DOOR!

THERE IS NO QUESTION that having a unique and superior product is a great way to enter the marketplace. In fact the Product Development and Management Association (PDMA) finds it to be the number one criterion for successful innovation.

However, it is definitely not enough to just have a better product or offering than anyone else. In *Marketing Myths That are Killing Business*, authors Kevin Clancy and Robert Shulman report that while consumer dissatisfaction accounts for fewer than one in three failures, poor targeting and positioning, together with less-than-stellar consumer awareness, account for more than half of all new product failures. We'll also add to this unfortunate list, the poor distribution and availability factors. If it is difficult for consumers to find a new product *when and where* they want to find it, you're heading into some big trouble.

Any firm that thinks that consumers will just walk into stores, see the new product on shelf, read the package, and then try the product is expecting way too much. Elsewhere in this book we refer to one hapless client who incurred product failure after failure despite going through concept testing and product testing, all because it did not have the funds to buy the advertising that would have made a required number of consumers aware of its offering. Marketing and communication efforts are so important that many new product-testing models, like BASES, factor in a company's planned marketing efforts in order to determine its volume estimates.

You can see from the above that in truth, it is a *myth* that if you simply build a better product, you're home free. It is not just the product offering that is critical; it is the full business plan—marketing, advertising and sales distribution—that makes or breaks the new product offering.

As obvious as the above statements are, we are now watching some companies so enamored with the Internet that they believe they can launch their products with nothing more than viral efforts, or an inexpensive, targeted banner campaign. While the Internet is definitely giving firms a new, well-targeted, efficient manner to get the word out, unless a company is willing to spend the necessary dollars on the Internet or elsewhere to capture the awareness of the huge number of consumers it needs to generate successful trial, the product launch will, in fact, fail.

Remember, too, "viral" marketing is just that—it is *viral.* And the funny thing about a virus is, you really can't control it. In fact, most viruses usually run slowly and unpredictably. The same is true for viral campaigns: for every one that makes headway (i.e., the ones you've actually heard of), there are also thousands that do little or nothing (i.e., the ones you've never heard of). So while a viral campaign can be very inexpensive, you generally get what you pay for.

THE TANGLED WEB WE WEAVE

Speaking of the Internet, we are seeing a recent flurry of innovative ideas for websites of all stripes.

Major firms are pouring hundreds of thousands of dollars or even well over a million dollars, to develop new and unique websites that all claim to be "like the next Webkinz, only better." The next epicurious. com, only with new, better, recipe tools. The next expedia.com, only with better bargains. And naturally they expect to make a profit. How? By selling advertising, of course. Why? Because millions of people will be coming to their sites and advertisers pay to get the attention of millions of people.

Here too, no matter how much better the website idea is, unless awareness of the site is communicated to enough consumers and offers them a compelling reason to visit, there will never be enough visitors. Without sufficient awareness and interest, there won't be enough eyeballs to generate enough advertising dollars. It's really that simple.

Just this year, a well-funded, celebrity-backed group that was developing a major new kids' web-based social community approached us. The graphics were solid, the story line was strong, and there was even a long-term plan on extending the site into an actual toy and craft line. Its revenue model called for a million viewers a month and for each viewer to pay a nominal annual charge. And, they were going to get these viewers via online advertising.

Okay. It's possible. But to get a million kids a month, whose parents were willing to pay even the smallest amount, would mean having to reach tens of millions of kids. How big was their communication budget? Under $100,000! For that you can't get enough exposure to enough kids to get enough eyeballs. We were not saying that this couldn't work; we were just saying that this couldn't work unless and until they addressed their communication model accordingly. Keep in mind, there are always possible answers, but it could never be through simple, infrequent on-line ads, we can assure you.

Let Marketing Open the Door to Your Heart

Everett Rogers, in his book *Diffusion of Innovation* reminds us that sociology and psychology may have more to do with the acceptance of new ideas than the merits of the ideas themselves. There are five factors that help define how quickly, and if, a new innovation can spread and be accepted by sufficient numbers of customers:

1. Relative advantage

What will consumers *perceive* as the advantage of the new innovation? This is where research and communication plays a critical part. Specifically, sometimes an idea is so simple it needs little explanation. For example, suppose a new food product has an attribute, and that consumers already know what the benefit will be, such as "low cholesterol." Consumers already know that lower cholesterol means better heart health, the ability to live a longer life, and so on. No need to spend a lot of time and attention explaining to the consumer why this product makes sense. However, with a very new, break-through idea, it may be far less obvious to consumers as to what the advantage of the new product is. *You* know the advantage, because you did all of the work and development. But you have to communicate what the advantage is to the consumers so they can easily grasp it. That's why advertising, and other marketing messages are crafted carefully.

2. Compatibility

How hard will it be to transition to the new innovation? Does it work easily with other items consumers now possess? Is the timing right?

3. Complexity

How much learning does it take to use the new innovation? Most consumers are lazy and everyone is time-stretched. Is it easy to understand, given where consumers are today?

4. Trialability

How easy is it to try? Is the cost too prohibitive, or is it so attractive the consumer has almost nothing to lose. The lower the perceived relative advantage, the less likely consumers are to risk spending any significant money in order to try it out.

5. Observability

The more consumers see others using the new innovation and how to use it, the more comfortable they are with trying it. Starting when we are about 8 years old, a strong motivational driver begins to take advantage of us: the need to "belong." Consumers have a strong desire to affiliate with others. Even non-conformists want to conform to other non-conformists. Here too, advertising and conspicuous sampling helps a lot. Think of this as showing "patterning" behavior.

In short, a company that has developed a new, unique, or better product, must also develop the appropriate marketing plans to ensure that the above criteria is adequately met if it is to maximize its chances for success.

Generally speaking, the newer and more different an idea is, the more you have to get the word out ahead of time to help take some of the "walls" down and grease the skids, as they say. Advanced PR, advanced "pictures," getting appropriate bloggers in on the "advance" notice, and sowing a pre-launch field of evangelists will all help open the door before opportunity can even begin to think about knocking.

Consider today's hybrid automobiles. The idea certainly existed well before they were introduced, but, even five years ago, there was no perceived relative advantage to them, let alone, little observability, trialability, and so forth. However, as the word began to get out in different ways, and as noted celebrities began to drive them and talk about them on chat shows, the doors began to open.

Also, there has long been an answer to the desire to commute in times of fuel shortages—the Vespa scooter! Italy's Piaggio filed a patent for the Vespa scooter design in 1946. The application documents referred to a "model of a practical nature" for a "motorcycle with rationally placed parts and elements with a frame combining mudguards and engine-cowling covering all working parts for a comfortable motorcycle offering protection from mud and dust without jeopardizing requirements of appearance and elegance." Attention to aerodynamics was evident in the entire design, in particular on the tail. It was one of the first vehicles to use monocoque construction (where the body is an integral part of the chassis).

It was first presented to the press at Rome Golf Club, where journalists were apparently mystified by the strange, pastel-colored, toy-like object on display. But the road tests revealed a "bike" that was more maneuverable and comfortable to ride than a traditional motorcycle—a "lesser" mousetrap, indeed!

The 1960's Mod youth revolution in the United Kingdom brought the appeal of the Vespa to the style conscious, similar to the way hybrid automobiles began to raise their profile when celebrities began to drive them. Mods enjoyed the fact that the Vespa provided some weather protection for their stylish Seville Row threads, while the "rockers" had to wear leather against both the elements and their oily big bikes. Mods went a step further by modifying their Vespas with lights, mascots, accessories, racks, and crash bars—and after the release of the Who film, *Quadrophenia*, profusions of multiple mirrors.

Today the Vespa is available for between $3,300 and $6,900 and gets 70 MPG! It is inexpensive to operate and fills a need, but it is still far from being a huge success in the United States of the 21st Century. Why? Despite its European legacy, trialability and observability in the U.S. is still too difficult.

MARKETING CAN BE MORE IMPORTANT THAN THE PRODUCT!

There have been many times where the marketing effort behind an innovation was actually far more instrumental to its success, than was the actual product itself. Many times, the superior marketing of a copycat product will enable the copycat to claim the #1 position.

Jeong Kim, president of Bell Labs at Alcatel-Lucent states: "You can [cite] numerous examples of companies that came up with [new] technology but eventually were displaced by somebody else." These "somebody elses" are companies with better funding or sharper management who were able to exploit a technology more quickly and effectively in the marketplace than the original creator. While it is nice to be the first to develop and launch a new technology, Kim warns us that: "the more flexible, the more innovative in terms of *business model* that the company is, the longer you can maintain advantage."

By now everyone has heard of the story of McDonald's. Ray Kroc became a huge success and McDonald's became what is now about a $30 billion company not just because of its original, unique product, but also because of the marketing. Dick and Mac McDonald developed the original "mousetrap." It was a hamburger stand that did so much hamburger and shake volume that Kroc, the exclusive distributor of the Multimixer Milkshake Machine, had to see for himself how one place could use so many of his mixers at once.

Once Kroc saw how fast so many people could be served at a McDonald's, he realized that if one McDonald's stand could do so well, what could more of them do? It was Kroc who struck a deal with the McDonald brothers to personally fund and open more of their stores. After all, each store would use more and more of his Multimixers.

By expanding the distribution and availability of the original McDonald's hamburger stand, he made it easier for consumers to observe and try. Its relative advantage of speed and taste became obvious and the rest is, well, McHistory.

A less well-known example is U.S.-based LensCrafters (a subsidiary of Italy's Luxottica Spa). It is the world's leading retailer of eyewear and has hundreds of outlets across the United States, Canada, and Puerto Rico.

Like McDonald's, LensCrafters owes its huge success to marketing. The original "mousetrap" was first built and offered by New Jersey-based Eyelab. Eyelab pioneered the eyewear concept, which featured mall-based stores, extended hours, onsite lens-grinding labs, thousands of frames, and rapid turnaround.

In 1983, Dean Butler, a 38-year-old former Procter & Gamble marketer basically took the original "mousetrap" concept begun by EyeLab, put some marketing know how and muscle behind it, and launched his first 7,500-square-foot Precision LensCrafters (later simply Lens-

Crafters) store just across the Ohio River from Cincinnati in Florence, Kentucky. Since LensCrafters had onsite lens grinding, Butler aggressively advertised the benefit of "glasses in about an hour," giving dimension to the relative advantage LensCrafters offered versus other traditional eyewear retailers who would routinely tell customers that they could pick up their glasses in three to four *weeks*. And, since Butler's stores were located in malls, customers could while away that hour shopping with other retailers. Money-back guarantees helped as well, since there was some early skepticism that glasses could be made in just an hour.

To help instill confidence in customers who were also accustomed to dealing with doctors, LensCrafters stores offered a "no risk sales guarantee." In a 1986 interview with *Forbes* magazine, Butler noted, "Marketing eyewear isn't much different from selling coffee. Retailing is what you do when customers walk into the store. But with a new idea, *marketing comes first.*"

Further, consistent with our overall message on the importance of innovation, on the occasion of its tenth anniversary in 1993, LensCrafters' CEO at the time, Dave Browne said, "Looking to the future, I'm sure of only one thing . . . the inevitability of constant change and our readiness to face it. It will be harder to stay on top than it was to get there. We will have to *recreate* ourselves continuously in order to maintain our leadership position in an ever-changing category." True to this statement, LensCrafters has since expanded into kiosks, continued to offer cutting-edge new products, new retailing formats, and more designer names, among other innovations.

Even Apple, with its phenomenal iPod, iMac, and MacBooks, has had times in its 30-year history where wonderful mousetraps turned into super flops due to issues with compatibility, complexity, trialability, and observability. Do you remember "Apple Cyberdog," the answer to Internet Explorer and Netscape Navigator in 1996?

How about the Motorola ROKR? That's right. Technically speaking, the iPhone is not Apple's first mobile phone. In 2005, Apple partnered with Motorola for the ROKR (say it with us: "rocker!") phone. As with any Apple product, it was widely anticipated. It featured an MP3 player with an interface similar to the iPod, and allowed users to play back music purchased from the iTunes store. The phone had great specs for its day (512 MB memory), plus Bluetooth, a bright display, and a Micro SD card for memory expansion. It was the best mousetrap in the history of phones, right? The marketing just didn't strike the right tone and within a year the ROKR was disconnected. Permanently.

WHO SAYS FIRST IS BETTER THAN SECOND?

Did you know that Johnson & Johnson actually created the first disposable diaper? It had the rather unfortunate name "Chux." This first generation managed to sell its radical new product to a whopping 1 percent of parents with small babies, which no doubt caused a rash of a different kind among J&J executives.

It would be a full decade later before Procter & Gamble launched Pampers. This second generation mousetrap managed to capture an incredible 95 percent of the available market. So, while J&J gets kudos for proving its mousetrap worked, it didn't prove to be as popular to say the least. Chux was overpriced and overcomplicated for a mass market, and the economies of scale didn't yet exist to drive down costs. The first to launch can be great, but only if you learn the valuable lesson that J&J had to endure. Being overpriced and overcomplicated for a mass market was not a problem at the beginning. The problem for J&J was that it focused on the customers it already had instead of the customers it needed. It was so used to the niche market for Chux, it didn't even realize that there was a mass market for the product. P&G did, and won.

Consider Xerox. It was, in fact, the first to launch a photocopy machine. And it dutifully created a multi-billion dollar company selling photocopiers to a niche market of big corporations. It became so good at selling to a niche market, that when competitors tried it failed to beat them at their own game.

Then Canon came along and created a photocopier for small businesses and home users. Canon was so successful at producing a copier that was less expensive and less complicated that it captured the mass market *and* significant portions of the niche market. Now *that* was a problem.

Amazon, eBay, Schwab, IBM, and Microsoft were not first to innovate, but over time they out-maneuvered their rivals. They were so successful that most people cannot even remember who was first. Innovation is a series of sprints. Winning the first does not guarantee that you will win again.

When Better is NOT Better!

Would you believe that there are opportunities to actually build a *lesser* mousetrap and the world will still beat a path to your door? In fact, if you are first to market, you should try thinking like someone who has entered the market second. We know that's hard because redeveloping a version of your product that is simpler and cheaper runs against everything you were ever taught as an innovator. But as you'll learn in the examples below, if you don't keep finding new ways of competing with your own product, the mass market will be difficult to sustain and vulnerable to competition.

Clayton Christensen and Michael Raynor's book, *The Innovators Solution: Creating and Maintaining Successful Growth,* points out how some of the most successful innovations are those that might not perform as well as the market leader (A.K.A., "better mousetrap") but are less expensive or more convenient to purchase. This is because there are times where the alleged "better mousetrap" overshoots what customers are actually able to use. In doing so, the cost of goods demands that the price at which the product is offered is high enough to cover these costs. Sometimes these costs are too high for many consumers who would love to buy the item, but cannot afford to do so.

It is not rare to hear about significant opportunities out there for someone to come along, offer a product similar to the "better" one, but price it more affordably because it is not made quite up to the standard of the original. The result is that the lesser innovation actually creates *new* consumption. When people are unable to acquire a product because it is too expensive, too complicated, or too difficult to buy, they can become ripe potential consumers of the new "good enough," but "lesser mousetrap."

Opportunities for lesser mousetraps exist when there are enough customers who have not had the money or skill, or had to go to an inconvenient location to acquire the "better mousetrap." If there are enough customers at the low end of the market who would be happy to purchase a product with less performance if it were priced lower and easier to acquire, then there is an excellent opportunity for innovation—as long as you can still make enough of a profit margin in making such an offer available.

One company that employs a version of this strategy is Tiger Electronics, a division of Hasbro. Tiger creates huge sales behind its "looks like-acts like" adult electronics line. Many adult electronics, such as MP3s, large screen projector TVs, and various mobile phones are too expensive or too complicated for today's older kids, so Tiger creates "good enough" copies of them designed especially for kids.

Importantly, sometimes the opportunities for lesser mousetraps are so good that these lesser products can actually drive the better ones out of business. One of our former clients, Cincinnati Microwave, is now precisely that (a former client) because it went out of business many years ago. When we started with this firm, it was the inventor and sole manufacturer and distributor of the Escort and Passport radar detectors. They were hot! They were pricey, at about $300 each, and they were only available through direct-response mail order.

Eventually, competitors such as Cobra and others entered the mar-ketplace. Their products were less expensive, at about $99 each, and they were conveniently available in retail stores. And since they were that much easier to acquire and were more affordable, they had two distinct advantages over the original, bigger, badder mousetrap. Cin-cinnati Microwave did what many other manufacturers under attack do. It felt that it was too good to go after a potentially lower margin business. Instead, the firm spent time and money to *improve* its product even further, unfortunately offering features that well overshot what people were looking for while driving up costs and eroding margins.

Of course it's easy to look in the rearview mirror now, but what they should have done is realize that it was okay to build a lesser mousetrap, price it lower, and make it more convenient to purchase. It could have done this under a different brand name, while endorsing it with something like "from the makers of Escort."

Anyway, Cincinnati Microwave suffered so much that its competi-tor, Beltronics, eventually purchased it. The Escort and Passport brands live on but the company did not. We are relatively certain that law enforcement agencies throughout the country applauded Microwave's ultimate strategy.

In conclusion, it is not necessarily the "better" mousetrap that gets the mouse. Rather it is critical that you build the "right" mousetrap. And no matter which type of mousetrap you build, it better have the right kind of *cheese* (marketing efforts) in order to lure the mouse into the trap in the first place!

MYTH #17

THERE'S NO SUCH THING AS TOO MUCH INNOVATION

WE HAVE CERTAINLY been warned that one must innovate in order to survive, or as we've heard: "Innovate or Die!" However, too much of anything is usually not a good thing, and this holds true for innovation as well.

Rushing to innovate too quickly, without due diligence, can cause a major disruption to any organization. Actually, most company innovation efforts suffer from a lack of focus, resulting in *too many* potential new product projects and not enough resources to produce them successfully.

Without proper planning, the company runs a much greater risk of going forward with a truly bad idea. Also, there are only so many innovations that the sales force and marketing team can handle throughout the year and too many product launches can easily cause them to take their eyes off the current business. And that's never a good thing!

When too much pressure is placed on innovation, the number of innovations goes up, but the quality of the innovations go down. That's because there is only so much time and money to go around. Rather than placing that precious time and money toward an innovation that might require a significant number of years, innovation teams pressured to launch a specific number of new products within a specific time frame naturally orient themselves towards small, closer-in, sustaining innovations, or line-extensions such as new flavor, size, or color alternatives.

So what's the problem with launching too many small, closer-in, sustaining alternatives?

Well, for one thing, each successive alternative gets less retailer distribution—making their returns smaller and smaller. Retailers only have so much shelf space available. They see these closer-in alternatives for what they truly are, minor business builders for the innovating company, but general*y not much, if any, extra business for their category or establishment.* Retailers can sniff out what are essentially just replacements for what is already out there versus true category growers.

As an example, Kellogg's Pop-Tarts, whose brand sports over 40 SKUs, now achieves distribution in only about two out of three retailers for every new close-in innovation to that brand. Why? Because most close-in-sustaining innovations tend to be new flavor varieties. After a brand already has dozens of flavors, a new one will most likely just steal its volume from an already existing Pop-Tart flavor. The chance of bringing in *new* consumers or *new* eating occasions is slim at best. And, if there are no new consumers and no new eating occasions, then there is no category growth for the retailer.

Closer-in alternative innovations tend to be somewhat cannibalistic and thereby derive their volume and revenue at the expense of the brand's *existing* business. So, not only do too many close-in, sustaining innovations get smaller returns due to lower retail distribution levels, but they also generate lower incremental revenue since they reside within the same category.

It's a common issue: More than half of all new brands brought to market each year are line extensions. For example, when Pepsi wanted to market a diet cola, it "extended" its brand equity—everything that has gone into building the brand that is the Pepsi Generation—into the product called Diet Pepsi. In this case, the line extension made total sense. While it might cannibalize some existing Pepsi business, it would also bring in new consumers and drinking occasions (meaning new sales volume to the category) from those customers who previously avoided drinking a lot, if any, higher-calorie soft drinks. But not every line extension has been as logical as Diet Pepsi. Some seem to have very little reason for being other than to just launch another item. Remember when PepsiCo introduced a new no-calorie soda and called it "Pepsi One?" What is Pepsi One exactly? Does it mean that it has just one calorie? No, it has zero calories, if you must know. It's sweetened with Splenda, but the average Joe doesn't know that. It's no surprise then, that Diet Pepsi was outselling Pepsi One by a 10-to-1 margin before sanity prevailed and Pepsi One was buried.

On the other hand, look what Pepsi decided to do within the lucrative and high profit-margin world of bottled water. It launched Aquafina. Can you imagine the disastrous results if it had decided instead to stay "within category" and launched an extension called "Pepsi Water?" No thanks.

Author Scott Bedbury offers the following brand extension rule in his book *A New Brand World:* "In creating bandwidth, always look around your core product category position before looking elsewhere, particularly when taking the brand into a new distribution channel. If you do it right, the new growth will strengthen, rather than dilute, your brand."

While done to take advantage of a strong consumer movement towards weight management and provide a defense against competition, the granddaddy of all brand cannibalization has to be Bud Light. It eroded sales from the parent brand, Budweiser, until it has now finally overtaken it. When measuring the growth of the extended brand, don't forget to consider (or subtract!) the lost market share of the core brand while you're at it.

So, in truth, you must innovate—'twas ever thus—but you must do it with proper balance and planning with the assurance that current business will not suffer. Innovation must be organized to occur in a timely manner.

We have seen plenty of firms move toward the development of an Innovation Calendar. The purpose of this calendar is to look forward and determine when during the year are the best opportunities for the company to launch a new product or service. Then, it determines which of the products in development it will choose to launch and how the company might accomplish this while protecting its base business.

Such calendars should extend several years into the future, and consider both closer-in and game-changing innovations, as well as existing business pushes. Calendars such as these not only help understand when a product can be launched, but also set up a target for the Innovation Team to know when a new product will be needed for launch at a particular point in time.

Beware of making your Innovation Calendar nothing more than an "excuse generator." We're reminded of the great Walt Disney's famous remark: "Disneyland will never be complete, not as long as there is imagination left in the world."

MYTH #18: CONCEPT TESTING IS A GREAT WAY TO MINIMIZE RISK

A CONCEPT TEST is a way in which firms secure customer reaction to an initial idea early in the process, so as to help determine whether to proceed in further funding, developing, and eventually launching the finished product or service into the marketplace. When done correctly, concept testing can weed out poor ideas before they wind up costing a company too much time and money. It may also uncover ways in which to modify initial ideas so that they become even stronger.

You would think that with these advantages, concept testing makes all the sense in the world. After all, why spend countless dollars, hours, and other valuable resources on developing something that, ultimately, too few consumers will want to buy? Yet, according to several studies by the PDMA and others, relatively few firms include consumer concept testing in their quest for innovation.

And, unfortunately, while concept testing **should** be a very valuable part of everyone's innovation process, many firms who do concept testing, make the *myth*stake of not realizing that the results are only as valid as the way in which the concept was presented.

Too often, very little thought goes into the presentation and communication of the idea to consumers—resulting not only in invalid consumer responses, but responses that mislead a company in a way that *increases risk*. As an example, a marketing director for one of our clients recently told us that she didn't have time to talk because she had to write *ten* concept statements (the written description of the idea that is tested with consumers) that afternoon. Let's make sure we understand this: she is going to be spending a whopping 30 minutes on each concept statement—each of which could result in millions of dollars being invested. Seriously?

We're reminded of one the greatest of Abe Lincoln's letters on display at The Smithsonian. It begins: "I apologize in advance for the length of this letter. I didn't have the time to write a shorter one." Lincoln's keen appreciation of the time required to do something well still shines forth today.

The truth is, more often than not, concept statements are written incorrectly. Some of the biggest mistakes include erroneously overpromising the benefits of the idea and, as a result, obtaining false-positive results that could lead a company to spend wastefully behind an idea that will ultimately fail.

Conversely, a concept statement may present a complex idea and fail to show how the new product is relevant to the consumer. Or, it may even confuse the reader. The result could be a very costly, negative consumer response that *would* have been a positive response if explained properly. In this case, this mistake could cause a firm to pass on an initiative that, in reality, might have turned out to be a huge success.

OVER-PROMISING

There is a lot at stake for savvy ideators, innovation groups, and new product departments. The pressure to come up with good ideas is intense. And what determines a good idea? Well, a great concept test score, of course. After all, a good concept test score *proves* to upper management that these people are doing a good job of coming up with ideas. A good concept test result furthers a company's interest, time, money, and enthusiasm toward the idea and, consequently, towards the people (and their jobs!) responsible for generating the idea.

Therefore, it is in the ideator's best interest to do everything possible to ensure the best achievable result for his or her concepts being tested. And, ideators are no fools. They know how to increase the likelihood of achieving good results. They inherently know that the more they promise in the concept statement, and the more people they appeal to, the better the outcome.

They'll use words and phrases that sell hard. They might include lots of "flavor" alternatives if it is a food, or include some pretty heavy handed persuasive language such as: "Tastes so great and delicious that *everyone . . .*"

In short, in their zeal to see their ideas score well, innovators could wind up testing a concept that promises something for everyone. However, the problem with this practice of stacking the deck is that realistically the ultimate product could never deliver *all* that is being promised in the statement.

Some might feel that promising too many things in an initial concept test does not matter. The theory, they reason, is that the weakest promises can be weaned out later by asking consumers what they liked most and least about the concept. This is okay so far as it goes, but only if the concept will be retested in its new, narrowed-down format. Because, some people who voted positive for the concept probably liked the promises that were later eliminated and now they will not buy the narrowed-down offering. Unfortunately, this re-testing is usually not done and as a result, the firm will go forward but will lack an accurate reading of the idea that will ultimately be introduced into the marketplace.

Finally, make sure to avoid the classic new-concept trap. It's easy to get so focused on layout and style that you forget that someone back at the office has to deliver on the technology that makes the concept so appealing. That's why after, or during the time that the concept is developed, the folks in research and development should get closely involved—not for style but for pragmatism. Can the product described really be developed and manufactured?

BEWARE THE DISRUPTIVE INNOVATION—CONFUSING THE CONSUMER

One of the most frequent complaints we hear about concept tests is that they cannot provide accurate readings on truly unique, break-through, disruptive innovations. A disruptive innovation is usually so unique and different that consumers just cannot get it.

Wow! This itself is a big myth! It is not the research, it is not the concept *test* that is to blame. Rather, it is the *concept* and the way in which it is presented.

Concept statements, especially those presenting radically new and different ideas, *can* confuse consumers to the point where they do not fully understanding the idea being presented. And, when consumers are confused or have unanswered questions, they respond negatively. So keep in mind that when you are going to concept test a new-to-the-world, never-before-seen idea, it is critical to do some up-front home-work to determine exactly what the consumer needs to know in order to make an accurate decision.

We can definitively state that in almost every case in which we found a concept for a promising disruptive innovation testing poorly, it was either because the insight was wrong, the benefit was not clearly and easily understood, or the reason to believe was not convincing. Oh yeah, and in some cases, the idea itself *was* pretty bad. In fact, we have made a nice little living in helping firms "optimize" concepts that had previously scored poorly.

One important step that firms can take to help ensure that any concept, let alone a disruptive innovation, is presented accurately and persuasively in testing is to involve consumers in helping to develop and optimize the actual concept statement. We actually find this step to be so important that we add this stage, called "Concept Explosion" in most of our innovation assignments.

Sometimes, depending upon how unusual a new idea is, additional steps must be taken to help the consumer understand the reasons for the product and its potential benefits. Remember, in the real world, unique and unusual ideas are likely to be backed with significant PR and advertising—tactics that marketers know are needed to help pre-sell consumers. Yet, in the concept test phase, too often consumers are just exposed to the naked unvarnished idea with no pre-sell and no definition, no matter how unusual the idea is. So, if marketing plans call for consumers to be exposed to specific communication and PR efforts to help them understand the idea in the real world, then consider using some of this in the testing as well.

A PICTURE IS WORTH A THOUSAND WORDS

Consumers are far more visual than verbal, yet many concepts are tested with neither a looks-like mocked-up product, or sample illustration. Some testers insist on not including a visual so as not to "bias" the consumer to respond in a different way. What? Aren't consumers going to see an actual product when it is finally in the marketplace? If so, you better give them some tangible evidence in the form of visualization. Our own research shows consumers respond far more accurately to a concept with looks-like elements because they are more likely to believe that the concept is real and thanks to computer technology, it is quite simple for us to develop a looks-like photo of what the product or package will be like. In fact, through the magic of 3-D wire framing, that non-existing product can "exist" on a kitchen counter or store shelf set.

BEWARE THE STATUS QUO

A cruel fact of concept testing is that companies and consumers have big problems evaluating fresh new ideas because many times they tend to do so using the status quo as their frame of reference. New ideas demand new perspectives. Therefore, when concept-testing new radical ideas, you have to describe the idea in a way that will enable the consumer to see it from a different point of view or context. Too often, companies tell us they have a *specific* way in which they test *all* of their test concepts. For example, perhaps only a simple statement is used or sometimes just a looks-like package or mock-up design is used to communicate the entire idea. When an idea is very different, how smart is that? We'll let you decide.

Remember, consumers (like fellow office-workers) listen through those same three types of "ears" and brain-filtration systems discussed previously. The goal is to talk about your new product in testing in enough ways (visual, verbal, written) so that all types of consumers can hear what you have to say in the way that appeals most to them. Every one of them listens in his own way. All you have to do is just make sure he can hear you.

OTHER CHALLENGES

Conducting a concept test that might be truly predictive of actual consumer responses has other challenges as well. For one thing, it depends on making what is normally an unconscious effort, like impulsively choosing an item, into a very logical, determined endeavor. Cognitive psychologists claim that as much as 95 percent of human behavior is controlled by the unconscious mind. How many times have you driven your car for let's say 30 minutes, constantly adjusting your steering, checking the rear-view mirror, changing lanes, glancing at the dashboard read-outs, responding to various conditions, only to realize once you've reached your destination that you can't quite remember much of the drive at all.

Further, in the real world, most consumers exhibit apathy toward many new product introductions, whether food, entertainment, electronics or something else. Yet, when a consumer is a respondent in a concept test, she is made ultra-aware of what is being offered and her involvement, information processing, and decision-making becomes very focused. The phenomenon of "over-thinking" begins to occur. Imagine if you spent the day *deciding* when to blink your eyes, or when to inhale and exhale, versus just organically allowing the process to unfold. It would soon become stilted and look unnatural.

Additionally, it is always good to remember that whatever is being communicated to the consumer in the concept statement, must *also* be communicated in the real world once the product is launched. So, the concept statement that is tested must describe the idea accurately enough for the consumer to fully grasp, but must also take into consideration that the idea will eventually have to be communicated in a simple package design or, most likely, a 15-second television commercial. Concept descriptions can contain hundreds of words, yet, when it comes time to take the idea to market, a 15-second TV spot is generally limited to about 35 words. A simple package front generally has room for only a few attention-getting descriptions. If you don't want to take our word on this, ask Honest Abe.

The point is that these challenges require a well thought out and thorough marketing and advertising plan. They scream for it. No matter what consumers tell you in concept testing, their emotions and overall excitement must be piqued at the time of actual product introduction (see our next myth). And no matter what the ad agency or package designers say about the need to create an ad and package that is "break-through," they better be able to also communicate the most important essence of the concept that was tested in the first place. Otherwise, whatever you have gained from concept testing is useless.

RULES OF ENGAGEMENT

Concept testing should help minimize risk, but only if done very carefully. Here are some suggested rules of concept construction that will help ensure concepts are presented in realistic terms. Naturally, the star of the show is the product idea itself. The best way to ethically improve test results (scores) is to improve the concept itself. Fortunately, we know what high-scoring concepts typically include:

- A headline that summarizes the product's ultimate benefit in consumer terms. For instance, "Make quick work of window washing and get more enjoyment from the fruits of your labor."

- A subhead that reiterates and elaborates on the ultimate benefit: "Introducing the most versatile garden tool you'll ever own, the new Garden Weasel makes short work of tedious lawn chores."

- Opening sentences of the product's story that engage the consumer by setting up the problem, the wish, or the desire: "Few things are more rewarding than admiring your beautiful lawn. Yet, maintaining your lawn can be time-consuming. Along with mowing, someone has to edge the borders and trim the hedges and cut back overgrown branches and tree limbs. And that someone is YOU!"

- Copy that explains what the product does, with reasons to believe that the product will perform as described: "The new Garden Weasel will save you time because now you have one tool instead of three. Without so much as swapping a blade, you can go from hedges to edges to tree limbs, because everything is built into one tool."

- A clear looks-like illustration, maybe two—one of the product itself and another of the environment the product is used in—to reinforce the copy and enhance the conversational feel of the concept.

- A statement producing a suggested retail price along with information as to where the product will be available for purchase, to reinforce its positioning in the market.

- As we like to say, "don't just sell it—tell it." Explain what the product is, how it works, and why the consumer should trust that it does what you promise.

- Most importantly, use a conversational writing style to make sure that your concepts engage consumers. The concepts shouldn't sound like an internally circulated marketing brief or a science report developed to satisfy the engineers or the food chemists or the lawyers—no matter what the lawyers may try to tell you.

Once you've developed stronger concepts, you should expect better test scores. And when the concept test results come back and the winner is chosen, everyone involved can pat themselves on the back and be happy, but not for long. The next key step is translating the successful concept into a comprehensive and actionable product brief that R&D can use to develop the final SKU.

See the pages 176–177 for a typical concept statement.

Concept Writing

Lorem Ipsum Dolor Sit Amet
*Consectetur adipiscing elit. donec quis enim.
etiam vitae ligula ac mauris.*

①

②

③

④

Pellentesque vel ipsum ullamcorper eros tincidunt tempor. Curabitur sodales, massa ac consectetur venenatis, magna mi mollis tellus, in suscipit ligula risus eu sapien.

⑤

Vestibulum ante ***ipsum primis in faucibus*** orci luctus et ultrices posuere cubilia Curae; Ut ligula eros, pulvinar eget, pretium et, malesuada id, nunc.

⑥

Praesent id lacus. Donec ut nisi. Quisque eu risus eu ipsum tincidunt venenatis. Etiam in velit at eros dictum vulputate. Sed sed sapien at nunc tempor blandit. Quisque in lorem sed turpis molestie eleifend.

Curabitur rhoncus tincidunt eros leo vel enim:
• Cum sociis
• natoque
• penatibus   **⑦**
• parturient montes

& Visualization

Objective
Develop the motivating ideas and make the unreal, REAL by expertly applying the art and science of concept development.

Process
Create ten (10) research-ready concepts using the following framework:

1 **product name**
Simple statement of product name.

2 **headline**
A clear, consumer-friendly statement that explains the *motivating idea* and states the benefit.

3 **visual**
Making the unreal, real, with life-like visuals of what the consumer will see on the shelf.

4 **accepted consumer belief (acb)**
Expresses the consumers' unmet need or unarticulated desire.

5 **benefit**
Primary advantage of the idea in terms of addressing the need in the Accepted Consumer Belief.

6 **reasons to believe (rtb)**
Provides the substantiation to the product promise in the benefit statement.

7 **specific details**
Provides the consumer with information on the overall offering such as flavors, price, location in store, etc.

Reality: What a Concept!

We conclude with our Top 10 List of Concept Writing Realities:

- Keep text as short as possible. No more than what would be communicated in a 30-second TV spot. Ideally, only what would be communicated on the package. No over-the-top marketing language.

- Treat the headline as if it's the only statement the consumer will remember.

- Benefit-based headlines are most effective (attention-grabbing headlines are not necessary).

- Keep it clear and single-minded.

- Express the target consumer's frustration, unmet need, or unarticulated desire. Remember, the solution will only be as important as the problem.

- Create a promise that answers the target consumer's question: "What's in it for me?"

- Provide distinctiveness vs. other products or services.

- Reassure consumers that their favorite product will still be available.

- Clearly show the size and price they will actually experience at their store.

- Make the ideas as concrete and credible as possible with an accurate visual representation of what consumers will see on shelf. (Color is ideal and recommended).

Finally, remember, if the idea is that new and radical and the consumer will be exposed to a significant amount of other information in the real world, consider exposing the consumer to this as well. Make the concept test as close as possible to what will really take place in the market.

MYTH #19   FACTS CONVINCE PEOPLE TO BUY

Oh, but if you feel like loving me
If you got the notion
I second that emotion
So, if you feel like giving me
a lifetime of devotion
I second that emotion
—Smokey Robinson & The Miracles, 1967

The Holy Grail for all brand managers or pipeline VPs has to be a "lifetime of devotion" for their brand or new product offering. However, one of the most-often repeated myths we hear is that if consumers could simply understand all of the *facts* about a new product, they would become loyal evangelists and repeat purchasers.

But Smokey Robinson was right about what it takes to turn a customer into a lifelong devotee. And the authors of this book unhesitatingly second that emotion, because it is emotion—not logic—that makes consumers' hearts race, and cash registers pump faster.

Admittedly, we innovators are constantly trying to anticipate every objection a potential customer might have about buying new products and services. It seems that if we could identify and address each of these objections and formulate a solution to each, we should be able to get them to buy almost anything. But that's the *myth*stake! The reality is very different and unpredictable.

Advertising and marketing strategies based on logic rarely do as well as strategies based on an understanding of people's emotions, desires, and needs. In fact, in the collective experience of the authors, you will only get the results you desire by appealing to both the logic *and* emotional needs of customers. We're all complicated creatures with hearts, minds, and souls and you can't ignore one just to please the other.

The truth is, consumer-buying behavior is generally motivated not on how one "thinks" about a brand but, rather, on how one "feels" about a brand. Several factors come into play including intellectual, physical, emotional or even (are you ready for this?) spiritual. A purchase decision can be based on beliefs, needs, or wants. Real and unreal. Other factors include knowledge, environment, peer pressure, past experiences, and the positive and negative thoughts of others. Even children have a significant influence over an adult's decision to buy. If you stop and think about it, we all buy things for basically two reasons: to solve problems we have, or to make us feel good. They don't call shopping "retail therapy" for nothing.

Louis Cheskin, a popular figure in 20th century marketing, understood how packaging, colors, and other factors contribute to how a consumer would *feel* toward a product. He took margarine, a relatively unpopular spread when first introduced, and made it wildly popular by changing its color from white to a golden rich yellow and its package to a premium-looking foil. Throw on the name "Imperial," and consumers *felt* absolutely different toward the brand.

Cheskin also helped E&J Brandy consistently outsell a far better tasting Christian Brothers brand. What could make people feel better about buying E&J Brandy when Christian Brothers had the better name and the superior taste (and that was a fact!)? Cheskin proved that bottle shape was the key emotional driver. E&J had nothing factually superior to the Christian Brothers product, but it's bottle shape made people *feel* that E&J was superior.

And what about our present coffee preferences? Howard Schultz, founder of Starbucks knows that he is not in the coffee business. He is in the business of creating emotional experiences. In Starbucks case, the product is the experience.

When working for our Borden Cheese client many years ago, we too got a surprise. You know that beautifully rich golden yellow American cheese that many of us find so cheesy and tangy and kind of rich? Well, it is really white! The yellow is added in the factory. Taste the same American cheese in white vs. yellow and see if they taste the same to you.

What does this all have to do with innovation? Plenty. So much time and effort is placed on coming up with and testing the actual idea, that when it comes time to turn it into a *buyer friendly* offering, mistakes are made. When a product idea is crafted and made ready for test, a lot of left-brain, logical-thinking goes into effect. When a consumer is asked to respond to the idea in test, she is almost always relying on her left-brain to carefully answer the questions posed to her. However, when it is time for a customer to buy the actual finished, packaged, colored, and advertised product, it becomes largely impulse—an action that is mostly right-brain. *Please* remember what we stated in our prior myth on concept testing—95 percent of human behavior is controlled by the *unconscious* mind.

Here is where the advertising agencies earn their keep. But, it is quite challenging for many marketers, researchers, and R&D personnel to take the logical, factual parts of a well-tested new product concept and allow an advertising agency to turn them into something that someone might actually buy in the real world. These people live so closely with the *product* that they have trouble understanding how all of the work that has gone into the details of the idea may not mean a thing to the *consumer*. A wise man once said: "Sell the sizzle, not the steak!" When it comes to line extensions and innovation with complex products like software, electronics, medical devices, and the like, many companies dwell on details that have nothing to do with what their customers really want. In fact, more often than not, the customer ends up bewildered, dazed, and confused.

I'm reminded of the 1990 movie, *Crazy People.* In the movie, Dudley Moore plays a former patient of a mental hospital who then recruits other mental patients to help him come up with advertising ideas for his ad agency. Well, what they come up with are "honest" ads that are hysterically funny—and crazy. Advertising slogans, like "Forget Paris. Come to Greece. We're nicer." for a Greek travel agency, or for the movie *The Freak*, "It won't just scare you, it will fuck you up for life!"

But *in the movie*, the clients love these advertising ideas, they go with them, and they are hugely successful. Working at an agency at that time I was often asked why real ad agencies can't come up with ads that are that funny and creative. Well, the truth is, of course they can, and of course they do, but the clients do not buy them. *In the real world*, the left-brain dominant thinking of corporate management cannot let them understand how or why ads like this could ever work.

On the other hand, the advertising agency has to do more than just take the tested idea and carefully craft it with the right emotions. The final, go-to-market product offering must certainly capture the attention and feelings of the target consumer but also, it must communicate the important elements of the idea that was tested. Believe us, this isn't easy. As we discuss elsewhere in this book, a major reason for a new product failing to live up to its tested results, lies in the fault of the advertising not adequately communicating the concept as tested.

In summary, at the end of the day, we all buy with our hearts, not with our minds. How else do you explain the mounting credit card debt in this country? Most buying decisions can be traced back to emotions that are only later rationalized by thought. There is no question that emotions motivate human actions far more than logical or rational considerations. People tend to base their decisions on emotional drivers and then rationalize those decisions or persuade themselves that they acted intellectually and with good judgment after the fact.

So when it comes to innovation and new product development, the earlier you can involve your ad agency, package designers, and other people on the "emotion" side, the better the potential outcome.

MYTH #20 BASES TESTING WILL SHOW THE WAY

PROPER RESEARCH is a significant help in reducing the overall risk associated with innovation. But, try as we might, research is not capable of removing *all* of the risk associated with innovation. Even one of the most frequently used and arguably one of the best providers of pre-market research, BASES, has its limitations.

BASES is the world's leading provider of pre-market consumer insights for marketers of consumer package goods, especially relatively inexpensive consumer package goods. Founded in the 1970s by Booz Allen Hamilton (and named for the Booz Allen Sales Estimating System), BASES has evaluated over 90,000 new product ideas in more than 60 countries.

BASES enables companies to obtain a sales forecast for a new product *prior* to launching it into the marketplace. Further, BASES can help a firm understand just how much a new product line extension may affect its overall brand franchise, who the core users of the new product will be, and even help determine the level at which the new product should be priced. And BASES can provide this information in just the concept stage (BASES SnapShot; BASES I), thereby saving a firm from having to actually develop the product. Or, for a more accurate forecast, from the product proto-type stage (BASES II), where consumers actually get to use and re-use or re-order a test version of the product.

BASES is almost a "fool-proof " way to determine whether or not your new product launch should go forward. It gives you a solid estimate of sales volume before having to commit bigger dollars in manufacturing, packaging, advertising, inventory build, and so forth. What could be better than that?

In fact, BASES has become so revered by many of today's leading consumer goods companies that we can't tell you how many times a client of ours has given us the order, "Just get us to and through BASES."

Ah, but here is the *myth*stake.

While many companies rely *solely* on BASES to decide whether or not to launch a potential new product, BASES results are only as accurate as the assumptions that go into the test. And too often the assumptions are way off.

BASES results are heavily determined by both the consumer reaction to the new product initiative *and* the BASES analysis of the market plan information the client provides. A basic model for determining consumer reaction to a new product involves:

Purchase Intent	How likely does the consumer say that she is willing to buy this product?
Liking	How much does the consumer report liking the product?
Value	How would the consumer rate the price/value?
Uniqueness	How different is this from other products?
Purchase Rate	How many would they buy the first time? How many times a year do they say they would buy this?

Remember what we discussed in our *myth*stakes about concept testing? Without very careful planning, concepts can easily over-promise or confuse the consumer. And the answers to the above questions will be largely based on consumers' reactions to the concept that they are presented with.

So if the actual new product will not be supported with much advertising in the marketplace, how much of the information in the "concept" will ever be communicated to the consumer in the real-world versus the BASES test? Conversely, if the concept presented is somewhat confusing, how much more clear or relevant might it be to the consumer in the real-world if in that world consumers see more publicity and descriptive advertising versus what they see in the concept presented in BASES?

Careful, in-depth, up-front thinking can help reduce some of this discrepancy. Specifically, you must take pains to try to present the concept in BASES as closely as possible to what the real world may be like. For example, if there is little advertising support being planned, make sure the concept is as brief as possible, perhaps stating only what can be placed on a package front. In fact, some companies do "pack-cepts," concept studies that are based solely on a proposed package front. On the other hand, when more information might be needed by a consumer to understand a concept, perhaps a test ad or video can be used to introduce the concept to consumers in BASES (if, of course, you intend this type of support in the real world). Additionally, going forward with actual product testing through a BASES II could minimize the risk of concept miscommunication.

Rest assured, BASES is a sophisticated organization and will no doubt assist its clients with understanding how to best present its concept to a consumer in testing. However, too often this is totally disregarded by the client in favor of client's own norms and processes.

Once you have determined the likely consumer reaction to the new idea in terms of who will want this product and what the probable trial, repeat rate, and frequency of purchase will look like, you are half way home to a solid sales estimate. "All" that remains is to determine what the real-world awareness will be among target consumers:

% AWARENESS X % TRIAL-RATE X % REPEATERS X FREQUENCY = ESTIMATE

Unfortunately, estimating true awareness requires huge assumptions.

- What will distribution and product availability be, by month?
- How effective will the advertising message be?

- How effective will the media plan and buy be?

- Where on the shelf might the product be?

Assumptions as to all of the above, and more, will go into the BASES model. What will the ad copy persuasion be? How many Gross Rating Points (GRPs) will you be running in advertising? Will you be running 15-second or 30-second TV spots, or print ads or some combination? What will your retail promotion feature and display level be? Will you be running coupons? What value? How often? How many? Lots and lots of planning. Lots and lots of assumptions. Lots and lots of *myth*stakes!

Perhaps, the toughest, most vulnerable and vitally important assumption you will make concerns product availability. All of the awareness in the world won't help if the consumer can't find the product on the shelf. A marketer can try anything and everything to capture distribution as quickly as possible but the truth of the matter is, it is largely in the hands of the retailer, and retailers don't get to play in the test.

And, it is not enough to assume what the annual distribution level might be. You have to assume what product availability will look like month-by-month, because if it takes a significantly greater amount of time to build distribution than what was assumed, the entire sales estimate for the first year will be considerably off. For example, if in the first three months you have only about one fourth of the annual distribution level you expected, you'd be getting only one-fourth the trial you expect early in the year. Think what this will do for repeat purchasing and frequency. If three-fourths of the entire base will not even be able to acquire the product until later in the year, how often can they buy or re-buy it before the first year runs out?

We learned the "distribution" lesson about ten years ago when a client of ours had a new product concept for an adult incontinence item. The product had some unique benefits and tested very well in BASES. A TV ad was developed and tested separately to make sure it was consistent with the concept and delivered persuasively. Based on the very encouraging BASES forecast, the firm was able to secure additional outside financing to ensure an aggressive, big-brand launch.

The new product was introduced into the marketplace and, just according to plans, heavy TV advertising hit full-force within six weeks after the brand's introduction. *Big Problem:* The product was, for all intents and purposes, not on shelf. Too many retailers still either had the product in their warehouses or had not even ordered it yet. By the time the product had finally been put on a reasonable number of store shelves, the company had finished its heavy up-front advertising spending and only moderate levels of advertising existed. Naturally, due to distribution varying considerably from an assumption given to BASES, the new product's annual volume came in nowhere near forecast. The company died.

If the above assumptions aren't complicated enough for you, there is at least one more that's very tough, and that's the supposition of competitive reaction. Because you just *know* there's going to be one. And anything a competitor does can significantly affect the sales estimate. Your competitor might quickly copy your new product idea and immediately cut your potential market size in half (or more, depending upon the power of its own brand and efforts). In those events whereby your new product is similar to others already in the marketplace, the competition can use aggressive price-reductions and other promotions to greatly delay or even impair your ability to gain trial.

Don't forget to watch out for potential retailer private label competitive moves as we've cautioned before. Unfortunately, today's retailers are becoming so aggressive that they, too, can quickly copy your new product as well as make their packaging look incredibly similar to yours and place it right next to the "real thing" on the shelf in the retail environment. Quite a few consumers may be "fooled" into buying the private label store brand *instead of yours.*

In reality, the real world winds up differing quite a bit from the initial assumptions that clients put into the BASES model. Distribution may be nowhere near the levels assumed. The advertising or packaging may not truly communicate the concept. The media effort may not be nearly at the levels planned. Displays, features, and retail promotion my be less than what is assumed. Competition may act in a totally unpredictable manner. Any or all of these can dramatically affect the initial "can't miss" estimate of projected volume.

And even in those cases where things basically hold true, where assumptions are not too far off, is BASES 100 percent accurate? No! And, BASES does not promise 100 percent accuracy either. BASES I promises that 90 percent of the time, it will be within plus or minus 25 percent of actual results. A BASES snapshot, less costly than a BASES I, promises only that 80 percent of the time, estimated volume will be plus or minus 30 percent. Even for firms that go to the expense of developing and testing prototype products, estimates can be improved to only plus or minus 20 percent—still far from risk free.

To make things a little more scary, we have seen over and over again that while BASES and other types of volume estimates will diligently report a *range* of sales, like plus or minus 25 percent, firms invariably plan for, and expect, the upper range. It is nice to be optimistic, but what happens is that so much is expected out of the new product, it is bound to disappoint.

BASES testing is as good as it gets and if handled diligently with careful time and attention placed on going-in assumptions, it can be a great part of a firm's innovation plan. But remember it is a tool and not an answer, *and it is only as good as the assumptions going in.* Remember too, BASES I estimates have an error range of 50 percent, which is far from miraculous. It makes us wonder how close to 50 percent of actual you can arrive at on your own? To be fair, we're relatively sure that no one will be upset in those instances where actual volume exceeds estimates, but for the half of the clients that come in less than anticipated, it can be a disaster of biblical proportions.

MYTH #21 — IT'S NOT WORTH DOING IF IT'S NOT INVENTED HERE!

*"When choosing between two evils,
I always like to try the one I've never tried before."*

—Mae West

Part of the cause for the "not-invented-here" culture is that too often, a company considers innovation to be strategy instead of a catalyst for fulfilling the goals and the strategies of the firm. What tends to happen when a company does not consider going outside for a new perspective is that the "insiders" go for the obvious low-hanging fruit to show some quick wins (which are usually pretty old and moldy fruit at best). Sadly, not only can these become quick "losers" in the hands of inexperienced innovators, but also, unless a firm also looks for the big, game-changer, results will always be marginal at best.

It's a shame more companies don't take their lead from Mae West! Instead, they prefer to keep things "in-house," play it safe, and close in. After all, let's face it, outsiders just don't understand our company the way that we do. Therefore, an innovative idea, or any innovation help coming from the outside really won't fit our company's needs the way that it should.

As a matter of fact, even if it *is* a good idea, why split the potential profits of a new innovation with anyone else on the outside?

And separately, how can we truly trust outsiders? Won't they want to sue us for stealing their idea if we talk to them and already have something like their idea on our docket? Won't they just go to our competitor with knowledge they gain from us if we don't do a deal with them?

Okay, okay! We get the idea. And in fairness, all of the above are valid concerns.

However, this does not mean that it is best for a firm to maintain a " Not Invented Here" (NIH) attitude. In fact, today, as a result of increased pressure to reduce costs and increase overall ROI, the need for speed, a rise in the number and quality of outside innovation consultants, and the ability the Internet provides for us to collaborate globally, the better way to innovate may well be to capitalize on the strengths of others.

Certainly, outsiders are not as strong as insiders in their understanding of what a specific company does or needs. But by being able to see a company from a different vantage point, without internal biases, outsiders can provide new innovative solutions that, a firm may never see from within. Further, while a firm certainly knows itself better than someone who is not within the organization, it cannot possibly know the world outside of itself, or the consumer as well as specialists in those areas. Actually, one of our responses to anyone who says to us: "You just don't know our business," is, "You're exactly right, we'll never know your business the way that you do. But, we will know the consumer and we can spot the opportunities better than you. So, let's work together to achieve phenomenal results!" As Mae West would argue, "try the one you've never tried before."

Hopefully, as we have shown in Myth #6 about "Consumer is King," you can see a benefit in getting outside perspective in order to gain true, unbiased insight about your customers—insight that provides true opportunities. Your own view, filtered through the lens of—your company can be skewed and stale. You can't call a stack of research "insight." Let's call it what it really is: a stack of research. Okay, a stack of observed facts and numbers. It really only becomes "insight" when you can apply some imagination and vision to that research to create the greatest areas of opportunity for game-changing ideas. Many times that comes from the outside.

When it comes to finding *new and different* solutions, you must consider taking advantage of the new and different opinions, experiences, and techniques that experts outside your company can bring. Think about it. Have you ever heard of the statement: "If you always do what you always did, you'll always get what you always got?" How can a firm come up with truly radical thinking if it uses the same project management tools, the same staffing models, the same team facilitation, the same meeting spaces, the same data, and the same perspectives?

Rick Neitz, a former professor of innovation at Vanderbilt University, explained it best when he instructed his class with the following bit of wisdom: "The world of innovation is like a big pie. I (or an individual) know just one slice of the pie. There is so much of the pie left that I don't know, but others do. To get the whole pie, we need to get as many of those slices on our plate as possible.

Seeking the right outside help throughout the innovation process can dramatically improve a firm's innovation results. A study of 700 firms by Booz Allen Hamilton reveals that experience in introducing new products significantly helps companies improve their new product performance. And, the simple truth is, outside innovation specialists have more experience innovating versus inside personnel who devote only a portion of their time, due to company constraints. Knowledge of the market, how to generate consumer insights, and how to develop opportunities along with the steps required to develop a new product brought in by outsiders can reduce cost and considerably improve performance.

The advantage of using outside innovation consultants can be seen in the old bromide that "practice makes perfect." Innovation consultants generally practice one thing and one thing only—innovation. We concentrate on uncovering consumer insights and ideation. And the more we practices the better we get. As Gary Player, famed PGA golf pro stated: "The more I practice, the luckier I get."

Want proof? Here's a simple exercise: How many things can you make with a spoon? Go ahead, be creative, think. The average person will come up with maybe a half dozen. But individuals that have been ideating more frequently will come up with maybe 100 or more! They'll think of everything from a shovel, spin-dial, weather vane, mirror for a midget, tongue depressor, little crow bar, lid opener, dirt pan, tiny bowl, backscratcher, light reflector, drum stick, weapon, catapult, paperweight, spinner, shiny ornament, and so on. Okay, stick a fork in me, I'm done! You get the idea.

As a benefit of working for many different companies in many different categories, under different market conditions, outside innovation consultants are constantly looking at consumers, gathering insights and seeing opportunities not just in one limited area, but in many areas. Consultants may look at areas completely unrelated to what the firm would look at. When a consultant's experiences and knowledge in areas unrelated to what a specific company may look at combines with the company's needs and objectives, true magic can occur.

As an example, as outside innovation consultants, we had the opportunity to study children and the way in which they ate various items. When working in the cheese category, we noticed how children love to pull apart and eat string cheese, one string at a time. When working in the confectionery category, we observed how children loved to wind and unwind certain taffies, licorice, and other confectionery items. This gave us the insight into how children loved food that they could unwind and eat piece-by-piece, strip-by-strip, string-by-string.

We were later able to bring this insight, along with many others developed over time to both a fruit-snack client and a frozen-meal client. The result? Kellogg's Twistable Fruit Snacks and Nestlé Hot Pocket Twists. Would these companies have found these opportunities by themselves? Probably not. But by partnering with an outsider they trusted and staying involved, magic happened.

In our ROI Myth #2, we discussed how beneficial Open Innovation (partnering with outside companies and inventors) can be in helping to reduce your cost of innovating. The fact is, this philosophy also has significant benefits in ideation as well.

Open Innovation can become crucial to companies whose need for continued growth becomes more difficult each year. We were at the P&G 2007 Global Alumni Conference where A.G. Laffley admitted, that his "connect-and-develop-open-innovation" directive was not exactly well received by his R&D people at first. But, when you considered the size of P&G and that a goal of just 5 percent annual growth would equal about $4 billion in new sales every year, you need some help.

While Open Innovation is talked about as a new and different way in which to do business, it has actually already been around for many years in some categories. For decades, toy companies openly looked toward inventors to present them with the next "blockbuster" toy. Hasbro's very popular SuperSoaker water gun came about from an outside inventor, Dr. Lonnie Johnson, a nuclear engineer. Kenner's Starting Line-up collectable figures came about from an NFL kicker, former Cincinnati Bengal Pat McAnally. Cabbage Patch, originally made huge in the 1980s by Coleco, was first thought up by an outside designer, Xavier Roberts and marketed as "Little People."

Today, toy companies still spend significant time and dollars wooing major toy inventors. The 2005 introduction of Spalding's highly successful Neverflat basketball came about when this industry-leading sporting goods manufacturer discovered a two-man (former Dupont) engineering operation that had invented a ball that could retain air longer. This past year, Wham-O even launched a contest to solicit toy ideas from kids.

Open Innovation is really nothing new in the area of retailing either. Retailers like Wal-Mart and Target aren't fashion kings. They use Martha Stewart, Isaac Mizrahi, Patrick Robinson, and Michael Graves to help them bring in customers.. The entire multi-billion dollar licensing industry is based on "licensing" an idea to someone else—a brand, apparel, toys, and so forth, so that the license purchaser can manufacture a product based upon it.

Other companies should open themselves up more often to outside inventors. All it would take to convince them is to learn a little from those companies and industries already doing this. It takes a process to screen for the right inventions or inventors and some appropriate, but not overburdening, legal protection. There are even companies, such as InventHelp and Creative Group Marketing to name a very few, that help firms find the right inventions/inventors and vice-versa. Also, for firms wishing to collaborate with partners to solve a particular business problem, there is Waltham, Massacusettes-based InnoCentive. It matches corporate "seekers" who have science, engineering and business problems with amateur "solvers" worldwide. The "solvers" then compete—for bragging rights and often token rewards.

Prominent examples of Open Innovation tend to focus on short-term transactions to access outside capabilities, but you should also be open to developing long-term relationships. SAP's developer ecosystem mobilizes more than 9,000 companies and engages more than 1 million individuals in sustained online interactions and discussions, for example.

In conclusion, while internal inventing still should play a part in corporate innovation, there should be no fear in remaining open to using outside consultants and Open Innovation to put your company in position to better develop out-of-the box, game-changing innovations both effectively and efficiently.

#22   R&D SHOULD LEAD THE WAY

AND NOW, a quick shout-out to our left-brained friends, the engineers. We love you guys, but you have to stay close to the market.

R&D quite rightly, is focused on technology, or how to get things done, and on better ways to get things done. R&D uncovers the art of the possible. It enables us to bring product improvements into our business. In short, R&D comes up with cool new solutions. But, here's a sobering fact of business for you: Technology, by itself, has no objective value.

Unfortunately, on its own, these cool new solutions can be solutions that nobody wants, at least, not enough to pay for. You know how it is, engineers are tucked away so far within a company that they don't see firsthand what customers really need. They become so focused on solving technical problems that they overlook the ways in which the customer actually defines value. If not careful, R&D–dominated innovation can get caught in a development dynamic where innovation is driven not by a focus on what the customer wants and is willing to pay for, but instead, on solving an engineering problem.

While R&D is certainly an important part of innovation, unless the technology is made, relevant to consumers and unless a strong business model supports it, the innovation will most likely fail. Even when R&D departments come up with great technologies, it takes marketers and consumer insight and innovation specialists to help make these technologies relevant, profitable, and successful.

Perhaps, R&D having responsibility for innovation may trace to the conventional view of product development that portrayed the inventor as hero. In reality, the inventor, whether a Thomas Edison or a Steve Jobs, has always been just a part of the process. Edison himself, hinted as much when he described the inventor as being a "specialist in high-pressure stimulation of the public imagination."

Whether it is the wizards in Menlo Park or Xerox PARC who come up with the concepts, the most effective product development and commercialization processes encourage dynamic communication and idea sharing among engineers, marketers and customers.

It is a *myth* that innovation is solely the realm of R&D. But, we're not saying that it should be solely in the hands of the marketers, either. While R&D focuses inward, marketing is focused outward, concentrating on customers, prospects, markets, and even analysts. Through analysis of external information, marketing can best decide if a product makes sense to consumers. Is it what customers are looking for or willing to accept? Where should the product go and how will consumers, retailers, and analysts understand it? However, this process of data collection and analysis rarely if ever leads to uncovering a revolutionary, game-changing idea. Also, let's face it, the best business model and best consumer insights don't mean anything if the actual product being marketed is junk.

Take a look at two very technology-driven companies and notice some profound differences. Contrast the successes of Bose, the Framingham, Massachusetts sound-system company, with that of Apple Computer of Cupertino, California. Apple, with its exceptional focus on customer insight, has been able to invent great products with great technology, which Bose does too. Apple, however, also creates vast *new markets*. Witness the way it has transformed the music industry with its hugely popular iPod. Interestingly, Bose has a new sound system specifically made for use with the iPod, and it has dramatically raised its marketing and brand identity push in the last few years. Anyone who's ever been on an airplane and flipped through a copy of *SkyMall* knows this all too well.

So how do companies maintain both a consumer and a technical focus? The use of cross-functional teams in product development is one way smart firms try to close the gap between technical know-how and customer understanding. You'll notice at Hewlett-Packard, for instance, the company requires that everybody on the team must go together to a prospective customer and personally hear the customer's comments.

Not only is the need for good cross-functional teamwork, especially between R&D and marketing, important in the development stages of innovation, but also it is also even more critical for ensuring that the new product isn't quickly copied and "stolen" by a competitor once it reaches the market. Jeong Kim, president of Bell Labs at Alcatel-Lucent and a successful tech entrepreneur, offered the following suggestion in a recent presentation titled, "Paving the Way for Disruptive Innovation." Mr. Kim stated that it is not enough simply to have brilliant engineers because without competent business side management and planning, even the most elegant technology can wind up on the scrap heap of business history, or even worse, usurped by a competitor.

Okay. So who should lead the innovation effort? If it is an individual, like a Chief Innovation Officer, or other appointed manager, there are four characteristics he or she will need to be successful:

1. Curiosity

2. Balance

3. Maverick

4. Math

Curiosity is at the heart of innovation. It is the key criteria for an innovative leader. It propels you to discover new things, lets you hear old ideas in new ways, and lets you see things differently than others. Curiosity is something we are all born with but, sadly, we seem to outgrow. We learned one of our favorite examples of this from our CFO (a very incurious kind of guy). He mentioned that one day his son, Ben, came to him and said: "Dad . . . Dad . . . let's look out the window, I'll bet we see ten deer!" We said, "That's cool," and asked him if he went to the window with his son. He said, "Of course not, there was no way there would be ten deer there." He was right, of course, but we wonder what he *would* have seen if he did go to the window. Who knows? One thing for certain, he'll never know.

Even though we want our innovation leaders to be creative, that doesn't mean we need them to be crazy. Most great innovators still know when it is time to go home and still know how to keep their teams fresh and not overworked. Overwork will cause teams to settle. Settling is the last thing we want when we are looking for that extra-brilliant unique idea.

We also want our leader to be a maverick because to be effective, he or she will need to have the guts and the ability to go against the grain, to buck the trends and most importantly to say, "Why not?" Since innovation involves meeting a need in a new way, it requires leadership from someone who welcomes the idea of doing things differently. And doing things differently, and getting others to follow means going against tradition and politics—a very tough test.

Finally, we need someone who gets the numbers. There is far too much risk in business today to invest money in an uncalculated dream. Sorry, but that old "trust me" plea doesn't work in today's tougher economy. For an innovation initiative to gain the support it needs, the key decision makers are going to want to know how much money they are going to make. And, of course, how much money it will cost.

So, in summary, we believe that the only way to really get control of the innovation process is to break down barriers between marketing and R&D and other corporate divisions, and create a truly collaborative process for innovation (our next myth will detail this for you). Then we recommend a solid team leader armed with curiosity, balance, the attitude of a rebel, and solid math skills, too. Neither Marketing nor R&D alone can bring enough to the table to own the process entirely. Add to this mix the distrust between marketing and R&D found in many organizations, and look out. It will be a miracle if innovation happens at all.

Are you willing to make like Gorbachev and "tear down this wall?" To survive, you may not have a choice. And that's no *myth*.

MYTH #23
You Don't Need a "Process" to Innovate

WELL THAT IS JUST MAD! And speaking of madness, you need a method to this madness. You are far better off to have a systematic approach to innovation if you are to be successful. PDMA studies show that best performing companies are more likely than others to have formal new-product-development processes (66 percent vs. 44 percent).

Innovation is too important and carries with it too much risk for firms to let it occur in a helter-skelter, or purely organic manner. In fact, without a well-managed process, those firms that embrace the increasingly popular "innovate or die" philosophy are more likely to fall victim to a less than thought-out, hurry-up-and-shoot, chaotic approach that virtually guarantees financial waste and unsuccessful innovation launches.

Companies can talk all they want about using innovation to grow and transform, but unless there is a true commitment to innovation and a structured process put into place, don't count on much of value really happening. Think about our government, for example. Every politician running for office makes dozens of promises. Not surprisingly, nothing really happens unless, because of some form of pressure, a process is put into place to ensure action. For years Americans have heard the promise that we would be looking for alternative fuels. Now, with the fear of being held hostage by oil producing countries, a goal has been set and a process is finally being developed.

Innovation can be free flowing and creative, *but* it should never be free-for-all chaos. That is why we heartily endorse a good innovation process that provides a method and a system that encourages as much creativity as possible while providing just enough structure to prevent the waste of time and money. It ensures that adequate new opportunities are uncovered and helps make certain that sufficient ideas are generated against the best opportunities. It guarantees that ideas are explored and those looking to be worthwhile to the customer *and* to the business are moved forward in a relatively fast-paced, but altogether efficient manner. It provides continuous checkpoints to help certify that important parts are not overlooked, and it provides for a careful way in which firms can monitor and control their investments to protect ROI.

Also, due to the relative unpredictability of innovation (since you can never really know what, or how big an opportunity will be until you find it) a good innovation process should have some degree of flexibility built in. Some companies, such as IBM, actually set aside innovation funds to support ideas arising from outside the normal planning and innovation process.

A solid innovation process should also understand that you should never be looking for the same old thing. Therefore, the testing methodologies, norms, and financial requirements may have to be more lenient for first-time, new products versus those demanded for existing brands. You cannot maintain status-quo methods and requirements while still expecting new game-changing results.

Further, a first-class process should also take advantage of several new technologies that are now available in order to maximize efficiencies and reduce uncertainties. Innovation technology includes newer methods for market simulation and modeling, better visualization capabilities, faster, easier, and more precise quantitative measurement tools, and rapid prototyping capabilities.

Additionally, an innovation process should provide for diverse thinking. A superior innovation practice provides for ways in which people from different departments and functions can interrelate. Innovations that are truly game changing are usually birthed by a collision of different ideas and domains that are not usually thought of as belonging together. For this to happen, diverse people with disparate experiences and backgrounds need to connect.

History shows that the big ideas of Thomas Edison, Ted Turner, Jeff Bezos, Steve Jobs, and others all came about through their interacting and networking with a talented, dissimilar community of people. Various experiments conducted by Scott Page, author of *The Difference: How the Power of Diversity Creates Better Groups, Firms, Schools and Societies*, found that distinct groups of problem solvers consistently outperformed groups of the best and brightest.

To get the best in uncommon thinking, smart firms will augment their innovation processes with outside people because even the most disparate team of employees will still share the same organizational DNA.

Finally, and importantly, a good-quality innovation process must make certain that sufficient time and effort is given to the development of the business rationale and marketing plan for the innovations' launch. A major analyses by the PDMA shows that what stands out most among new product failures is the lack of time that was spent up front, in pre-development activities, determining market size, potential volume, profits, and costs.

ESTABLISHING A PROCESS

Establishing and managing the right innovation process for any company is far from easy. Since every organization is different, there is no one-size-fits-all process that will work perfectly for everyone. Many leaders that are used to managing efficient processes in their business wind up struggling with innovation's need for creativity, intuition, out-of-the box thinking, and activities that might or might not rely on outsiders. Many leaders have trouble starting with a totally blank slate without a specific target in sight.

The specific format and timing of the steps in a company's innovation process may not be that important. What is most important is that all functional teams involved in the process understand and agree to the steps and maintain a consistent understanding of the metrics.

A first-class innovation process should ensure:

- Searching for and uncovering real opportunities.

- Good quality, prolific, problem-solving ideation.

- Proper screening of ideas based on consumer and business needs.

- Appropriate checkpoints used throughout to minimize mistakes and protect ROI.

- Flexibility to take advantage of the unforeseen.

- Diversity of thinking.

- Due diligence in business/marketing planning.

- Continued communication between all relevant departments.

And it should do this while allowing for top, unbiased creativity, and reasonable speed.

The Stage-Gate Approach

One particular process that is often cited is Robert Cooper's *Stage-Gate*. Stage-Gate or other phased development processes are used in one form or another by probably half of the companies developing new products. The Stage-Gate Process provides an orderly way to move a new product project from idea through launch, via various predetermined stages and steps. Built within each stage are pre-agreed criteria for go/no-go decision making. At the conclusion of each stage, the project must be determined by management to have successfully met pre-determined criteria in order to pass through the "gate" to the next stage.

Typical stages listed are:

1. Idea development and screening.

2. Building the business case.

3. Development of the product.

4. Testing and validating.

5. Launch.

Stage-and-gate processes have appeal to management, because they do a great job of managing risk. Basically, they restrict investment in the next stage until management is comfortable with the outcome of the current stage. The "gate" can be effective in controlling product quality and development expense. For those wishing to learn more of the details of Stage-Gate, we encourage the reading of Cooper's *Winning at New Products: Accelerating the Process from Idea to Launch.*

But, managing risk should not always be the prime objective or certainly not the only objective. When speed to market is also important (and it usually is), the sequential, step-by-step pathways can make it difficult to move quickly or simultaneously. In fact, sometimes speed to market is so important that a much more open, parallel process must be designed. In these cases, it is almost essential that organizations dedicate a separate staff just for the innovation effort, so that other day-to-day challenges do not get in the way.

The Stage-Gate Approach

An option to the traditional stage-and-gate process that allows for quicker action and faster-to-market executions is the bounding box approach. This method basically applies a management by exceptions technique in which, as long as the project continues to remain within certain critical parameters, the team is free to move ahead on its own. Key parameters or boundaries must be limited to the critical top few and must be objective and measurable to avoid team confusion.

An example of "Bounding Boxes" could include:

CONCEPT ACCEPTANCE – MINIMUM TOP TWO BOX SCORE OF _____ ;
UNIQUENESS SCORE OF _____ .

FINANCIAL ASSUMPTIONS – COST OF SALES LESS THAN + _____ % OF PLAN;
ENGINEERING EXPENSE IS LESS THAN + _____ % OF PLAN.

MARKET SIZE AND WINDOW – TIMING TO MARKET IS =/– _____ MONTHS
WITHIN OBJECTIVE; MARKET SIZE IS _____ .

Other boundaries established could include product performance, key retailer acceptance, value proposition, target market, or whatever is critical to management's acceptance of the project.

Sufficient time should be taken in order to design a stage-gate type of process that allows the next stage to begin in at least a limited capacity, before the prior stage passes through its own particular gate. Or, for that matter, a process could be designed that in theory would allow for parallel gating. It is up to the individual firm and its specific circumstances to determine what speed and risk level is acceptable.

Whether the decision is to use a Stage-Gate process or not, the important learning is that you would best be served to agree upon and adhere to a step-by-step path that takes a project from ideation through product launch, specifying go/no-go deliverables or boundaries throughout the course. The agreed-upon path should encourage good quality of execution, demand a strong market and consumer orientation, enable sharper focus and prioritization, and encourage speed in both implementation and decision-making.

OUR PROPOSED METHOD: THE LAUNCHING PAD

We wanted a process name that tells it like it is, that reinforces the need and desire for exploration into uncharted worlds, that demands precision in its execution, that strives for flying as high as you can yet recognizes the dangers and takes all steps necessary to ensure a safe flight, that is thrilling and makes a lot of noise when it is ready for ignition. Oh yeah, and it goes so well with our company's name, LaunchForce.

We propose a process that entails three equally important stages:

1. **Stargazing** This is where it all starts. It is the part of the innovation process where we gaze at the universe, immersing ourselves in and exploring new worlds—the three worlds of innovation (interior, consumer, and visionary). Initial opportunities or missions are uncovered (CIFAs), ideas are generated, refined, polished, and validated. And finally, the light plan is made, a.k.a. the business case for the product.

2. **Countdown** Here is where the dreams come to life. The concept(s) chosen for potential launch must be carefully but speedily developed, optimized, and manufactured and the flight plan, a.k.a. the marketing plan, is firing up and propelling us toward the final stage.

3. **Blast-off** Now it's time to launch and fly this baby! All must come together at the right time. The combination of fuels must all be brought together just right. We must have proper, timely ignition. And, we have to fly our product safely into the stratosphere.

Stargazing	Countdown	Blast-off
Interior World	Sourcing	Sales Meetings
Consumer World	Constructing	Start of Sales
Visionary World	Package Design	Start of Advertising
CIFAdeation	Consumer Testing(s)	
Mapping	Market Planning	
BrainGaming	Sales Materials Complete	
Concepting		
Concept Testing		
Business Case		

Note, the above represents just a suggested list of tasks for each stage. Each company will no doubt have its own specific requirements, and each task has many other sub-tasks that must be accomplished. Each company must determine what is needed in order to proceed to the next stage based on its risk tolerance and need for speed.

Stargazing

The deliverable of this stage is the identification of a well-defined new concept that is confirmed to be useful and desirable to users as well as technically feasible and attractive to the business. It all starts with generating a good idea because, try as we might, the simple truth is that no process, no matter how well executed can save a bad idea.

There are no guarantees that your exploration will lead to a great, validated, technically feasible idea each and every time. However, experience has taught us that what we *can* promise is that the right people looking in the right places with the right frame of mind will invariably come up with great new opportunities and ideas again and again. It may be hard to believe for some, but new product ideation in the hands of those who have done it frequently, is not too dissimilar from joke-writers never running out of new jokes, song-writers always coming up with the next song, or novelists and poets creating newer and better works. The more experience you have with something, the better you generally get at executing it.

A well-loved story is often told of Pablo Picasso about the day an admirer of his bumped into him at an outdoor bazaar on a sunny afternoon. The man was dumbstruck to meet one of his idols. He finally worked up the courage to ask Picasso for his autograph. Without hesitating, Picasso reached over to tear a piece of brown paper from the bag the other man was holding. After producing an ink pen, Picasso quickly signed his name on the piece of scrap paper, but not before doodling a one-of-a-kind original sketch to go along with it. The entire action seemed effortless and totally organic. The man reached for the paper when Picasso withdrew it in an instant and said: "That will be

$50,000 dollars." Stunned, the man said: "$50,000? But that only took you ten seconds!" Nonplused, Picasso answered: "My dear boy, that took me sixty years!" The story has been told so often that it is known as "The Picasso Effect."

The idea is that whereas a particular skill or talent may appear effortless and second nature, it is, in fact, the result of decades of learning, training, skill, honed intuition, and discernment. That's the reason there is a difference between the absolute "cost" of something, and its "value." It may have "cost" Picasso about two cents worth of paper and ink to create something that has a value worth thousands. Bottom line: experience is invaluable in innovation and just about any other walk of life. If you were about to undergo a heart operation, ask yourself this question: Would you want to be the heart surgeon's "first" operation, or her 300th operation? That should tell you all you need to know about the importance of experience.

Okay, let's assume that you have within your own organization, (or with the help of outside experts you have recruited) at least some creatively gifted, intuitive individuals on your innovation team. Even if you could actually bring a group of qualified, diverse people together, encourage them to converse and interrelate, with the hope that they could produce new ideas, the chances of getting anything unique coming out of them is quite unlikely if these people start with the same old data and the same old orthodoxies and the same old perspectives. It's the ultimate "garbage-in-garbage-out" scenario.

That is why we call for *true* stargazing, or exploration if you will, at this stage. Just like explorers of old, if everyone in Columbus's time explored in exactly the same place, let's say Latitude 40° 47' and Longitude 73° 58', then *everyone* would find exactly the same thing— America! Even more specifically, they would all find what is now New York City. No wonder it is so crowded! But seriously, this is the main reason that so many competitive companies wind up creating, testing, and introducing exactly the same new product ideas. It is also the main reason why so many companies charged with coming up with new ideas year after year always come up with the same ones many times over. It is because everyone is exploring in exactly the same place. True exploration means setting off in uncharted waters and uncharted worlds. How else can you hope to discover something new?

So what is also required is a process for this front-end phase that significantly improves the likelihood you will find those elusive great, new ideas. That process is FutureCaster, which is fully discussed in our "Consumer is King," Myth). Followed by BrainGaming, which is discussed in our "Brainstorming Works!," Myth #10.

An important part of this stage is to validate that what you have discovered is truly a worthwhile, new discovery and that's where concept development and testing comes in. To understand how best to go about this, consult "Concept Testing is a Great Way to Minimize Risks," Myth #18.

Last, while concept testing will help you determine from a *consumer* point of view whether or not you have a potentially solid new product candidate for launching, it is worth pursuing only if it makes sense for the *company* as well. So while the results of the concept testing will indicate who might want the product, how many of them might want it, how often they will use it, and so forth, you should do a preliminary market assessment including estimated sales and profit ranges, competitive situation, technical feasibility, and company fit. A more complete budget detailing estimated cost to manufacture and market the item is also of great importance. In reality, much of this assessment can begin prior to the results from concept testing. The conclusion of this assessment must clearly communicate why it makes sense for the company to undergo the expense of development and eventual marketing of the potential new product.

While we stated that all three stages are equally important, we must realize that the first stage, stargazing, is probably the most important of all stages. It is this stage that is supposed to minimize the likelihood of an eventual, expensive failure. It is difficult for a firm to stop an initiative once it gets going and picks up steam. Plus, mistakes in Stage I can lead to serious delays in the Countdown stage.

Yet, despite the importance of this front-end work, it receives by far, the least amount of time and funding of any other part of the innovation process. The PDMA reports that the reason for most new product failures is insufficient up-front marketing and business work. Reportedly, 75 percent of new products were never tested to determine if consumers wanted or needed them and only one in five companies ever took the time to consider the potential market size for a new product with which it was moving forward.

Countdown

Here is where the money really starts flowing, so communication between the "stargazers" and those "counting down" is essential. And, communication between those who are "counting down" and the original target consumers is equally essential.

We have cautioned elsewhere in this book about the critical role that communication can play in new product success or failure. One of the key areas in which internal communications can breakdown is in the handoff of the fully tested concept from those involved in the upfront work to those who are now tasked with development and production of the actual item for consumption. This can lead to the production team incorrectly translating the concept, which would be a disaster.

Two things must be done to help minimize the likelihood of the developed product not living up to consumer expectations based on the concept. First, a careful product definition must be established for R&D, which will clearly state the *key must haves* of the product and any other mandatory elements, including the product's position, benefits, features, costs, and even timing. Second, frequent consumer "checks" must be done along the development route to ensure that the product, as it is being developed, is in sync with what the consumer expects.

Finally, consumers' wants and needs can change quickly in the marketplace, so you must take steps to ensure the production occurs in a relatively timely (i.e., fast) manner. There's an old saying that "you can always make a product better," but you need to ask yourself how long that will take, and what is the opportunity cost, versus launching a "good enough" product that fully meets your consumers' expectations? Remember what we cautioned in Myth #3: "Don't Bother Unless It's Perfect." R&D can be instructed to look for potential ways in which to save time. Perhaps the addition of a piece of equipment, or outside help can speed the process that much more.

There must also be clear and continued communication between the "stargazers" and the "countdown" team responsible for development of the marketing plan. What insights were uncovered during exploration that might help marketers understand barriers that might hurt consumers being able to easily adapt the new item? What other assumptions were the consumers making that marketers must be careful to address? What must the advertising and packaging clearly communicate? What can the sales force tell retailers about why they should carry the new item?

Blast-Off

Everything must come together for a perfect launch. The sales force must be totally briefed. The advertising and collateral must be ready to go and, hopefully, pre-tested. The sales calls must be effective and made on time. The new product must be shipped and stocked to be available to a sufficient number of consumers so that the advertising is efficient and effective.

It all starts with the market plan developed during the Countdown stage but the first hand-off between "Countdown" team and "Blast-Off" crew is also critical. This is where the company's first line of fighters, the sales force, must be armed and absolutely "sold" on the idea. The sad truth of the matter is that many people by nature are negative. It is easier to say that something won't work and then be in position to say, "I told you so," than it is to stick your neck out to say, "This is great!"

As we cautioned earlier in this book, it is getting more difficult to persuade retailers to give up precious shelf space to carry what they may see as just another, "only slightly" better, or even worse, copy cat product. So, much attention must be placed on how the new product is introduced to the sales force. It must be done with all of the confidence, supporting facts, excitement, fanfare, and noise that will ensure that each and every salesperson fully believes in his or her heart that their customer *must* agree to accept this product.

In Summary

As you have no doubt gleaned, the idea that you can simply assemble a team and start innovating, or that any kind of "process" would get in the way of innovating, is certainly one of the biggest myths going these days. Innovating in a purely Blue Sky manner without having all the steps laid out beforehand to get to that hallowed Wild Blue Yonder is absolutely fraught with peril. As with any journey, you should have a map ready so you don't have to stop to ask for directions, especially when you're reaching for the stars.

MYTH #24 Stick With the Plan, No Matter What! (Case Study)

JUST ABOUT EVERYBODY has heard this one. As if by sheer force of will you could alter the facts in a given situation. But keep in mind, there's a big difference between the virtue of "determination," and simply being flat out "delusional," though. It's ironic that when it comes to innovation, we talk so often about the "pipeline." You know, that ubiquitous conduit that is continuously primed to bring new and better ideas, products, and services flowing into the marketplace (or at least keep those new ideas in development).

It's ironic, because one of the biggest *myth*stakes in the history of U.S. innovation was trying to stick with the original plan on the construction of the Alaska pipeline.

The Alaska pipeline is a wonderful example of innovation in action. It reminds us that nothing speeds up the need to innovate more than a competitive threat. Action to innovate requires a top management directive. The best ideas and solutions can come from looking outside the category and from a change in perspectives. BrainGaming helps solve problems. And, experience helps.

Back in 1968, when Atlantic Richfield prospectors struck oil at Prudhoe Bay, they stumbled upon a massive strike, the largest oil field ever discovered in North America. Other oil companies joined in and started drilling their own wells. But that wasn't the innovation. In fact, that was the easy part. The biggest need for innovation anyone could foresee was how to get 10 billion barrels of oil out of Alaska. The call went out for innovators of every stripe. That's because there wasn't even a road within 400 miles of the wellheads. The Arctic Ocean was frozen solid most of the year. The oil companies considered ice-breaking tankers, nuclear-powered submarine tankers, and twelve-engine jumbo jet tankers. Eventually, they agreed that the only possible solution was a pipeline.

In February 1969, the oil companies announced their pipeline plans. They ordered $100 million worth of steel pipe from Japan. The project would cost 900 million dollars, they said, and be finished by 1972, even though they did not yet have a single design drawing or construction permit.

The shortest route anyone could come up with would still run 800 miles through the heart of Alaska, from Prudhoe Bay on the northern coast to the port of Valdez in the south, almost equivalent to building a pipeline from Chicago to Dallas, except you have to account for an Arctic wilderness in between. It was country so fierce; some of it had never been mapped.

The pipeline would cross three mountain ranges, 790 streams and rivers, and some of the world's most active earthquake zones before reaching the ice-free water in the south. It was an audacious plan, even for the oil industry.

Getting that oil out of Alaska would take nine years, employ some 78,000 people, cost more than $8 billion, and require threading 800 miles of steel pipe through America's most pristine wilderness. That's where the innovation comes in, and lots of it.

Film producer Mark Davis of PBS's *American Experience* made a documentary about the entire undertaking, including the unprecedented innovation it required by *not* sticking with the plan—sometimes on a daily basis. And if innovation means change, then the Alaska pipeline is the very definition of the word. "It changed just about everything and everyone it touched," says Davis, "from the people who opposed it to the people who supported it, the people who built it, and the state of Alaska." There are great lessons to be learned about remaining flexible throughout the innovation process. And while we've pointed out elsewhere that it is always necessary to have a plan to begin with, sticking with that plan as unforeseen events occur can be an epic **myth**stake.

There were, of course, incredibly detailed plans for the Alaska pipeline to be sure. But before the first mile of pipe could be laid, the project ran into unexpected opposition from native Alaskans who had been waiting for more than a century for Congress to settle ancestral land claims. Since the proposed pipeline would run directly through land they considered theirs, they believed that the government should settle their claims before construction began. Oops! Time to come up with a new plan. But wait, there's more. Another formidable challenge came from environmentalists, who feared that the colossal project would wreak havoc on America's last untouched wilderness. Native Alaskans and environmentalists both sued in federal court to block government approval of the pipeline.

Now what?

With the oil industry lobbying on their behalf for a quick resolution, the Native Alaskans received 44 million acres of land and one billion dollars from the Federal government. Okay, check. Now can we start building this thing? Not so fast. The environmental battle took much longer. A new law required the government to consider environmental impacts before authorizing any project on public land. Taking advantage of this, environmentalists used the law to force studies of everything from caribou migration in the far north to fish spawning in the streams and rivers the pipeline would cross.

They pushed for detailed plans to limit pollution from construction camps, prevent oil spills, and survive earthquakes. One legal challenge followed another, as environmental groups tested the limits of the new law. Years passed with the pipeline stuck in legal limbo.

It probably didn't help that the project also faced criticism from the government's own scientists. That's right. They warned that the traditional pipeline construction method that was specified in the plans ("dig-a-ditch-and-bury-the-pipe") wouldn't work in Alaska. That's because beneath a thin, insulating cover of tundra and vegetation, much of Alaska sits on permanently frozen ground called permafrost. In some places, it's mostly gravel, but in others it's mostly ice. If ice-rich permafrost is allowed to thaw, it turns into loose mud that cannot support any weight. Prudhoe Bay oil would come out of the ground hot, and as it flowed through a buried pipe, it would thaw any ice-rich permafrost along the way. From there, it doesn't take a genius to realize that the unsupported pipe would eventually buckle, break, and start leaking oil. The only option was to build more than 400 miles of the pipeline *above* ground. That wasn't in the original plan, though.

Environmentalists still had the pipeline tied up in court in 1973 and things weren't looking so good when all of a sudden the Arab states declared an embargo on oil shipments to the U.S., plunging America into a serious energy crisis. The price of oil doubled overnight. Shortages led to gas lines, gas rationing, and sometimes no gas at all. Pipeline supporters said that Prudhoe Bay would produce two million barrels of oil a day, cutting imports by one third.

Time to capitalize on a trend, right? Alaskan oil became a national security issue. President Nixon signed the Trans-Alaska Pipeline Authorization Act, which prohibited any further legal challenges, and the pipeline forged ahead. Environmentalists were painted in dire terms with the *Anchorage Times* once describing someone in an editorial as being an "admitted" environmentalist.

But oil historian Joseph Pratt recalls that permission to proceed is not the same as permission to succeed: "The industry was somewhat beyond confidant that they had the know-how and the money to solve any engineering problems they encountered; they believed. And when you think of that kind of confidence, it does border on arrogance, and it does border on hubris, given what happened next."

No matter where you work, as you develop new product ideas, you probably feel that working with R&D can be tough. But imagine forming a company to design and build a pipeline. Now add to that fact that your job now entails drilling 15,000 soil samples along the route to locate all the areas of ice-rich permafrost. We've all faced some tough deadlines in our career, but with the energy crisis of 1973–74, there was enormous pressure to get the pipeline built quickly. And, the pressure from oil company owners was even greater. They had already spent billions at Prudhoe Bay, and they were losing $22 million dollars a day in revenue while the oil sat in the ground.

They made it clear that the pipeline had to be up and running in three years, no matter what. Once again: calling all innovators, calling all innovators.

After almost six years from the original oil strike and first set of plans, construction crews finally went to work at the end of January 1974. They had to haul in road building equipment and temporary housing while the ground was still frozen. By spring the tundra would be too soft to drive on. Cargo planes flew in more freight, landing on frozen lakes.

The first job was to build a supply road through the trackless northern half of the state, from the Yukon River just north of Fairbanks to Prudhoe Bay, and then build 29 construction camps along the pipeline route to house the workers.

By fall, the 360-mile-long, gravel road was finished, and the race was on to be ready for construction the following spring. Three million tons of pipe, machinery, spare parts, fuel, and food would be hauled in over the next two-and-a-half years.

At the end of March 1975, it was time to start putting the actual pipe in the ground at long last. No one had ever attempted construction on this scale in such an extreme environment, under such intense scrutiny, or on such a tight schedule. The only hope of finishing on time was to divide the route into five segments and build them simultaneously.

The man in charge of getting it done was Frank Moolin, a veteran big project engineer who had just finished BART, San Francisco's rapid transit system. He was a tireless worker who knew how to motivate as well as innovate. Moolin would live in a helicopter for the next two years, trying to keep the sprawling, complicated project on track. There were hundreds of streams and rivers to cross, twelve pump stations to build, plus a tanker port on the coast at Valdez. And then there was the pipe (800 miles of it) to be welded together 40 feet at a time. If the ground was stable, it could be buried like any other pipeline. But remember that about half of the pipe would have to be built above ground and then insulated to keep the oil fluid in cold weather. Nothing like it had ever been done before. The massive scale of the operation made everything more difficult. We're sure you remember the phrase "innovate or die." Well, no one worked harder than Moolin did. And friends believe his relentless style contributed to an early death at age 48 not long after the pipeline was done, but for the record, we are not advocates of "innovate *and* die."

Nonetheless, innovating on the fly had its own share of challenges. Housing, telephones, electricity, everything was in short supply, or no supply. There were times when aircraft had to be hired (at a cost of $10,000) just to go get a $50 item for a Caterpillar tractor to get it started so they could keep moving. But when you're spending $25 million dollars a day, holding up production for a "widget" is not an option. It doesn't matter at that point how much it costs to get the widget, just get it!

One noteworthy innovation was the division of labor itself. Keep in mind this is the mid-1970s. It wasn't at all common—even on the nation's final frontier—to have women doing jobs typically performed by men. But the task was so massive, new perspectives on gender roles had to be examined. Thousands of women got into construction for the first time on the pipeline driving busses, flatbeds, whatever they were asked to do.

Naturally, Alaska's got some of the worst environmental and weather conditions in the world. It's not unusual to get down to −45°, −50°, −60° in the wintertime. And while workers were provided Arctic gear and some training in how to use it, nothing could prepare a person for the North Slope, where the sun never rises for two months in the winter, and wind chill temperatures can reach 100° below zero.

Somehow though, the pipeline was getting built. One innovation was the fact that Moolin took the unusual step of negotiating no-strike clauses with the unions. And what he gave in return were high wages, and tolerance for a certain amount of bad behavior, which was something quite new. He recognized the value of labor peace, and he bought it. With all of the ever-changing plans the job required, the one thing he didn't need was labor troubles and he was willing to pay for it. And it worked. Despite more workers than were needed, despite waste, despite incredible theft, in the end, it got done. Simply seen as a feat of engineering and construction and project management, the pipeline was really our nation's second moon shot.

But a new crisis was about to hit, and this one threatened to take down the entire project. Early in 1976, the national media reported that thousands of welds made in the previous year might be fatally flawed. Every one of the 108,000 pipeline welds was supposed to be X-rayed, inspected for flaws, and certified, an enormous task that quickly overwhelmed the companies hired to do the job. One of the subcontractors got behind and pulled a trick that had been learned in the industry long before: if you find a good weld and you X-ray it 10 or 15 times from a different angle and then call it ten or fifteen different X-rays, you could then claim the next 15 joints are in good shape, which would allow you to move ahead and get caught up.

When the deception came to light, it was disastrous. The whole quality control program was now called into question. Until Frank Moolin's people could sort out which X-rays had been faked, all 30,800 field welds done to date were under suspicion. By laboriously crosschecking every X-ray, they were able to find all the duplicates and narrow the number of suspects to 3,955.

More than half were in buried pipe, some beneath rivers. In the end, some 1,900 welds needed minor repair. Another 37 had to be cut out and re-done. It was an expensive setback. But the schedule suffered the most damage. Moolin was told that he could spend up to an additional $10 million dollars a day as long as what he spent it on would save a day. Wouldn't you love your boss to give you that directive.

Two of the most difficult sections remained, the rugged mountain passes of the Brooks Range in the north, and the Chugach Mountains in the south.

In the Chugach, the problem was the roller coaster terrain, and the difficulty of getting machinery and pipe where it had to go. One spot in particular presented problems that no one in the pipeline business had ever confronted before: the near-vertical 2,800-foot south face of Thompson Pass.

Time for some serious BrainGaming, and on-the-spot innovation, as well. The Pass was so steep, there was seemingly no way to get material up one side and down the other, let alone operate machinery on it. Eventually, the engineers finally innovated a tower and cable system to fly the 80-foot pipe sections into place. The cable operators had to maneuver the nine-ton sections into position with nothing but radio communication to guide them. It worked well until the time came to position and weld the final sections on the steepest part of the slope, at which point, the welders cringed and began to shy away, one by one. A co-worker had already been injured by a falling rock, and most of the others decided it was too dangerous to continue.

Elsewhere in this book, we have mentioned the value of experience when it comes to innovation. And the Alaska Pipeline is yet another example of this axiom in play. With time running out, the managers turned to one of the oldest and most experienced welders on the job to save the day, while all of the younger upstarts were backing off and allowing fear to get in the way of a solution.

The welders were ready to quit. The last thousand feet of the Alaska pipeline had to scale an almost sheer cliff. It looked impossible, and no one was willing to risk his life on that rock face, until Hugh "Junior" Leslie, the oldest man on the job, volunteered. Without knowing it then, he said one of greatest innovation mantras of all-time: *"I was going to do it because so many of them told me it couldn't be done."*

On the Alaska pipeline, as with any company you may work for, there was always something that couldn't be done—that had to be done. And after "Junior" volunteered, other workers decided to follow his lead and worked in a place where only rock climbers had ventured before. They said it felt like trying to wash the windows on the Empire State Building, but like any great innovator, they were fearless.

A little more than twenty months after work began, the 800-mile steel pipe through the heart of America's last untouched wilderness— the biggest, most expensive, and most controversial private enterprise in American history—was completed.

By late spring of 1977, the pump stations were ready to start moving oil. On June 20, the valves at Prudhoe Bay were opened, and the first Alaskan crude began to flow south. The safeguards environmental-ists fought for produced a pipeline as green as almost anyone could have hoped. The final cost was $8 billion dollars, almost 10 times the original estimate.

The pipeline is a brilliant example and a marvel of innovation, because the builders had to constantly adapt to the new needs of environmental quality, by spending more money, and changing the design as they progressed. As a result, more than 15 billion barrels of oil have been delivered so far—50 percent more than predicted. And Alaskan oil has been the biggest resource bonanza in U.S. history, transforming Alaska from one of the poorest, to one of the wealthiest states in the nation.

The pipeline did exactly what it was supposed to do. Whether you consider that good or bad, it's the case, and like the best innovations do, it has changed the face of Alaska forever.

So as you find yourself working on an innovation project be it large or small, and the plans need to change, keep in mind the words of senior Alaska pipeline welder Hugh "Junior" Leslie for inspiration:

"When I did that I didn't do it to be glorified or anything. I did it because it needed to be done."

MYTH #25 INNOVATION MEANS NEVER LOOKING BACK (CASE STUDY)

BECAUSE INNOVATION, by its very nature, is future-focused, it's easy to make the time-honored *myth*stake of only looking forward. We're all about the "what-can-be," so who cares about the "what-was," right? Well, to be sure, we want to avoid retreads and also-rans. But in looking forward, it is always a good idea to also take one last look over your shoulder. For two reasons: to learn from history, so you don't repeat it, and to draw upon the past for inspiration.

There are so many great ideas, technologies, and concepts that are worth taking a second look at, not because they are moldy-oldies, but because they were actually based on an opportunity, or as we've called them, a CIFA (Consumer Insights Focus Area). And as we have said before, any opportunity can yield a significant number of ideas. Innovations like the mobile phone, the Internet, television, and MP3s were all ideas that didn't "catch on" when first introduced, but when the timing and execution was right, they were launched with great fanfare.

In the case of these products, the original opportunity insight was still there—the desire of consumers to have "real life" entertainment experiences. However, while the idea to solve it was valid, the original execution missed the mark. That does not mean that the opportunity went away. It means that a different way in which to approach it might yield a winner. Eventually technology provided a new and much more acceptable way in which to deliver the idea, and the results were far better

We all know those people who keep their bell-bottom pants, or their skinny ties, or their platform shoes in the back of the closet because, as they will attest, "Just wait, these are gonna make a comeback!" Some have been proven right. Thanks to the haute couture of AMC's *Mad Men* series, dapper suits and hats for the workplace are a staple of this year's runway and designer lines, but they've been improved with better fabrics for 2009. The same is true in media and entertainment.

When DreamWorks Animation chief executive Jeffrey Katzenberg (the movie mogul behind mega-hits *Beauty and the Beast* and *Shrek*) took the stage at the Intel Developer Forum stating that he was about to show the "greatest innovation to occur in the movie business in 70 years," I'm sure the audience was skeptical. By the time he left the stage, they were sold.

"The movie theater experience has not changed in many decades," Katzenberg said. "Meanwhile, the home experience has gone through extraordinary innovation in just the last decade. To some degree, people have stopped coming to movie theaters." The innovative solution? "Immersive story telling," Katzenberg said. The innovative method? 3D filmmaking.

Hold on, you say. I thought that was around in the 1950s? "This is not your father's 3D," according to Katzenberg. In fact, he predicts that 3D "will reinvent, redefine and completely transform not only how we make movies, but even more excitingly, how audiences experience them." Katzenberg likens the latest innovations in 3D technology to the third revolution in movie making. First, movies transitioned from silent films, to sound, followed by the change from black-and-white to color. Katzenberg argues that 3D will be the third revolution because the latest technology will make the audience feel like "they are leaping buildings with Spiderman."

Technology has advanced since the days when 3D films frequently induced nausea. Just look what DreamWorks (as well as other movie studios) are doing to bring innovation to the movies by looking backward—in order to be future-focused. No longer does the 3D movie experience involve two projectors working in conjunction (but not always perfectly in sync!) and those odd red and blue glasses. That was the past. Today it's been re-imagined for the future, with Intel's InTru3D technology that takes 3D filmmaking to new heights. Now it's a single projector doing advanced computing to render an image that is viewed as three dimensional with the much more sleek RealD glasses with polarized lenses (think Tom Cruise's glasses in *Risky Business*—or the Blues Brothers). By the time you read this book, the next innovation will be Italian-made sunglasses that become 3D movie glasses in a darkened theater.

During his presentation, Katzenberg had a giant movie screen wheeled out and asked everyone to reach under his or her seats. Taped under them were the RealD glasses, which he then asked the audience to put on. He proceeded to show a clip from DreamWorks' hit film *Kung Fu Panda*—fully rendered in 3D.

The crowd gasped in amazement. Everyone felt totally immersed in the film. No one was thinking about drive-in movies, or the hokey 1950's box office bombs. This idea may be a blast from the past, but the innovations made from that source of inspiration were all about the unprecedented future. But Katzenberg wasn't done. After talking about filmmakers such as Robert Zemeckis, Steven Spielberg, Peter Jackson, and James Cameron, and their commitment to three-dimensional films, Katzenberg had the lights dimmed again. This time he showed off the new film *Monsters vs. Aliens.* "3D is the next great frontier," Katzenberg said. Now *all* of DreamWorks Animation films will be both authored and offered in 3D. And this is how looking back for inspiration can lead to such wonderful innovation going forward.

Of course the fascination with producing 3D objects dates way back to the ancient Greeks. They understood the ability to perceive objects with perspective and depth depended on the brain's ability to process two separate images, one from each eye. When we look at something, the brain is able to merge those images to create a field of vision that is three-dimensional and also allows the viewer to focus on specific areas within any given scene. It's simply taken this long to perfect the innovation. Good things come to those who wait. The stereoscope—a sort of 3D image viewer—was invented in 1844 and was popular with middle-class families right up until the Second World War. The Lumière Brothers (among the earliest filmmakers and often credited with the "invention" of cinema) patented a color film process in 1903, but were experimenting with 3D tests in 1934 when they were in their 70s. Of course they once notoriously stated, "The cinema is an invention without any future." Not so fast, fellas! What would they have thought of IMAX, which helped bring 3D back into the public's consciousness?

As we know it today, three-dimensional technology—the ability to add the appearance of depth to a flat image, typically when viewed through special viewing glasses—has been the movie industry's answer to outside competition on and off for more than 50 years. Scott Kirsner, author of *Inventing the Movies,* tells us why 3D first became popular in the 1950s: the movies needed a competitive advantage over television, which was an upstart technology at the time. Kirsner adds that the movie industry is in a similar situation today, as it tries to fend off encroachment from home theater systems. For the next five years, he says, "You'll have to go to the theater" to see movies in 3D. Even though the 3D fad in the 1950s died quickly, Kirsner is more optimistic regarding the current generation of 3D movie technology. "The technology is better this time around," he explains. And if consumers consider the theater experience demonstrably better, then movie theaters are not just different from the TV and DVD experience, but superior to it. That potentially eliminates the erosion of ticket sales to alternative media.

However, as we've seen before, nothing spurs innovation as much as your competitor becoming innovative. So the thought that TV would stand idly by and let its audience slip away to movie theatres is ludicrous. Typical TV fare like football games, are already being shown experimentally in 3D at select theaters across the country. The Oakland Raiders vs. San Diego Chargers game in late 2008 and 2009's BCS championship game are recent examples. Now the Super Bowl has gotten in on the act, but not with the game. 2009 marked the first Super Bowl *commercial* to be shown in 3D. DreamWorks Animation and Pepsi's SoBe beverages teamed up with NBC and Intel Corp. to create a 3D ad break set that not only included an eye-popping trailer for the DreamWorks film *Monsters vs. Aliens*, but also a 60-second ad for SoBe Life Water that featured the popular SoBe lizards, which appeared during the game in 2008, alongside NFL stars and characters from the movie.

In an event known for producing once-in-a-lifetime ad moments, the SoBe-DreamWorks idea was certainly innovative. More often than not, Super Bowl advertisers put the spotlight on themselves, not anyone else. (Pepsi has, on occasion, taken potshots in Super Bowl ads at its rival, Coca-Cola). But SoBe and DreamWorks determined that highlighting multiple brands represents a better strategy than flying solo. Viewers were also told to hold on to their glasses so they could use them to watch a 3D episode of *Chuck* that aired the next day.

Intel had to produce more than 125 million pairs of 3D glasses, which were distributed by PepsiCo though 25,000 SoBe Life Water retail displays in grocery stores, drug stores, and other retail venues as part of a "Don't Chuck Your Glasses" promotion.

While no one really believes that 3D will give theaters a permanent technology edge, that's what innovation is for. For now, it is clear 3D movies are an audience draw. Carmike Cinemas reports that they showed *Journey to the Center of the Earth* in 3D on 327 screens and generated five times the per-screen revenue compared with regular films. They also had no customer pushback from their two dollar 3D surcharge. That's good news, because there are 23 movies expected to be released in 3D in the next year.

Disney's *Hannah Montana & Miley Cyrus: Best of Both Worlds Concert*, a 3D movie, pulled in $31.3 million in its opening weekend, an impressive feat because it played on only 683 screens, compared with many wide-release films that open on more than 3,000 screens and make only half as much. The total ticket sales are a box office record for a Super Bowl weekend (surpassing *Titanic*). The equally successful *Jonas Brothers in 3D* concert film followed this up in 2009.

Naturally, not all innovations in films have been as enduring. Some were merely exploited as gimmicks. Do you remember "Smell-O-Vision" and "AromaRama," which dispersed scents into the theater? If not, you didn't miss much. Some innovative movie technologies did live on past the gimmick phase to become a standard part of the movie viewing experience, however. "Sensurround," used powerful low-frequency speakers to add ground-shaking effects to movies like 1974's *Earthquake*. And while it came and went, innovators looked back toward Sensurround and emerged with slightly less intense low-frequency subwoofers which became a standard component of multi-channel theatrical "surround sound" systems and home theater systems today.

So what's next for 3D? First is obviously a broader range of movies that appeal to older audiences. Currently, 3D is largely focused on animated offerings where the 3D technology can better amaze, thrill and sometimes, even scare the audience. But, while this is appealing to younger audiences, not many senior citizens and retirees would readily put aside their reading glasses to don 3D spectacles. Further, unless this happens, theatres located in areas whose population is largely older may be reluctant to undertake the expense to upgrade to 3D technology, thereby limiting this format's distribution opportunities.

More exciting still is the prospect of holograms floating around your own home. This is still some way off, but last year the journal *Nature* revealed a breakthrough that has allowed scientists to create an updateable palm-sized holographic display. The displays, which were produced by a team at the University of Arizona and show a car, brain molecule, and skull in three dimensions, have raised hopes that a prototype holographic TV system will be available in five to ten years. Holography involves using laser beams to create 3D images. Just as a moving picture is actually a series of stills shown in quick succession, a moving hologram would be a series of still holograms run together to fool the brain. Imagine how holograph innovations could help in other fields such as air traffic control, surgery, or advertising. Moving holographs will no doubt come first to mobile phones and hand-held consoles, then to television, and then we will watch them on a more traditional vertical-standing TV set with the images sitting out somewhere in front of it.

Katzenberg agrees, but adds that most creativity has largely been something that has been only on the screen, and that the next round of innovation will be more behind the scenes. Returning to Intel's inventive InTru3D as an example: It's not just the end product you see that is truly innovative; it's the way in which these 3D films are, and will be made. InTru3D gives animators and filmmakers the tools to render 3D images in real time and manipulate them to make the clip they want. Before Katzenberg took the stage, a montage was shown of how animation was done in the old days—by hand. An animated film could take months, sometimes years. But he found it necessary to look back at how it *was* done first, before pondering the next innovation. Now it's just a question of having enough computing power to render images.

The opportunity always exists to look back at a new technology (like improved 3D) in order to bring it forward into your home as well. As you read this, Intel executives aren't quite sure yet about how 3D would work at home, because the format still requires glasses, and they said much work was being done to remove that restriction. They'll figure it out—and they'll do it by looking back, in order to look forward.

A bevy of theater chains, including AMC, Regal, and Cinemark, among others, are exploring or installing digital cinema and 3D systems as you read this. And Intel and others are innovating new tools for companies like Dreamworks to make the next generation of 3D animation films. Experts at Wharton say with 3D movies back in vogue, they may yet save the movie theater from extinction. Guess what's helping to pay for all of this capital investment? More innovation, of course. For example, instead of the old-school laborious method of printing and shipping giant canisters of film for each reel to thousands of locations, movie theaters are installing 3D projection technology and digital cinema systems, which streamline movie distribution by using digital media or satellites to "download" the films.

Cobb Theatres, a leading motion picture exhibitor in the Southeast, upgraded its locations to include all-new DLP digital projection systems coupled with RealD 3D technology. The extensive installations were planned and implemented to accommodate the flurry of new 3D movies that will be arriving in theatres; dozens are now in the Hollywood pipeline!

Innovation is driving the decisions. And Jeremy Welman, chief operating officer of Cobb Theatres says it best: "We have always tried to be at the forefront of industry innovation, and this is a major statement that we are making to the communities in which we do business." Their upgrades feature new Barco DLP 2k digital projection systems, RealD 3D technology, and a new, specially designed silver screen.

Who would have ever thought famous movie moguls, theater CEOs, and even R&D folks would all be pioneering the latest innovations in entertainment by looking backwards for inspiration? Could anyone have imagined that forgettable 1950's 3D fare like *Bwana Devil* or *Taza, Son of Cochise* would someday serve as connective tissue for Hollywood blockbusters and giant leaps forward in technology? And yet, they do, and they will continue to do so. In fact, box office figures have shown the immersive effect of 3D can attract two to three times more movie-goers who are willing to pay as much as $3 more per ticket, so this is one innovation platform with long legs—and twice as many eyes!

MYTH #26 — YOU HAVE TO PLEASE YOUR AUDIENCE (CASE STUDY)

YOU'VE HEARD the expression, "You can't please everybody," and while that certainly is true, this particular myth is almost the opposite side of that coin. Some audiences aren't worth pleasing in the first place. In fact, it can be wonderful to forget one audience while simply creating a new audience entirely and enjoying it all to yourself.

One of the grandest examples of this is the case of the Nintendo Wii and how Shigeru Miyamoto tried not to please the hardcore "gamer" demographic, but rather the very folks that gamers make fun of—the novices, the greenhorns, and the (gasp!) older people of the world. Not bad for a company that began life in the late 19th century as a play-ing-card manufacturer.

Miyamoto may not be a household name, but his video-game designs are. The list reads like a Who's Who of Pop Culture: Donkey Kong, Mario, Zelda, et al. Miyamoto also happens to be the general manager of Nintendo's Development Division, so he knows a little something about profitable home-entertainment-console games. Some people began to question that at one time, as Nintendo's GameCube fell behind Sony's PlayStation and Microsoft's Xbox. His plan to turn that around meant he couldn't buy into the myth about trying to please the gaming enthusiast audience with something they would like better. Maybe there's only one Coke in the world, and one Pepsi. He didn't care to play the part of Royal Crown Cola, trying to persuade Coke and Pepsi drinkers to switch.

"Hit 'em where they ain't," as Pittsburgh Pirates infielder, Wee Wil-lie Keeler, used to say! How else to explain Miyamoto's decision to launch a peculiar wireless device that senses a player's movements and uses them to control video games? And how brilliant it was to recognize that the gamer audience is as stagnant as it is devoted—to the point that he could ignore the core market gamer audience instead of trying to please it.

Miyamoto also followed a principal we outline in our chapter about trends, in the sense that he "capitalized" on the fact that games were becoming so expensive to create, he knew his competition would be risking less and less money on fresh ideas. So he was content to let them spew out a series of uninspired sequels and spin-offs. And the most fascinating and myth-busting move of all was that Miyamoto, fully aware that both Xbox 360 and Sony PS3 had a plan to "please their audience" with faster chips and better online service, decided to go counter. He knew that with the right innovative approach he could reinvent gaming and please the much larger, not-interested-in-games audience that Microsoft and Sony were ignoring. This was sheer genius. But it seemed insane to everyone else that rather than chase the "gamer," Nintendo would decide to pursue the non-gamer. Now all Miyamoto needed was the impossible. How on earth do you get people who don't care about games, to suddenly care about games?

First, he began by asking why people don't play games in the first place? The answer that started to emerge is that to the average non-gamer person, playing games looks kind of difficult and hard to master—like learning a foreign language. If you are new to the concept, all the joysticks and buttons, and triggers and toggle switches are too intimidating. Typical non-gamers would observe two people playing a game and miss what could possibly be so fun about it. It looked like work, and with a learning curve, too!

He knew at once that the game interface would have to be changed so that players could tell the machine what they wanted to do. There would simply be no other way to get non-gamers interested. So they did it. Out went the "game-controller" and in came a white wireless wand that at first glance resembled a TV remote.

Now, if you want your character on the screen to swing a golf club, you just swing the controller—between the laser pointer and the motion sensor, and it knows what you're doing, and how fast you're doing it. Instead of passively playing a game, you physically perform it by acting it out, and that's the secret to the magic: it's almost like theater. You forget there's a glass screen between you and the game because you are so immersed in the illusion of personally being a part of the game's world. With all of this acting and movement comes another side benefit: it instantly creates a "party atmosphere" in the room. Instead of sitting on a couch staring at the screen, you're jumping, dancing, running, swatting. Unlike "old school" gaming, anyone watching two people play this kind of game would be convinced they were having a great time.

But that's only half of the innovation. Let's take a moment to talk about the software. Nintendo created a task force to come up with a list of games *for people who don't play games*, including the elderly.

And believe it or not, there was a segment of the population even less into gaming than the elderly—namely, school-age girls. No worries. With the introduction of *Nintendogs*, an entire demographic that had never bought a video game before marched out to buy their first one.

You want more innovation? How about the name Nintendo gave to this revolutionary new controller: Wii. Something unreadable, unintelligible that no one was sure how to pronounce. The name not wiithstanding, Nintendo paid no heed to two myths that its competitors were slavishly loyal to. The first is, always listen to your customers. The hard-core gaming community are some of the most vocal bloggers out there, but if Nintendo kept trying to please them, hard-core gamers would be about the only audience it would ever have. As an innovator, you must know that if you are simply listening to your customers and giving them what they ask for, you will never surprise them. No one in a focus group ever asked for an iPod. Or a chainsaw, for that matter. They didn't know they needed one—until it was invented. Again, "Consumer is King" is a myth.

The other myth Nintendo shattered was the idea that cutting-edge technology is more important than cutting-edge design. Not so much. And yet, the myth persists among engineers that consumers want more power and more features. It's simply not true. Going back to the iPod example: as a pure device, it didn't and doesn't do much more than the competition. But it became a sensation because it was easier, and quite frankly, sexier to use. In the world of cars, the one that you look the coolest driving is often better than the one that is the fastest. Remember our myth on facts vs. emotions.

Sure enough, the Nintendo Wii has managed to be the best selling last generation console, despite PS3 and Xbox 360 having "better" hardware and sheer power. But power alone is not enough if it is not coupled with innovation. Controlling a character on PS3 or Xbox 360 can be downright boring—and difficult, as we mentioned earlier. All the hardware improvements in the world couldn't fix that. It took Wii's "weaker" hardware, but brighter imagination, to change the rules and bring back the *fun* to gaming through interaction vs. complication and visual effects.

Today, the Wii is basking in the glow of having accomplished its goals of bringing a larger audience into the tent. Now "non-gamers" who used to fall asleep watching their children play video games are playing Wii with their peers. The same phenomenon is occurring with Trailing Boomer and Gen-X women, who formerly had no use for video games, but are now becoming intrigued via the Wii *Fit*. This isn't new for Nintendo. A few years before, *Brain Age* on the DS platform convinced thousands of aging baby boomers, (including my Auntie!), to buy the DS in order to give their brains a work-out and stave off the onset of Alzheimer's. In any case, Nintendo has perfected the method of breaking from tradition, and blazing a trail into the untapped non-gamer, general population.

Wii *Fit* could also be accurately described as an innovation in marketing. It's part yoga video, part bathroom scale, part personal trainer and all with a natural feel. The VCR was only in existence for a year or two before a plethora of fitness tapes were released to play on it. In marked contrast, video games have been in homes for over 25 years, but only now with the Wii *Fit* are they taking advantage of the need for health and wellness from a huge audience that was being ignored by the competition. Thus "exergaming" and the marketing push that goes with it, was born.

It has often been said as a left-handed (or left-brained!) compliment to Nintendo that the Wii is "gaming for the masses." Perhaps. But that didn't stop Nintendo from adopting that very line as their slogan in an ad campaign.

The Wii case study also offers a valuable lesson, in that everyone at Nintendo set their fears aside to get completely onboard as a team in order to defy (i.e., not follow) the trend in the industry. Instead of following the technology "roadmap" by trying to make something faster and flashier, they went "off-road," in order to make a bigger impact on a new customer base. Mainstream technology at the time could have never predicted the emergence of the Wii. It was simply too off course from the direction the industry was heading, which is exactly what makes it such a brilliant innovation. It takes a lot of courage to deviate from roadmaps, but in doing so, the Wii discovered what we like to call "new values." For example, there was a time ("old values") all the automakers were competing over more horsepower. Then hybrids came along and created a new emphasis on environmental performance, while creating a "new value" along the way. The Wii accomplished the same feat.

Gaming Makes Strange Bedfellows

Continuing with its impressive string of engaging (and in some cases befriending) new markets with the Wii comes news in 2009 that in an effort to boost interest in music among kids, Nintendo is now partnering with The National Association for Music Education to bring Wii *Music* to classrooms across America. Now think about that one for a minute. A gaming company being *invited* into schools! It's truly remarkable. With all of the bad press that gaming gets from parent groups and teacher associations, and with pressure from juvenile diabetes organizations that sitting on your duff playing games is the problem, who could imagine the two sides sitting down to broker a peace? Well, it helps that with the Wii you don't sit on your duff, and that Wii games have less to do with themes like stealing cars and shooting guns and more to do with harmless pursuits and sports.

Wii *Fit* opened the door to fitness, and Wii *Music* now quite convincingly stakes its claim to educate youth. It will not exactly teach kids how to play music, but it will at the very least create an interest in music by engaging them with some key concepts in a format they find appealing, in much the same way that Wii *Fit* didn't provide jogging instruction, but rather, convinced folks that jogging could be more fun and immersive in the first place.

Teachers are already lauding Wii *Music* because it requires students to use language skills, spatial awareness, and hand-eye coordination. It's the ultimate win-win because it's educational, but adds a love of music to children's lives as well, since it is a memorable, hands-on experience. We like to call these kind of activities "accidental learning" occasions, because when you're having so much fun, you don't even realize you're being taught something new. Not a bad way to help kids discover their own creative voice, either—all of which adds up to another hit for Nintendo—by *not* trying to please the audience, but finding a new one.

So why don't more companies and organizations take Nintendo's lead and shatter this "please your audience" myth once and for all? Good question. Maybe they lack the imagination. Because, as they like to say at Nintendo, "Innovation is not easy, but it starts in the mind."

MYTH #27 — WE'LL INNOVATE WHEN WE NEED TO

BY NOW IN THIS BOOK, we hope to have persuaded you that innovation is absolutely essential for long-term corporate growth, if not survival. In fact, looking at the modest, (if that) growth rate of existing brands and categories, it is easy to see how innovation is probably *the most* critical driver of growth. Without it, you are almost certainly doomed to the whims of your category.

But with innovation, you can outgrow the boundaries. You can steal market share from competition and even better, you can move outside the category.

Yet, it is extremely difficult to be able to set aside the extra time and money needed for on-going innovation. Today's times demand that companies try to operate as efficiently as possible and keep staffs lean and mean. As a result, most personnel already spend their entire workday filled with activities needed to take care of their normal daily responsibilities. How can they make the time to take on responsibilities to generate "future" growth through innovation as well?

So, while companies realize that they must innovate, it is totally understandable how tempting it is to put it on the back-burner and do so only when it is desperately needed. The *myth*stake here is that a company's need to innovate *is not a once-in-a-while situation;* it is an ongoing one. So, yes, it is appropriate to only innovate when needed, but it is actually needed all of the time.

Despite how difficult it might be to operate a firm profitably in the short-term, the fact is, companies operate in an increasingly dynamic environment. Consumer needs continue to shift. Competition remains intense. And for your competitors to grow, they must try to turn *your* customers into their customers. As a result, the offerings, processes and business models can quickly become obsolete, and with it, so goes the business.

The only answer is to maintain a *continuous*, accelerated innovation pace. Or as has been said, "The only way to predict the future is to create it."

The bottom line is that innovation is just too important to leave to chance, or to turn on like a light switch on a moment's notice. Isolated, sporadic innovation projects just won't get the job done. Large, once in a while initiatives take too long and can't react to market shifts or sudden opportunities.

SETTING UP A CULTURE FOR CONTINUOUS INNOVATION

Companies need to cultivate innovation as an integral part of their on-going day-to-day operations. Okay, but how? Simply put, it must come from the top. That's really the only way in which it can happen. The firm's top executives must demonstrate a sincere interest in finding new breakthrough ideas. And, they must demonstrate this interest by setting aside adequate resources to do this and making appropriate managers and personnel responsible for achieving it. They must demonstrate this by clearly exhibiting the right attitude toward innovation.

Central to a firm's ability to continuously innovate is a corporate culture that encourages its people to be connected and to openly communicate. Remember, "Two heads are better than one." Top managers must try to establish systems that encourage the sharing of customer data, supplier relationships, discoveries of new technologies, and other learning among product teams and other appropriate personnel. With proper communication, a new invention or learning for one product can quickly be integrated into other new products, as witnessed by Toyota Motor Company's moving parts and inventions used in one year's Lexus to the next year's Camry.

Remember too, that innovation is an expedition. This is why it is critical for companies to build a corporate culture that encourages personnel to look in many places, and create many ideas. It also needs a culture that realizes that several projects are needed to surface, not just one. As we have seen, a good, new innovation process enables companies to weed out the less-than-worthy ideas throughout the entire process, because you never really know if a product is going to end up going to market—until it actually does.

Perhaps the most important move that key executives can make to better ensure continuous, company-wide innovation, to not just talk about it, but also establish plans and measurements to *guarantee* that it gets done. The best way to do this is to set goals that actually *encourage* and applaud risk-taking. In setting goals, some firms like P&G and 3M have objectives detailing exactly how much of their future business will come from products that are currently not in existence. GE has a well-earned reputation for holding its business leaders responsible for submitting at least three major game-changing proposals per year.

Interestingly, some firms judiciously place such aggressive growth requirements for each line of business, or brand, that the only way in which the business team can hope to achieve its goals is by building innovative initiatives directly into its business plan. These companies realize the simple truth of this old bromide:

"If you always do what you always did, you'll always get what you always got!"

So their business teams *must* do something new and innovative if they are to ever achieve their new growth objective.

Setting goals that automatically require innovation helps a company "pull" innovation through an organization. When teams realize that they must build innovative programs into their plans in order to make their numbers year after year, and then are measured and rewarded accordingly, innovation becomes an important on-going part of the business. As a result, there is much less need on the part of upper management to "push" for innovation to happen. In other words, the boat moves faster when every one onboard is rowing in the same direction.

The companies that are the most serious about innovation tend to set up separate innovation departments. Whirlpool reportedly sets aside 75 people from its operations to do nothing but innovation for a set period of time. Kellogg's and Wal-Mart have hired separate innovation brand managers, leaving the administration of on-going businesses to other brand managers. This separation is particularly effective. Not only is it the sole role of the innovation managers and departments to innovate, but also because they tend to be further away from the day-to-day business, they are more likely to be unbiased in what a brand can or cannot do and therefore come up with truly game-changing ideas.

MANAGING THE PIPELINE

To have continuous innovation, means to have several projects working at the same time. Ed Sullivan never booked an act that had only one plate spinning in the air for a reason: It wouldn't be compelling enough. In the case of innovation, any plate can fall and break at any time. The same is true with simultaneous innovation efforts. The more you have, the more exciting it is, *and* the safer it is, even if the time to market can be longer for some (since the chance of success might be lower for others).

The bottom line is, companies need to track innovations along various stages of their innovation process. How many are in the upfront stage? How many validated ideas do we have? How many are moving into development? What does the launch calendar look like?

Naturally, it all begins with the idea. There must always be enough of them at the start in order for firms to get enough *validated* ideas (validated from both a consumer and corporate viewpoint) into development. Research shows that it takes nearly 300 ideas to achieve a single successful product. And, you must have enough projects in development to ensure that at least some will make it all of the way through. And by all the way through, we mean that it has to be technologically possible to achieve while delivering what the consumer is expecting at an appropriate price point.

Most pipelines resemble a funnel: Lots and lots of well-focused ideas at the top, yielding a few products that will actually get launched at the bottom.

All the traps you have to run to keep the funnel full have been discussed elsewhere in this book. But if you look for opportunities and ideate against those that have been uncovered, you'll be in good shape. A key point is that *several* potentially strong ideas can surface against every single opportunity that has been uncovered. Therefore, keep in mind that any single exploration can yield many potential new product ideas. In fact, all too often once we help clients uncover consumer insight focus areas, and help them in their initial ideation, they have so many ideas that we are no longer needed for several years because their pipeline is full. This is certainly a great compliment, but the kind that doesn't exactly help *our* business model.

On the serious side though, always remember that consumers and markets shift quickly. Smart companies try to uncover new opportunities and new ideas over and over again, thus ensuring that they have a significant number of the very best new product opportunities in their pipeline. Innovation must be continuous, and so must be the ongoing search for new and fresh perspectives.

In summary, continuous innovation starts with the top management.

- They can make obsolescence a goal. Rather than wait for competitors to displace a firm's products, they should do it themselves. Set specific goals as to what percentage of future revenues should come from "renovating" products introduced within the previous two to three years.

- Be ready to reward failures. Innovations require trial and error, so personnel need to be rewarded for taking chances. As long as they follow the right steps and procedures, their attempts should be celebrated no matter the outcome.

- Try to encourage innovation. Set aside the time for people to innovate. Create a specific process. Set goals that "pull" a manager's desire to innovate as a way to achieve business goals.

- Ensure that steps are being taken to continually uncover new customer insights and opportunities.

- Create and manage an innovation pipeline.

With this, our final myth of the book, we'll send you off to do your job, which is to innovate, to change your firm, your life, the lives of your customers, and to be better and better!

It's not "Innovate or Die"

It's . . . **"Innovate & Live!"**

References

Anon., *2008 Best Practices Study: The Making of World-Class Innovators*, Prophet.com.

Anon., "Business Leaders Call for Progress in Advancing U.S. Innovation by Strengthening Science, Technology, Engineering, and Math," *WSJOnline*, July 13, 2008.

Anon., "Expanding the Innovation Horizon: The Global CEO Study 2006," IBM Global Business Services.

Anon., "From Problems to Ideas through to Innovation—capturing Ideas and Creating the Right Culture to Maximize the Value of Intellectual Property," Quocirca.com, November 2008.

Anon., "How Companies Approach Innovation," DeRiff India, December 18, 2007.

Anon., "How Companies Approach Innovation," McKinsey survey, 2008.

Anon., "The Fifty Most Innovative Companies," *BusinessWeek*, May, 2007.

Anon. "The Missing Link in Open Innovations: Where Product Managers Should be Looking for New Ideas," InventHelp.com

Anthony, Scott D., Mark W. Johnson, Joseph J. Sinfield, and Elizabeth J. Altman, *Innovators Guide to Growth: Putting Disruptive Innovation to Work*, Cambridge: Harvard Business School Press, 2008.

Avishai, Bernard, "Why Detroit Can't Keep Up." Innovation Nation, WashingtonPost.com, November 23, 2008.

Berkun, Scott, *The Myths of Innovation,* Sebastapol, CA: O'Reilly Media, Inc., 2007.

Boag, George, "Innovation the key to success in fast-moving worldwide economy," NewScottsman.com , August 30, 2008.

Davila, Tony, Marc J. Epstein, and Robert Shelton, *Making Innovation Work How to Manage It, Measure It, and Profit from It,* Philadelphia: Wharton Business School Publishing, 2005.

Day, George S. and Paul J.H. Schoemaker, *The Peripheral Vision: Detecting the Weak Signals That Will Make or Break Your Company,* Cambridge: Harvard Business School Press, 2006.

Chesbrough, Henry, *Open Innovation: The New Imperative for Creating and Profiting from Technology,* Cambridge: Harvard Business School Press, 2006.

Christensen, Clayton M. and Michael E. Raynor, *Innovator's Solution,* Cambridge: Harvard Business School Press, 2003.

Clancy, Kevin and Robert Shulman, *Marketing Myths that Are Killing Business,* New York: McGraw-Hill, 1994.

Cooper, Robert, *Winning at New Products: Accelerating the Process from Idea to Launch,* New York: Basic Books, 2001.

Erstin, Judy, "Innovation: Crucial to our Future," *Huffington Post,* September 5, 2008.

Heath, Chip and Dan Heath, *Made to Stick: Why Some Ideas Survive and Others Die,* New York: Random House, 2007.

Jaruzelski, Barry, Kevin Denhoff and Rakesh Bordia, "Smart Spenders: The Global Innovation 1000," *Strategy+Business,* Booz-Allen Hamilton, 2006.

Kantor, Rosabeth Moss, "Innovation: The Classic Traps," *Harvard Business Review,* November, 2006.

Keim, Brandon, "Obama answers your science questions," *Wired* Science Blog Network, September 2, 2008.

Keller, Ralph, "Continuous Improvement—A better way of developing new products," *Industry Week.* June 1, 2008.

Lafley, A. G. and Ram Charan, *The Game Changer: How You Can Drive Revenue and Profit Growth with Innovation*, New York: Crown Business, 2008.

Maddock, Michael G. and Raphael Louis Vitn, "What to Look for in a Chief Innovation Officer," Newsfactor.com, November 20, 2008.

Martin, Neale, "How Habits Undermine Marketing," *Financial Times*, July 1, 2008.

McGrath, Rita Gunther and Ian C. MacMillan, *Market Busters: 40 Strategic Moves that Drive Exceptional Business Growth*, Cambridge: Harvard Business School Press, 2005.

Mootee, Idris, "The Four Areas of Innovation: Beyond Just the Fuzzy Front End," Innovation Playground (blog), September 6, 2008.

Phillips, Jeffrey, "Creating Innovation 'pull,'" Innovate on purpose (blog), September 2, 2008.

Pittinsky, Todd L., "An innovation national once more," CSMonitor. com, September 15, 2008.

Rogers, Everett M. and Everett Rogers, *Diffusion of Innovations*, New York: Free Press, 2003.

Skarzynski, Peter, and Rowan Gibson, *Innovation to the Core: A Blueprint for Transforming the Way Your Company Innovates*, Cambridge: Harvard Business School Press, 2008.

Smith, Preston G. and Donald G. Reinersten, *Developing Products in Half the Time: New Rules, New Tools*, New York: John Wiley & Sons, 1998.

Smith, Preston G. and Donald G. Reinersten, "Shortening the Product Development Cycle,"*Research-Technology Management*, May-June, 1992.

Sood, Ashish and Gerard J. Tellis, "Do Innovations Really Pay Off? Total Stock Market Returns to Innovation," *Marketing Science Journal* (online edition), January 12, 2009.

Tapscott, Don and Anthony D. Williams, *Wikinomics: How Mass Collaboration Changes Everything*, New York: Portfolio, 2008.

Vitale, Dona, *Consumer Insights 2.0*, Ithaca, NY: Paramount Market Publishing, Inc., 2006.

Whitwell, Tom, "Tiny Music Makers: Pt 4: The Mac Startup Sound," *Music Thing*, 26 May, 2005.

Wladawsky-Berger, Irving, "The Challenges of Innovation," *Business-Week Viewpoint*, August 22, 2008.

Innovator's Guide to the Myths

Which *myth*stake to review when you need to respond:

	Myth #	Page #s
That's the job of R&D.	4	46
	22	195
	23	199
As long as we follow the trends, we'll be okay.	5	50
	6	59
	11	121
	12	125
Let's just brainstorm and see what we come up with.	10	104
	17	164
Let's just make our existing product in new colors.	1	11
	3	41
	25	220
Who needs to advertise when you have great innovations?	11	121
	13	133
	14	139
	16	152
	19	179
It costs too much to be innovative.	2	31
	3	41
	18	167
	21	189
We have to "focus group" everything.	6	59
	8	92
	10	104
	11	121
That's an old idea.	25	220

	Myth #	Page #s
Innovation doesn't work.	1	11
	2	31
It will take too long to make it perfect.	3	41
	16	152
	17	164
	20	183
Nobody here is creative enough to innovate.	7	87
	8	92
	9	95
As long as our customers like us, our products will sell.	15	146
	17	164
We don't need ideas from outside the company.	21	183
	22	189
	27	234
What exactly is an "insight"?	6	59
My CEO says to innovate. How do I do this?	23	199
	27	234
Unless we get a great top-two box purchase intent score, we don't go.	15	146
If we're not first, don't bother.	12	125
	16	152
Who needs to keep innovating?	The Situation	1
	2	31
	27	234
We already have lots of ideas.	The Situation	1
	2	125
	13	133
Failure is unacceptable.	1	11
	27	234
We only launch new products that test above the norm.	1	11
Why innovate?	The Situation	11
	2	31

	Myth #	Page #s
Innovation is risky.	2	31
	23	199
We can't afford to innovate.	2	31
	3	41
	4	46
What does brand positioning have to do with innovation?	6	59
	16	152
Why not just rely on traditional research methods for innovation?	6	59
	23	199
What does the consumer say about it?	6	59
	8	92
	14	139
	18	167
Just write up a concept statement and test it.	14	139
	18	167
We always come up with the same ideas.	6	59
	10	104
Encourage all employees to give us new ideas.	11	121
How do we know a good idea from a bad idea?	12	125
Why go for the home run?	12	125
	15	146
	17	164
How much will this cost?	12	125
Why, after all of the research, did we fail?	14	139
	16	152
	18	167
	19	179
	20	183
Consumers cannot accurately judge truly different, unusual ideas.	18	167
Why do so many competing companies come up with the same ideas?	23	199
I thought about 80 percent of innovations fail.	1	11
	3	41
	25	220

	Myth #	Page #s
Listening to the customer is the best way to innovate.	6	59
	11	121
	12	125
	26	228
Aren't research findings and insights the same thing?	6	59
	18	167
	20	183
	22	195
A Focus Group will tell you what they really want.	8	92
	10	104
	11	121
We should focus on quality over quantity	3	41
	9	95
	10	104
I'd rather share a big idea than own a smaller one.	5	50
	15	146
	16	152
A bad test score is the "final word" on a new idea.	18	167
	19	179
	20	183
Shouldn't a concept look more like a mini-ad?	18	167
	20	183
The more you spend, the better you'll innovate.	2	31
	18	167
A great idea can overcome bad marketing.	2	31
	14	139
	18	167

About the Authors

Timothy J. Coffey

His father an engineer, his mother a choir director and teacher, and himself, a musician turned researcher turned marketer turned entrepreneur, ever the Gemini in both spirit and mind, Tim is the quintessential left and right dual-dominant brain-type.

This nature-and-nurture-forged makeup may explain why he is sometimes referred to as "The Consumer Whisperer" who conjures visions of new products and innovations that have captured the hearts and minds of consumers all over the world. During the first decade of his career, he learned the fundamentals of consumer insights and marketing at Procter & Gamble. Then, in a siren call from an American icon in need of re-imagining, he turned his skills to the re-making of Tupperware. Finally, his true calling was realized when he founded WonderGroup,® a digital marketing firm and, LaunchForce,® an insights and innovation consultancy.

Leading those companies has allowed Tim to bring his innovative vision to scores of companies including such global leaders as Kellogg, Johnson & Johnson, Kraft, ConAgra, Heinz, Tyson, Nestlé, and Purina. Most notable inventions are the patent-pending Consumer Verité,™ Interactive Portal and Hypno-Imaging,™ both of which came to him in a dream. In addition to *Innovation—Myths and Myth*stakes, Tim co-authored two books: *The Great Tween Buying Machine* and *Marketing to the New Super Consumer—Mom & Kid*.

Undoubtedly, Tim's greatest co-creations, together with wife Jill, are his four daughters: Sara, Kathleen, Shannon, and Elizabeth.

DAVE L. SIEGEL

Thirty-five years ago, Dave Siegel wrote a Master's Thesis on "Why New Products Fail." Who knew that *this* would be his ultimate calling? He is a sought-after expert by the national and international media and is co-author of *The Great Tween Buying Machine*, and *Marketing to the New SuperConsumer—Mom & Kid*. He has spoken on innovation to conferences as far away as Singapore, Australia, and Brazil which means he must be smart—or at least he must have lots of frequent flyer points.

Right out of grad school Dave landed a job at Procter & Gamble on the marketing team that was readying the company's launch of a super-secret, highly important, *new* Liquid Detergent product—ERA. From there, his sweet tooth got the better of him and Dave joined Cadbury-Schweppes, a major confectionery company, where he directed the development and marketing of *new* confectionery products, quickly launching such sinful items as Cadbury Eggs, Caramello, and other decadent sweets. Unfortunately, while he was gaining business he was gaining weight even faster! So on he went. During his career, Dave helped develop and launch dozens of other hits. Among them, the first bathroom cleaner to turn toilet water green! Speaking of green, let's add Heinz Green Ketchup to the line-up along with a top-selling board game, the world's #1 selling leisure product, a new business model for ad agencies, an award-winning new media model, lots of different foods, and lots and lots of toys.

After co-founding the WonderGroup, Dave joined Tim Coffey as the President of LaunchForce.

Dave will admit that many of his best ideas come from his wonderful wife Jan (just ask her!) and very talented children Adam, Lauren, Robin, and Tiffany.

MARK A. SMITH

Mark Smith started his career in new product ideation by taking a chainsaw to a dictionary, just to see what would happen. He continued on this path for years, wearing spiffy suits, while learning how to turn insights into ideas, ideas into innovations, and innovations into new products. From the "One Show Pencil" to The Pro Awards, he's got the honors to prove it.

Twenty years removed from his Bachelor of Fine Arts from the University of Cincinnati's College-Conservatory of Music, Mark's creative influence and strategic management have touched a wide range of clients, from Corona beer to Folgers Coffee, ConAgra, Keebler, Kraft Foods, Pepperidge Farm, Walt Disney World, Kellogg's, Nestlé, P&G, Purina, Hasbro, Heinz, Chevrolet, and everything in between.

Prior to becoming the VP Executive Creative Director for Launch-Force, Mark had ultimate responsibility for the creative product at some of Los Angeles' top advertising agencies until his inability to tan forced him to flee California for the verdant Ohio Valley. But not before becoming a published poet, as well as a trained hypnotist and a member of the Screen Actors Guild and the American Federation of Television and Radio Artists.

Throw in an amazing wife (and former account executive), a brilliant and gorgeous daughter, a love of Elvis Costello, a weakness for Route 66, talking in the third-person, and an unhealthy dependence on cheese pizza, and you get Mark's life.